Robert S. Kricheff
That Doesn't Work Anymore

MW00355466

Robert S. Kricheff

That Doesn't Work Anymore

Retooling Investment Economics in the
Age of Disruption

ISBN 978-1-5474-1682-0
e-ISBN (PDF) 978-1-5474-0075-1
e-ISBN (EPUB) 978-1-5474-0077-5

Library of Congress Control Number: 2018960087

Bibliographic information published by the Deutsche Nationalbibliothek
The Deutsche Nationalbibliothek lists this publication in the Deutsche Nationalbibliografie;
detailed bibliographic data are available on the Internet at http://dnb.dnb.de.

© 2019 Robert S. Kricheff
Published by Walter de Gruyter Inc., Boston/Berlin
Printing and binding: CPI books GmbH, Leck
Typesetting: MacPS, LLC, Carmel

www.degruyter.com

Praise for *That Doesn't Work Any More*

Kricheff explains why so many of the broadly used economic and financial tools need to be reconsidered in the face of rapid technological change. *That Doesn't Work Anymore* highlights the unique challenges that industries and companies face as technology changes the world—particularly in the emerging markets.

— Eraj Shirvani, Vice Chairman—Emerging Markets,
Credit Suisse AG

Bob Kricheff is the Malcolm Gladwell of investing. He rightly forces you to question the stalwart theories and rules of economics during a time where technological disruption across all industries has become the norm. *That Doesn't Work Any More* analyzes everything from Keyes vs. Hayek to the impact of music streaming, and even the food industry. It is a must read for anyone serious about capturing alpha in a rapidly changing economic landscape.

— Judy Joo, Chef, restaurateur, TV personality, and author

An entertaining and enlightening book that expertly questions the status quo of investment economics during this present period of rapid technological innovation. Bob challenges core economic assumptions and provides a great, and often humorous, guide for navigating investments through an environment of constant disruption. Well done Bobby K!

— Patrick Dyson, Partner, GoldenTree Asset Management

We are surrounded by data, and we must learn to use new forms of information to make better decisions. *That Doesn't Work Any More* illustrates how modern technology has changed the data we use, and the context for how we use it. This book is a helpful guide of novel ways to analyze the economy and our businesses.

— Charles Rivkin, Chairman and CEO,
Motion Picture Association of America (MPAA)

Business in the 21st century requires a different lens to interpret trends and construct approaches to investment and management. *That Doesn't Work Anymore* is a splendid prism through which economic data and developments can be viewed and understood. Robert Kricheff has written a clear and concise volume that frames economic concepts in a contemporary light.

DOI 10.1515/9781547400751-202

It is easy to read with robust examples that enrich one's understanding of particular topics. His insights are entertaining and invaluable.

— Robert I. Grossman, M.D.,

The Saul J. Farber Dean and Chief Executive Officer,

NYU Langone Health

To my brothers, David and Mark, personification of brotherhood and family.

About De|G PRESS

Five Stars as a Rule

De|G PRESS, the startup born out of one of the world's most venerable publishers, De Gruyter, promises to bring you an unbiased, valuable, and meticulously edited work on important topics in the fields of business, information technology, computing, engineering, and mathematics. By selecting the finest authors to present, without bias, information necessary for their chosen topic *for professionals*, in the depth you would hope for, we wish to satisfy your needs and earn our five-star ranking.

In keeping with these principles, the books you read from De|G PRESS will be practical, efficient and, if we have done our job right, yield many returns on their price.

We invite businesses to order our books in bulk in print or electronic form as a best solution to meeting the learning needs of your organization, or parts of your organization, in a most cost-effective manner.

There is no better way to learn about a subject in depth than from a book that is efficient, clear, well organized, and information rich. A great book can provide life-changing knowledge. We hope that with De|G PRESS books you will find that to be the case.

DOI 10.1515/9781547400751-204

Acknowledgments

Most importantly thanks to my parents, Irv and Marge, who by word and deed have been the most wonderful of parents and grandparents to me as well as my brothers, our wives, our children and occasionally to some of my friends. Without them nothing would have been possible.

My good friend John Lutz, managing partner of the New York office of McDermott Will & Emery LLP, was a good sounding board on early book ideas and was most helpful with legal advice for this and my other books. He continues to combine a great legal mind and a sense of humor. Jessica Brewer Donofrio and John indulged me when I threw out ideas about this book, well before it was written.

A special thank you goes to Mark Shenkman and Justin Slatky, the co-CIOs of Shenkman Capital, for giving me a wonderful opportunity at a great firm and being so supportive. I have benefitted from their knowledge, experience and especially their friendship. Also thanks to Adam Kurzer, vice chairman of Shenkman Capital, who has put up with me through several decades at two firms and always done so with a distinctive laugh and great advice. Over the years I have gotten a bevy of great insights from these three people.

It is not an easy task to be able to consistently develop unique macroeconomic concepts while seamlessly and entertainingly connecting them to very specific investment markets; that is what Dr. Neal Soss has done for decades at Credit Suisse. I am very grateful that I have had the chance to learn so much from him about life, the world and a pragmatic approach to economics and all its interconnections. The lessons usually included a good laugh too. I have never seen him take an economic number at face value. I am sure we have discussed many of the ideas in this book and I hope he will read it and let me know all the parts he disagrees with or that I got wrong.

For the much needed help with mind, body and soul over the last few years, whether it involves hitting a pad, a target or the right mental state, thanks to: Juan Berrios of Englewood Krav Maga (who gets the most out of our scarce resources and leaves no doubt if he is happy with your work or not), BK Lee at JCC on the Palisades (who forces efficiency through insisting on proper form and smiles at pain) and Ivan Rosas at Mendez Gym, NYC (who gets the maximum utility of each day by bringing energy and a smile at 5:00 A.M.).

Finally, I want to give an apology to all my co-workers, friends and family who unsuspectingly listened to me bounce ideas off of them that are in this book, and many that are not.

DOI 10.1515/9781547400751-205

About the Author

Bob Kricheff is a senior vice president, portfolio manager and global strategist at Shenkman Capital. He has 30 years of investment research and strategy experience in leveraged finance. Prior to joining Shenkman Capital, Mr. Kricheff was managing director and head of the Americas high yield sector strategy for Credit Suisse. During his tenure at Credit Suisse, he has overseen U.S., European and emerging market credit research as well as high yield sector and portfolio strategy. He also worked as a high yield analyst where he covered the media, cable, satellite, telecom, gaming, and entertainment sectors. His work covered bonds, loans and CDS. Additionally, Mr. Kricheff has published two textbooks and two e-books on topics related to leveraged finance and its analysis. Mr. Kricheff received a BA degree in economics from New York University and a MS in financial economics from the University of London's School of Oriental and African Studies.

DOI 10.1515/9781547400751-206

Contents

Part 1: **Introduction**

Chapter 1: The Economy Is Running the Data Is Walking and Trends versus
Cycles —— 3
Macroeconomic and Microeconomic Trends —— 7
Using Data Wisely —— 8
Chapter 2: An Approach to Economics—Bottoms Up —— 11

Part 2: **Disruption, Culture, and Indexes**

Chapter 3: Disruptors or Just Progress —— 19
Chapter 4: Cultural Changes Make Economics Change — 25
Chapter 5: Goodhart's "Underappreciated" Law and Benchmarking —— 29

Part 3: **Math Moves—Remembering That Everything Changes**

Chapter 6: Means Move——Analyze the Averages —— 37
Chapter 7: Rethink Regressions and Resist Correlations —— 43

Part 4: **Big Economic Data Points 53**

Chapter 8: GDP—Overrated —— 55
Chapter 9: Unemployment versus New Employment —— 65
Chapter 10: Wages Are Different Now —— 71
Chapter 11: Inflation—Just a Little Bit —— 75
Chapter 12: Interest Rates and Falsehoods —— 79
Chapter 13: Currencies—Chicken and Egg — 85
Chapter 14: Expectations Theories—Always Changing, Always Relevant —— 91

Part 5: **Old Capital, New Capital**

Chapter 15: The New Role of Capital and Capital Formation —— 101
Chapter 16: International Capital Flows—Increasingly Critical —— 107

Chapter 17: Human Capital—The Real Data to Watch —— 111
Chapter 18: Aristotle, Infrastructure, and Capital —— 115

Part 6: Tonight the Role of Government Will Be Played By...

Chapter 19: Government's Role: Past and Future —— 123
Chapter 20: Government's Job —— 129
Chapter 21: Funding the Government: Taxes and Debt—Good, Bad, and
Completely Lost —— 133
Chapter 22: Expense Management and the Government—
A Misnomer? —— 139
Chapter 23: More Gray and Purple, Less Gridlock —— 143

Part 7: Business is Different Now, But It Always Is

Chapter 24: Business Structures—Think Again —— 149
Chapter 25: Business Investment—What People Watch and Should
Watch —— 155
Chapter 26: Business Cycle Theory: It's Wrong and Slow —— 159
Chapter 27: Tearing Down and Running Around the Barriers to Entry —— 163
Chapter 28: Incumbents Can Fight Back —— 167
Chapter 29: Food and Energy —— 171
Chapter 30: Supply Chains, Outsourcing, and Innovation —— 177
Chapter 31: Measure of Trade —— 183
Chapter 32: The Invisible Consumer: Customer Retention,
Big Data, and Customer Service —— 189

Part 8: Value, Volatility, Uncertainty—Different Arrangement but the Song Remains the Same

Chapter 33: Value —— 197
Chapter 34: Volatility and Risk Measures—A Point of View —— 203
Chapter 35: Uncertainty—The Opportunity —— 209

Part 9: **Random Ramble and Concluding Topics**

Chapter 36: New Industries and What to Do about Them —— 215
Chapter 37: Emerging Economies—New Paths —— 219
Chapter 38: Socially Responsible Investing and Environmental, Social, and Governance Factors —— 223
Chapter 39: Trends, Data, Correlations, and a Few Other Things—Again —— 227
Chapter 40: Never Close Your Eyes or You Will Miss Something —— 231

Index —— 237

Preface

When you sit back and go through all the amazing changes in technology and society that have occurred through the beginning of the twenty-first century it becomes clear what an incredible time of innovation we are living in and how it is dramatically changing every aspect of life. With such massive transformations at all levels of the economy, you must question how valuable it is to base investments on historical economic data and relationships. Investing really requires rethinking about what theories and data are applicable for today. Notably, historical data has become less valuable to use in analysis because so many rapid dramatic changes have occurred that in many instances past experiences are not applicable to the current environment. Additionally, there appears to be increasing differences in how the macroeconomy is going to act in this environment when compared to the micro and mid-levels of the economy. The macrotrends are behaving very well as they broadly benefit from innovation. However, at selective microlevels there are competitive disruptions, shifts in revenue models, changes to industry, and regional dynamics, which are sending asset valuations in varied directions and causing some types of jobs to disappear and others to emerge.

This book is not about broad financial economics, but specifically investment economics. It is based, in part, on the concept that you understand things better if you question them. This book should make you reconsider typical theories in textbooks, not necessarily to reject all these concepts, but to know that it is okay to throw them out if you need to or develop new ways to use them better. The book attempts to address some of the impact on the economy due to technology-driven transformational developments. It tries to outline how these factors are impacting the value of data that is regularly used in making investment decisions. It discusses how the economics for industries and individual companies are transitioning. Hopefully, the book gives some guidance on how to apply these changes in your decision making process.

The book covers a fair number of topics and moves through them quickly—a bit like a series of conversations you might get circulating through a cocktail party of economic geeks. While hopefully some people will read the whole book, each chapter should be able to stand well on its own. It can be read in order, cherry-picked, or you can skip around. The goal is that the reader comes away rethinking and talking about the value and usage of traditional investment tools in today's economic context and about how asset valuations are increasingly and rapidly being reshaped by innovation.

Thank you,
Robert S. Kricheff
:()

DOI 10.1515/9781547400751-208

Part 1: **Introduction**

Chapter 1
The Economy Is Running the Data Is Walking and Trends versus Cycles

Sending a document cross-town, trading millions of shares of stock, ordering groceries, and manufacturing a car all happen much faster than they have at any time in the past. The acceleration in the speed at which you can get things done in this era of digitally driven innovation is not like anything seen before. New technology is also getting adopted much more quickly than at any time in the past. If everything is moving with such greater speed, economic theories and measurements need to keep pace. Should traditional business and credit cycles move faster than in the past? Why should investors react to data such as gross domestic product (GDP), which was developed in the 1930s and contains data that is sometimes six months old if the economy has evolved while waiting for the results? If you are an investor, of any kind, you need to rethink how to use popular economic data and traditional economic theories, consider other newer data points to use and reevaluate the relevance of all this data that is available in the current environment.

This era of technical and societal revolution is impacting how investment decisions need to be approached. First, these developments are so extreme and rapid that historical economic data is not as good a tool as it once was when trying to predict future asset values. Secondly, that the multitude of technologically driven improvements in efficiency should lead to an extended period of macroeconomic expansion with recessionary dips potentially being very minor and fleeting when compared to the past. However, these same developments are likely to cause select industries and regions of the economy to go through much greater distortions leading to dramatic differences between winners and losers at the micro level. The value of historical data has declined. Investing is about deciding on where you believe the future value of an asset will be. This decision is usually made using historical data as a significant input. However, since technology and related sociological changes are making historical information less relevant in predicting the future, investors must adapt. With so many aspects of economics and business being different now, historical interactions between data and asset valuations often do not work the same anymore.

What once may have been a very valuable data point to use in analyzing asset values may not work so well today. One of the common reasons this occurs is that the components in the data set may have changed. For example, you can discuss how high the current average price/earnings ratio for stocks in an index are com-

DOI 10.1515/9781547400751-001

pared to historical averages. However, today the largest stocks in the index are likely to be very different companies in very different types of businesses than they were ten years ago. How valuable is it to compare the historical average ratios versus the current ones if the underlying companies are so different? The second common reason a data point may become less valuable for your investment decision process is that interactions have changed. The music industry is a good example; in the late 1980s through the 1990s you could track a relationship between the sale of music CDs and the revenue for companies that produced and sold recorded music. By the mid-2000s services like Apple's iTunes had disrupted this correlation and using the number of digital music downloads was a more important data point relative to industry revenue. More recently streaming services have changed the paradigm for downloaded music sales. Tracking sales of CDs or even downloaded music is not as useful in understanding the business today. Relationships between different data points are not constant; the introduction of new technologies is causing relationships to change more frequently. You can not ignore the old data. It still has value and markets still react to it, but you must adjust to how you use it and find other tools to use as well.

It is not just technology but also social change that is transforming investment economics. Some of this social change is due to the data driven era. People are communicating differently and using different types of entertainment. Demographics are also driving social change. There is a large population bubble in the United States and some other developed countries, referred to as millennials. This demographic will be transforming the economy and public policy over time. Many millennials were just getting ready to enter the work force when the great recession hit, and that experience may influence how they invest. Many of them are drawn to different employment structures and have consumption patterns that vary from prior generations. All of this will shift the value of old data and theories and will influence asset valuations in the economy.

The economy is made of people and their individual choices, technology, education and societal developments change how those choices are made over time. However, there is always an effort by investment decision makers to quantify and formulize the aggregate data of these individual choices as if they are mathematical constants. The use of averages, regression, and correlation seem to be the most popular ways to formulize data. Most often this is done with time series which are driven by old data that comes from time periods that may not be applicable to the current situation. The overuse of these techniques without the application of logic can be significantly misleading.

With economic change happening at a much faster pace using more market-based data can often help to give a better picture of the current environment, market prices change much more often and have greater fluctuations than economic data. Market data sends critical signals as to how demand and valuations may be moving. When there is so much change afoot utilizing market data, and more heavily weighting more recent information, can help give a much better sense of the current and future outlook for valuations than over emphasizing out of date historical analysis.

It is easy to get lost in all the data. Just because some data is widely used doesn't mean it is a good signal. It might just be noise. It is good to have confidence about what is and is not a good signal. However, even if you think a data point is just noise and has no bearing on your investments, if people are talking about it, it matters and can move market prices. If markets are reacting to some data that you believe is now useless in the modern economy, it may create an opportunity to either buy or sell. The media and markets often react to new data at least temporarily, but also often have the attention span of a cat in a yarn factory and quickly move on to the next data point.

While one theme is clearly that technological advancements are changing the value of using historical economic and market data to make decisions, a second theme is that these developments are also altering how long-term economic trends and cycles are acting. People are constantly trying to apply the laws of natural science to economics—it often does not work. In the natural sciences there are highly predictable cycles; like how sound waves move and the timing of the sun rising and setting A cycle is supposed to be a series of events that gets repeated in the same order. People try to apply cycles to economics all the time. However, this does not always work; because the patterns and the context in the economy are not always the same as in the past, there is always a significant difference. For example, in the United States some recessions have lasted six months and some eighteen months, these are meaningful differences and not that predictable. It is not that boom and bust cycles do not sometimes occur in economics, but each one has its own nuances and differences and too often people try to squeeze and manhandle data to fit into a specific definition of a cycle that they have seen before and not factor in what might be different now. With everything from data to capital moving so much faster, cycles may start to look very different than in the past.

While cycles are usually thought of as somewhat circular, trends tend to be linear. A trend occurs when something is developing in a specific direction. Major economic driven investment themes are usually best to think of as trends. This is when, over a reasonably long period of time, selected data moves in the same general direction and impacts asset valuations. Over time some factors driving the trend are likely to change, and eventually trends end, but they often last longer than some people realize, and the current technology driven trend looks like it has some significant way to go. During any long-term trend there are likely to be some bumps and dips in the trend line. These shifts could be viewed by some people as cycles, but if you are a long-term investor do not lose sight of the trend when these bumps occur, they can create opportunity. The increasing velocity of economic change and financial flexibility should make these dips in the economy last for much shorter time periods than in the past and the declines in economic activity may be less extreme. If these economic dips are shallower and of shorter duration, they will matter less.

Long-term trends account for the bulk of the time periods in which you will be investing, as opposed to periods of big bubbles and bursts that diverge from trend. Bubbles and bursts do not occur that often, and it is better to prudently invest along trends you believe in than constantly be trying to call the next great crisis or rebound while missing a current trend. To get a sense of some trends over time we can look at the economy of the United States. In the United States there have been eleven post-war recessions through 2017[i] with 130 months of contraction and 722 of expansion. The odds have been with you if you focused on the expansionary trends for 722 months rather than trying to call the eleven recessions. Trends and cycles can be tricky things to define and predict in real life. Figure 1.1 shows interest rates since 1981 in the United States using the five-year Treasury bond as a benchmark. This chart shows a major trend of declining interest rates. You can also see that there are certainly some periods where money could be made by going against the trend and positioning for rising rates, and some of these could be called cycles, but the long-term trend is pretty clear and if your investment thesis was for declining rates and you stuck with it long term you would have done very well. Lots of money can be made in booms and busts, and the potential for these to occur should not be ignored, but the bulk of time economies are following a much less cyclical pattern and following a more linear trend.

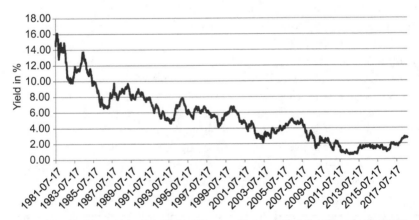

Source: Board of Governors of the Federal Reserve System (US), 5-Year Treasury Constant Maturity Rate [WGS5YR], retrieved from FRED, Federal Reserve Bank of St. Louis; https://fred.stlouisfed.org/series/WGS5YR, September 2018.

Figure 1.1: Yield on the Five-Year U.S. Treasury Note—Constant Maturity

Macroeconomic and Microeconomic Trends

Various parts of the economy can have their own trends and cycles that differ from aggregate economic data. Economics is typically divided into macroeconomics and microeconomics, even though the two are incredibly intertwined. Macro examines the broad economy, micro focuses on decisions by individual agents in the economy such as people and businesses. In investment economics, perhaps there should be a separate level of economic analysis, medi-economics (medi being Latin for middle). This field would include the studies of how macro and micro decisions influence subsectors of the economy such as an industry or a region. This medi arena currently seems to fall into discussions on both macro and microeconomics, but it really has its own unique dynamics. While the broad economy can be going in one direction at the medi levels there can be very different trends and this divergence is likely to be more common during this current era. Technology is transforming different industries and regions in varied ways, so sector and regional analysis is critical. Decisions at the medi-economics level are what drive key rotations in investments and decisions on how to weight different factors in a portfolio, such as the decision within an investment portfolio to overweight stocks of software companies while reducing exposure to the stocks of microchip manufacturers. With industry disruption so prevalent understanding the changes happening at the medi-level and making the right choices can be as valuable as the decision at the macro and micro level.

The changes wrought by this digital era should change how you think about investing at all levels of the economy. Technology innovation is leading to greater flexibility in corporate structures and capital movements as well as greater operational efficiencies. This should keep the overall long-term macroeconomic trends in most developed economies on a positive trend for a significant period of time. Historically, we may look back and see that we are currently in the very early stages of this technologically driven era of growth. The biggest risk to this trend would appear to be poor decisions by government entities that could stifle or distort the potential benefits accruing to the economy from innovation.

Technology is having a very different transformative effect at the medi and microlevels. It is changing the equation for many aspects of business, such as, barriers to entry, the ability to attract capital and corporate structures. This is going to continue causing significant disruption and swings in asset valuations at the regional, industry and corporate levels of the economy. People will need to reevaluate historical data and relationships at the medi and micro levels. While the general economy should perform well, at these other levels we are likely to see a meaningful number of recessions that stay contained in an industry or regional pocket. These pocket recessions are often likely to get nasty and cause significant divergence in asset valuations, but, the impact should generally stay within the pockets and not lead to larger more troublesome economic malfunctions. This will mean that sector rotations and individual investment decisions matter more in this era.

Using Data Wisely

Understanding the data you are using to make decisions and how it fits into the current world should lead to better investment results. It does not mean things need to be complex; as a matter of fact, simpler is often better. In the era of big data with the capacity to run enormous rapid calculations it is easy to be persuaded to use more data when a smaller series of data might work fine. With the value of data changing rapidly you need to constantly monitor the relevance and the interactions of each data point you are using. More data does not always create a more robust answer and using too many different data series can create problems as it increases the probability of dirtying up your conclusions with information that has become irrelevant as the economy has moved on. A quote sometimes attributed to Albert Einstein sums it up as, "Keep everything as simple as possible, but not one bit simpler."[ii]

There are some major biases to guard against when using any data, and particularly when more market based data is used. These include anchoring, confirmation and recency biases. Anchoring occurs when you base too much of a decision on one initial or older piece of data and disregard other signals in favor of your initial data point. Confirmation bias happens when you are too wed to your current position and any new data is manipulated to rationalize your current investment holdings. Both are dangerous in an environment of constant innovation. Recency bias also needs to be guarded against. This can happen as you try to be more reactive to market data and place too much emphasis on the most recent data point, often assuming that this one data point is a predictor of a massive new trend, when it could just be an anomaly. Rapid innovation may be the only constant in the current economy, in such an environment it is vital to look at all data, and the conclusions derived from it, with a very cynical eye. Questioning the consensus views and the data used to reach those views is a good thing, it does not always mean consensus is wrong, but be sure to poke it. Just because certain data points usually interact a certain way does not mean that they always have to act that way. This book is not supposed to provide all the answers, but should expand the angles from which you examine data used to make investment decisions. A good quote to keep in mind as you examine any data in this period of evolution is attributed to the nineteenth century writer Oscar Wilde, "To believe is very dull. To doubt is intensely engrossing."[iii]

---

i Energy Information Agency, Crude oil production, www.eia.gov, September 2018.
ii quoteinvestigator.com/2011/05/13/einstein-simple/ This references a 1962 letter from *The Publisher in Time Magazine* that references the Einstein statement.
iii Winokur, J. (1992). *The Portable Curmudgeon*. Plume.

Chapter 2
An Approach to Economics—Bottoms Up

Economics is sometimes described as a social science that focuses on decisions about the allocation of limited resources. This definition is broad and acknowledges that economics may not always only involve commercial decisions. It could study the decision process of someone with a limited amount of time that has to allocate between going to a party or to the gym. This book takes the approach that finance and the study of investments are subsets of economics. Finance focuses on investments, assets, liabilities, uncertainty and risk over time and is sometimes defined as the science of managing money and funding activities.

The economic philosophy that influences this book is that all economics starts with the choices that individuals make.[i] Individuals have different needs and wants, and this leads to different priorities. The hierarchy of needs will change from person to person and will even change for the same individual over time. These priorities may not always be purely driven by financial considerations. It is easy to forget about nonfinancial factors when considering economic and investment problems, but they often play a major role in the outcome of investments. This is especially important in the face of the large millennial population boom and changing demographics, which may lead to a large portion of the population having very different priorities than prior generations, this will cause them to value assets differently.

Many theories assume that all decisions are made on sound economic principles to maximize profits and that everyone will act as an "economic man." This is clearly not true. There is a myriad of motivations for people's actions. Individuals have limited resources and they apply these resources to meet their needs and wants where they can get the most satisfaction for them or in other words where they get the best "utility." An individual's decisions are based on the amount of utility they think they will get out of each decision. However, that utility is not always based on making more money. Simply put people are looking for the most "bang for their buck" but each person may define their "bang" differently. We have all seen instances where the pursuit of a nonfinancial goal leads to decisions that may not be considered the most financially sound. Think of some of the financial decisions that are made in pursuit of a physical relationship. These decisions may not maximize a person's financial situation, given what they might spend on their hair, clothes, and dinner. However, it is clearly an economic decision because they are choosing to apply a limited resource (time and money) toward a goal that they believe they will get the most utility out of at that time (even if that utility might be fleeting).

DOI 10.1515/9781547400751-002

Macroeconomic data is just an amalgamation of people's decisions. Gathering of large amounts of economic data is destined to have flaws in the process and most macroeconomic data is flawed in some ways, if a large group of people are pursuing careers or starting businesses that are not included in the traditional counting methodologies, the economic numbers will get even more distorted from reality than usual. This is more likely to happen when an economy is seeing constant innovation. There are large swaths of the economy that get lost in these big numbers and are not properly represented in the averages. Sometimes the individuals or companies that are not acting in line with the averages are the more exciting part of the economy. Think about a sports analogy, in the 2016–17 Spanish soccer league on the championship team, Real Madrid, among goal scorers the average was six goals for the season. However, Cristiano Ronaldo scored 25.[ii] His goal total was not near the average and he certainly brought a bit more excitement to the team than the average player, but the "average" figure did not capture this.

The concept of marginal utility is important in understanding demand and asset prices. Marginal utility is based on the changes in the benefit that a person gets from getting more units of an item. For example, the "utility," or benefit, that someone gets from buying the first three tires for a car may be less than what they get for the fourth tire, the difference between the value of tire three and tire four is the marginal utility. Similarly, their marginal utility for the first four tires for their car is probably much greater than for the sixth tire. Analysis of marginal utility can be applied to business decisions such as product pricing or a decision of where to reinvest in a business. This is what drives an amusement park to offer lower prices during slack seasons and this is also the tool that a company might use to decide if it could make more money by adding another manufacturing shift or hiring more sales people.

Institutions and structure are critical to an economy. The financial and legal institutions that are in place and through which people must make their economic decisions (e.g., stock markets, legal systems) can make a big difference in how well an economy operates and how well it can adapt to changes. From an investment point of view, the laws and institutions that are in place to control markets must have a high level of consistency, clarity and fairness. Rules-based economies help people to have greater confidence, which creates less uncertainty, and usually attracts diverse streams of capital. To operate properly, markets need rules of law and fairness. The institutions that control markets are so important because markets are a critical part of any economy. Markets are any place where transactions occur. Information from markets can help tell you what the value of your home is or can tell a distributor which products are in demand. Markets are the way individuals express what they want and do not want. This does not mean that markets are always right about asset values over time, but when a transaction happens, and an item is bought and sold, that price is the value of the item at that moment, even if the value changes a second later. The price where something transacts in the market is a signal given at a precise price point in time.

Security market systems provide some of the most important sources of data, they are the purest and most real time data points you can use to make investment decisions. Markets often react first and lead the economy, but markets also give off lots of noise and false signals. Markets are not always right about the ultimate value of assets, but they can not be ignored. Many securities markets respond to corporate news and this data is usually released more rapidly than economic news. Corporate news releases are valuable data to monitor. For example, if during one month half of the companies that report earnings state that they are not hiring anyone for the foreseeable future, markets can react and they do not need to wait for the employment numbers to come out. Monitoring corporate data can give you great insight into the broader economy, especially if you group some of the individual corporate data into segments and track trends.

The markets give important signals about trends in items like valuations and interest rates. However, the value of this data can change over time or be distorted. For example, there are fewer public companies now than in many prior periods; the impact of stock market signals, therefore, may be based on much narrower information than in the past. Additionally, index driven buying and momentum driven algorithmic trading may increasingly be distorting valuations of public stocks relative to the value that an actual buyer of a company might be willing to pay.

Markets are important because value is subjective. No matter what asset you are looking at, if it is a guitar, real estate or a stock, the valuation is not based on what it cost to make or where the seller wants to sell it. The valuation of an asset is what someone is willing to pay for the asset. A person telling you what an item cost to make should not make you want to pay more. When it comes to valuations on things like stocks and bonds, many people use similar methodologies to determine what they will pay, but their assumptions and the nuances in their methods will cause differentiation in the final price each person will want to pay. No set of data will always work because the economy is dynamic not static. There is no single best economic and investment theory that can be applied universally and have it always work. Economic data that might drive investment decisions in one place or time, does not necessarily work in other places or times. This means that economic theories that work well for a small agrarian society do not necessarily work well for a modern industrialized economy. Similarly, the data points that are correlated with increased asset valuations in an industrialized economy do not necessarily translate well if that economy transitions into one that is service and technology-oriented.

No economic or business concept is timeless or ubiquitous. A key economic concept is that there is constant creation and destruction in healthy economies. There are an endless number of examples of how great successful ideas eventually run their course. The big box retailer Toys 'R' Us was once an innovative disruptive force in retailing and the toy industry. Charles P. Lazarus was the pioneer in retailing that founded Toys 'R' Us. He had come back home from being a cryptographer in World War II and saw service men coming home and marrying. He assumed this trend would lead to a baby boom and an increase in demand for baby furniture quickly opening a store specializing in it. He soon realized parents usually bought only one set of baby furniture but many toys. In 1957 he opened the first Toys 'R' Us store in Rockville, Maryland. It was a pioneering firm offering a huge number of products and as it expanded it began to crush the local toy stores. It was an innovator in the use of computer inventory tracking and pricing systems. Video games and the sale of toys on the internet rapidly changed the dynamics in the industry. After several tough years and a buyout, the price at which Toys 'R' Us debt was trading at in the market signaled they were in trouble and many years after Mr. Lazarus had left the company, it filed for bankruptcy in 2017. In March of 2018 reorganization seemed unlikely and a liquidation of the entire company was being proposed, Mr. Lazarus passed away the same week.[iii,iv]

These types of failures due to industry transformations are lessons and at some firms they are not ignored. Mark Shenkman, a pioneer in the leveraged finance market and founder and chief executive officer of Shenkman Capital, holds a morning meeting each day with his investment team. At these meetings, Mr. Shenkman shares his views and opinions on the credit markets, interest rates, and the economy, and his comments are frequently peppered with history lessons. Shortly after Mr. Lazarus passed away, Mr. Shenkman related, how as a young analyst at an equity firm in Boston, he was impressed with Toys 'R' Us innovative marketing. He also commented that Mr. Lazarus was a driving force in the retailing industry. However, Mr. Shenkman ended his remarks by pointing out that no concept or business model can prevail forever, because every idea or business must adapt, change, or die.

No investment or economic model works forever. The economy is ultimately driven by individuals. Individuals do not act like mathematical formulas, they change. All economic data starts from the bottom up, and the data may change each time a decision is made.

i Many authors have written on this topic, marginal utility and subjective value that are all mentioned in this chapter, but these concepts as expressed here are often most associated with Carl Menger and Ludwig Von Mises who are associated with the Austrian School of Economics.
ii Foxsports.com/soccer/real-madrid-team-stats
iii Corkery, M. (2018, March 22), Charles P. Lazarus, Toys 'R' Us Founder, Dies at 94. *The New York Times*. Retrieved from NYTimes.com
iv Silverman, E. (2018, March 22), Charles Lazarus, who turned Washington Bike Business into Toys 'R' Us, Dies at 94. *The Washington Post*. Retrieved from Washingtonpost.com

Part 2: **Disruption, Culture, and Indexes**

Chapter 3
Disruptors or Just Progress

Disruption is part of life; little to no innovation or economic progress happens without it. In this century much of the economic innovation has come from digitally driven computing technology. This has been utilized to make new products and revolutionize various processes and services.

It is difficult to predict and track all of the various disruptions that have been occurring in the economy in recent decades. Most of these developments help make the overall economy more efficient and more flexible. This should allow for longer periods of expansion. However, it will also lead to more distress and distortions within selected regions, industries, and corporations.

One of the reasons for the dramatic impact from these innovations and why they are having a different effect at the macro, medi,[i] and microlevels of the economy is because of how quickly they are being adopted compared to the past. Electricity took thirty-five years to reach 10% of the United States population, the telephone took twenty-five years, but it took computer tablets just five years to reach the same level. The cell phone took only five years to reach 50% of households.[ii] This rapid adoption creates constant gains in economic efficiency while potentially enhancing job creation and consumption for the macroeconomy. However, it also represents rapid and sudden competition to incumbent businesses giving them little time to react.

One of the problems with economic data is that it is always from the past. The faster changes happen in the economy, the more rapidly historical data depreciates in value as an analytical tool. Therefore, understanding where and what kind of disruption is occurring, what the multiple layers of potential consequences are, and how current conditions differ from the past are all necessary if you use any kind of economic data to make investment decisions.

In the 2010s every time there is an innovative change to a business it is referred to as a "disruptor." Disruption has been around a long time. Pants apparently came on the scene about 1000 to 1300 B.C. in China. It was a major change for horseback riders. Pants improved riders' comfort and their stamina to stay on horseback.[iii] While you can not prove it, it is probably safe to assume that the media at the time had stories about how the pant innovation would wear down horses and create a horse shortage, and would reduce the need for riders and give pants-wearers an unfair advantage over other riders. This did not even begin to touch on what pants might do to the incumbent loincloth manufacturing industry. Clearly, disruption has been around for some time and innovation has economic ramifications. Also note that there is no evidence that the inventor of

DOI 10.1515/9781547400751-003

pants created a great company based on the invention of pants. This is a good reminder that sometimes a good innovative idea survives even if the companies that created them do not.

Innovation that seems ground breaking at first may often evolve into being common place. However, sometimes an invention that seems relatively mundane can shake the global economy up as much as a break through like the smart-phone. Sometimes the ideas even come from Newark, New Jersey.

Malcolm McLean was not tech savvy; he did not even like to do business over the phone. However, Mr. McLean developed one of the most impactful disruptors in the world as he sat in a truck waiting to load cargo onto a boat. He watched as each item was unpacked from the trucks, reloaded on the boat, and then repacked. He came up with the idea to put all the goods into one container, load the container on to the boat, and then unload the container at its destination. If planned right the container could be taken right off the boat and put onto a truck for delivery to its destination. This innovation was the intermodal transport container. From this innovation Mr. McLean grew his company Sea-Land into a transportation logistics giant. His first container shipment went out in 1956 from Port Newark in New Jersey. Forty years later it was estimated that 90% of world trade moved by container.[iv] This massively disrupted the role of the longshoremen that loaded and unloaded ships but reduced shipping time and costs and was a major step in the development of global supply chains. The improvements and use of technology in logistics have been a huge part in making economies more flexible. This was a major innovation, it could be argued that it was as simple as deciding to put things in a box.

Relatively simple developments in efficiency and process can vastly impact economies, especially if they are in segments that are very far reaching and touch all aspects of people's lives. Logistics is one of those subtle industries and so is energy. They are both so ubiquitous it is easy to not think about them. Recent technological innovations in the oil and gas industry has reshaped global supply

The evolution of fracking has appeared to change the global dynamics in energy more than any development in sustainable energy so far. Fracking is not a slick, clean, or green business, it has almost nothing to do with Silicon Valley but it has been a disruptor. Large scale use of fracking is a relatively new way of extracting oil and gas from subterranean deposits. It uses modern technology that applies high pressure to force water, sand, and other chemicals into underground rock formations to open fissures (or "fractures") to gain access to more oil and gas in shale structures. While the process can be controversial, it has changed the energy business. From 2008 to 2018 it is estimated that shale oil production went from 450,000 barrels of oil a day to 5 million.[v] These wells can be used to increase the rate of extraction of oil and gas more quickly than traditional drilling. This extraction from shale structures lends itself to a more "manufacturing lite" process that is able to be toggled "on and off" more easily than conventional wells, making it more responsive to market prices for oil and gas. This technology has changed the balance of power in global oil supply and impacted prices for energy around the world. In addition, the technology is not standing still, there have been continual improvements in drilling wells and extraction. It is not as cool looking as a new iPhone, but it has been a global disruptor of epic proportion.

The increased United States oil and gas production has also changed several dynamics in economic data. It makes extrapolation of historical oil imports and exports somewhat meaningless. It means inflation models for the United States that may have been heavily dependent on the price of oil shipped from the Middle East or the North Sea now must factor in the price of domestic oil. It can impact the cost of shipping and employment.

Anytime there are disruptions there are also typically derivative "disruptions." Amazon disrupted the retail environment, which hurt brick and mortar retails stores like Toys 'R' Us. A derivative disruption occurred in the real estate market because values for shopping malls suffered as stores struggled to compete with the internet. This could then put pressure on some banks with loans to shopping mall owners. On the flip side, the internet retailers have increased the demand for delivery services and packaging. Fracking has spurred demand for new equipment manufacturing, however, if it keeps oil and gas prices down it could hurt the development of alternative energy sources. To try to invest properly in disruption you must look at multiple layers of analysis.

Great ideas can be very disruptive but they do not always create great businesses. While the idea may live on, the business may fail. When thinking about disruption it can be helpful to try to categorize the type of innovation you are looking at, the opportunities and challenges. Figure 3.1 shows a simple way of laying out some of these issues. Do not just be a believer, be a cynic too.

Product Focus			
Consumer	Business	Government	

Type of Innovation			
Process	Product		
Entirely New	Enhancement	Replacement	

Competitive Edge			
Price	Quality		

Opportunity Considerations			
Target market size (TAM)[vi]	Scalable beyond target	Profitability horizon	Good idea or good business

Internal Challenges			
Capital	Management	Expertise	Distribution

External Challenges			
Incumbent bites back	Barriers to entry	Government suppression	

Derivative Opportunities			
Who else benefits	Who else gets hurt		

Figure 3.1: Sample Grid of Disruptor Considerations

The bottom box in the figure can often be the most impactful on your investment decisions; the derivative impact of true innovation is very far reaching. In the great book *Economics in One Lesson* by Henry Hazlitt, the author outlines that economics consists of understanding not just the immediate but the long-term impact of economic policy and then tracing the impact of it not just on one group but on all.[vii] Mr. Hazlitt's emphasis was on public policy, however, the same concept can, and should, be applied to economic developments in the private sector. This is especially true when there is disruption afoot.

Following the multiple trails of what a truly disruptive innovation will do, and keeping in mind how it changes historical data may lead you to successful shifts in investment strategy.

i Medi is Latin for middle.

ii McGrath, R.G. (2013, November 25), The Pace of Technology Adoption is Speeding Up. *Harvard Business Review*. Retrieved from HBR.org

iii Chayka, K. (2014, June 3), These Are the World's Oldest Pants. *Time Magazine*. Retrieved from Time.com.

iv Pearson, R. (2001, May 21), Malcolm McLean Dies. *Washington Post*. Retrieved from WashingtonPost.com

v Owyang, M.T., and Shell, H. (2018, May), The Rise of Shale Oil, *Federal Reserve Bank of St. Louis on the Economy*.

vi Total Addressable Market is an overly quirky term for business opportunity.

vii Hazlitt, H. (1988, December 14), *Economics in One Lesson: The Shortest and Surest Way to Understand Basic Economics*. Crown Business.

Chapter 4
Cultural Changes Make Economics Change

Despite the math that people throw at economics, it is still a social science. That means that how people decide to act influences results. Cultural changes can disrupt the value of historical economic data just like technological changes can. Many times, investors focus too much on the financial and business data and then get blindsided by cultural change.

Cultural changes can come from shifts in demographic, events that can impact social consciousness, evolution in thought, or changes in education and the evolution of institutions. Events like the opium wars in China during the nineteenth century, the World Wars, the legalization of birth control, and the terrorist attacks in the United States on September 11, 2001, have all caused social change that ended up impacting economic behavior and relationships. For example, Mr. Lazarus, the Toys 'R' Us founder, rightfully predicted an increase in household formation and the baby boom after World War II. This was a social change that impacted the economy, skewed real estate values and purchasing data for decades.

In the United States and many developed countries there has been a population bubble referred to as millennials[i] made up of people born after 1980, and this age group is influencing and changing the economy. In the United States estimates put this generation at about 72–73 million people. They have had different experiences than other generations, which will impact their economic activity. They have more likely been raised in a divorced family and grew up in an all-digital era. They spend more on dining out and more on mobile phone service than other generations. Many surveys show they prefer to spend money on experiences rather than things (e.g. thus the increased level of spending on dining out). A significant number of millennials were also just starting to invest and get there working life underway as the great recession hit, which may influence how they invest in stocks and bonds or think about real estate. They also tend to have different political views than other age groups, which may influence policy over time. They appear to have views about work that differ from earlier generations, some expect more structure and nurturing as many have grown up in an era of coaches, tutors, and extra help (for people who could afford it); some are happy to switch jobs so they can learn more. They have also seen the incredible success and growth of companies like Google, Apple, and Amazon that did not exist a few decades ago that may inspire more entrepreneurship.

The millennial population bubble is already changing economic data and will likely lead to changes in how various economic factors interact. Overtime we

DOI 10.1515/9781547400751-004

may see that the high level of job changing limits wage growth or spending on out of home dining becomes a meaningfully larger portion of household expenditures; this may be accelerating a trend of restaurants replacing stores in America's shopping malls.

New trends are often most prevalent in younger people; this can often be seen in changes in music, or fashion, the switch from board games to video games or even trends in which sports are popular. Sometimes the shift permeates society and moves beyond just younger people, such as the demise of newspaper want-ads and the move from printed to online news. However, young people are, well, young. Sometimes what may look like a long-term trend among younger people disappears as a generation gets older and takes on more responsibility and outgrows the latest fad. There are a fair number of octogenarians that text, but not many using hula-hoops.

Immigration and immigration policies can have many obvious impacts on an economy and society as well. Countries that are attractive to immigrants and have a successful history of immigration have a unique opportunity to shift and reverse demographic trends in their country. If a population within a country is aging rapidly and the percentage of working age is too low, immigration can change that much more quickly than the amount of time it takes to make a baby and have it grow into adulthood.

Immigration also adds to the diversity of a country, which can lead to more creative thought and impacts the country culturally and economically. For example, a few years back in the United States salsa sales surpassed ketchup sales as Americans' tastes expanded thanks to immigration.[ii]

The cultural changes from immigration can impact and skew economic data. According to one study from 2010 to 2015 immigration from Asia, including the Indian subcontinent increased into the United States by 72% and these ethnic groups accounted for approximately 20 million people by 2015.[iii] For many people from these cultures the most important holidays do not necessarily fall into the fiscal fourth quarter around Christmas but are focused around Lunar New Year (Chinese New Year) and Diwali (Hindu festival of lights). Spending for gifts and family gatherings increase around these holidays for people that celebrate them. As this population has grown they are likely influencing seasonal spending patterns. Seasonal adjustments in economic data may lag and be less accurate over time, and the subtle distortions in the data may increase, thus making the data further from being an accurate depiction of the real world.

Major events effect how a culture acts and can impact data. The terrorist attacks on the United States in 2001 caused dramatic changes in U.S. government spending habits; it impacted the travel industry and shifted resources to security measures from other projects in the public and private sector. The great recession also appears to have left some economic scarring. Some studies have shown there were declines in the fertility rate and household formation, whether these are long-term behavioral changes or simply short-term deferrals due to economic setbacks will take time to see.

Cultural changes can redirect trends and make extrapolation from old data meaningless. However, not all cultural trends necessarily have wide-reaching economic impact. For example, it used to be commonplace if a person met a celebrity to ask them for an autograph, and many people had autograph collections. Nowadays the request is more likely to be for a selfie photo. This is a technological driven cultural change and may be long lasting. However, it probably does not have far reaching economic impact outside of the autograph collecting market. On the other end of the spectrum, the internet has changed the world in obvious and subtle ways. It has given people immediate access to information on items like celebrity gossip from places like the *National Enquirer* website, to information on health and education that can help individuals better themselves and allow an economy's human resources to improve and transform more fluidly.

Cultural shifts in the economy can be an invaluable lead to investment ideas, if you can catch the distortion caused by cultural changes early. They can come from population changes, life changing events, technology, or the arts. However, there are many false starts in this arena. The key is to get a sense that they appeal to a broad diverse range of the population and that these trends are sustainable.

———

i Fyr, R. (2018, March 1), Millennials projected to overtake Baby Boomers as America's largest generation. *Fact Tank News in Numbers*. Pew Research Center Retrieved from www.pewresearch. org/fact-tank/2018/03/01/millennials-overtake-baby-boomers/
ii O'Neill, M. (1992, March 11), New Mainstream: Hotdogs, Apple Pie and Salsa. *New York Times*. Retrieved from Nytimes.com
iii Lopez, G., Ruiz, N.G., and Patten, E. (2017, September), Facts about Asian Americans, a Diverse and Growing Population. *Fact Tank News in Numbers*. Pew Research Center. Retrieved from www.pewresearch.org/fact-tank/2017/09/08/key-facts-about-asian-americans/

Chapter 5
Goodhart's "Underappreciated" Law and Benchmarking

It is impressive when you have a law named after you, even if it is a somewhat obscure law. If you study finance you may not have come across Goodhart's Law. However, it is increasingly relevant as computers help to create more indexes, investors benchmark their investments off the indexes, and this distorts market data and corporate valuations. Charles Goodhart is a British professor of economics at the London School of Economics. He has done extensive and distinguished work on regulation, banking and financial systems. He has served governments and published textbooks on monetary economics.

He wrote a paper in 1975, which among other things, discussed the consequences of monetary management. From that paper emerged what is known as Goodhart's Law. The quote from which the law is derived is, "Any observed statistical regularity will tend to collapse once pressure is placed upon it for control purposes."[i] There are numerous adaptations of his statement. For example, one summation states, once a social or economic measure is turned into a target for policy, it will lose the features that drove you to choose that target in the first place, as people try to anticipate that policy. Another interpretation is, when a measurement becomes a target it ceases to be a good measure.[ii]

One of the most famous stories used to explain Goodhart's Law is believed to be a bit of a fable that involves the nail industry in Soviet Russia. The central planners wanted to measure the productivity of the factories so they told the managers they will be measured by how many nails they make in a given year. To meet its goal a factory made the smallest nails possible to make the most nails out of each iron delivery. The nails were so small they were unusable and there was a great nail shortage in the Soviet Union. The next year the central planners tried to correct their mistake and set a goal that the nail factories would be measured by the weight of the nails they produce. The same nail factory then proceeded to order as much iron as it could get and produced one giant nail. The story does not tell what happened to the factory manager. This is a good illustration of how peoples' actions to achieve a target distort the value of the target. This is also a pretty good story of why central planning fails.

Goodhart's Law was derived with a focus on the impact of regulation, but it can be rephrased and reworked for many other things. For example, there are numerous mapping programs now that show drivers how to beat traffic back-ups, however, if too many people use the same program it can then create a traffic

DOI 10.1515/9781547400751-005

back-up on the alternative route. Near the George Washington Bridge that connects New Jersey to New York City, this became such a problem and drove so much traffic to one town that the mayor of the town tried to ban cars from out of town from cutting through their neighborhood streets.[iii]

As there is more focus on measurable metrics for business and investments, Goodhart's Law has become increasingly important in the investment world. On a trading desk the law might be simplified to the phrase, "there isn't any value in a crowded trade."

Market and valuation distortions happen when everyone is using the same benchmarks to measure investment success. Computing power and data storage have helped to create a proliferation of indexes and investment performance measurements. This has led to more demand from investors that money managers perform within a band relative to a benchmark (i.e., limiting tracking error to the benchmark).

Benchmarking has become a bit of an obsession. Trillions of dollars track benchmark indexes.[iv] The desire to copy these benchmark indexes has driven a whole industry of passive investing. This strategy involves investment managers simply trying to mimic the performance of an index. The goal is to do no better or worse than this index, no best ideas, and no specialized focus to meet the ultimate investors' specific goals. Many of these passive investments are being made through exchange traded funds (ETFs).

One of the problems with benchmarking is that indexes often base their investment weighting on the market capitalization of the company. Therefore, stocks with bigger market capitalizations get a bigger portion of any new money that comes into the fund. This can create more momentum in the stock of the large capitalization companies, thus increasing their weighting in the indexed funds. Paul Woolley of the London School of Economics has done several studies in this area and is quoted as saying "When used as a benchmark for active management, market cap indices carry perverse incentive that impair fund returns, distort prices...."[v]

The process of chasing benchmarks can create risks in a portfolio. The benchmark chaser can end up running after investments where capital flows have gone, such as momentum stocks. These investments are made without analyzing or factoring in the potential cash flow of an investment or its value. Momentum investing can have success but it also has risks.

When market distortions happen, speculators and arbitrageurs weigh in to the market to exploit miss-pricings and opportunities caused by poorly structured investments. Assume that high risk investors see a stock that is in an index that has a high likelihood of having a positive near-term event; they may buy the stock, even though its long-term prospects may not be that good. Their purchases will likely push the price up. They know that this will make it a larger part of the index. Passive investors and benchmark huggers will have to buy that stock to stay balanced relative to the index. This passive buying will create a floor price for the risk investors and a potential exit after the news occurs. The passive investors may not realize they have just increased the risk in their portfolios.

As higher volatility stocks gain upward momentum benchmarking creates more of an upward bias in these higher volatility stocks (the same obviously can happen in bond markets, too). Mr. Woolley and Dimitri Vayanos have published models and studies[vi] that show that benchmarking distorts prices of stocks. If a positive shock occurs for a company and the stock rises based on the merit of the news, it can get a second boost when benchmark driven funds realize they are underweighting the stock and their buying adds to the momentum.

This benchmarking not only distorts prices but long term can create misallocation of capital to companies that may be performing better in the stock market regardless of how they are performing operationally. This trend may cause the equity markets to stop functioning as a gauge of success or underlying value and just as a measure of the size of a company's market capitalization. The value of stocks now often moves not just on the inherent value of a company's cash flow generation power, but on whether the company's securities are included or excluded in an index.

Benchmark Inclusion and Risk of Manipulation

Benchmark indexes have become big business. This can be seen by how much acquisition activity has occurred involving index families. Three of the largest index companies have accounted for some of the consolidation as they bought competitors; Dow Jones, FTSE Russell, and MSCI.[vii] Some of the largest index families had been owned by banks and been viewed as relatively independent, but they have all recently been bought. These include the indexes of Citibank, Bank of America Merrill Lynch, and Barclays.

There is a large industry dedicated to promoting and increasing the use of benchmarks and indexes. This is a for profit industry. As an example, MSCI, is one of the leading companies in the space and one that is most purely focused on this part of the data industry. In 2017 it had revenue of about $1.3 billion, this was up about a 10% from the prior year. This revenue stream also benefits from the relatively "sticky" nature of their revenue as large institutional allocators incur a cost of switching indexes and having to rework their systems and there is an understandable desire for consistency.

There has been a reasonable body of academic work looking at whether inclusion of a security into an index leads to abnormal stock gains, regardless of any fundamental change.[viii] Most seem to show a meaningful increase in security prices from inclusion in an index.[ix] From a practical sense it appears that the inclusion/exclusion effect is real, there have even been publications that outline trading strategies around securities before and after index inclusion.[x]

Work done by Bloomberg has shown that when American Airlines was going to be added to the S&P 500 index, some traders bought the stock as soon as it was announced, four days before it was included in the index. The stock moved up by 11% prior to the actual inclusion date. The trading volume in the two minutes before the close of trading was more than the typical two-week volume for the stock.[xi] This legal advanced buying increased the cost for any late buying index funds, increasing the cost of the securities for their investors. While there appears to be no reported incidences, this type of data trail raises the potential for conflicts and abuse of the system.

Well run indexes have inclusion and exclusion rules and must be transparent. As the markets and the economy change the indexes revise their rules periodically. Indexes often socialize these potential index changes with their clients. While there does not appear to be evidence of it occurring, there is clearly the risk that investors try to buy or sell securities ahead of any index rules change and then try to influence index revision rules so that their investment benefits. The biggest financial investment institutions are likely the largest customers of the index companies and therefore could have more impact on them than smaller firms. The chief executive officer of FTSE Russell was quoted in 2015 in a *Financial Times* article by John Authers saying, "If we do a rule change, we have to consult with the institutions. The power is with them. We only make changes with their support. They do have the ability to choose between us and MSCI."[xii]

Using an index's return as a target for investment portfolios does not create the same problems as the Soviet nail factory but there are several risks if you chose a specific index as a "target." Indexes are not static, they change, and you need to stay abreast of the rules. Index's rules usually lead to changes in the make-up of the constituents over time. Indexes also can change their inclusion and exclusion rules periodically. Therefore, the targets that you had found attractive in each index may change. You need to carefully monitor the changes to an index, to make sure it is still a target you want to pursue as an investor.

Benchmarks have other idiosyncrasies that differ from trading real world portfolios. Benchmarks do not have transaction costs included in their returns. These costs occur when an investor trades the securities that are in the index. If other investors start to "game the system" and run in front of the benchmark inclusions and exclusion rules, as there is some evidence of, the costs of the investments can go up for the passive indexers and their respective benchmarks. Indexes also do not include any management or administrative fees that need to be incurred in a real-world investment. A strategy that just tries to copy or "hug" a benchmark can not outperform it meaningfully, especially after transaction costs and management fees.

Gains in computational power and access to digitized data coupled with the desire to develop better measurement of investment performance have led to an explosion in indexes and benchmark analysis. Understanding and analyzing investment performance is a necessity for asset allocators so that they can understand returns relative to risks and properly allocate capital. However, too much emphasis on benchmarks can lead to distortions and investors losing sight of what their real investment goals are.

Index creation has boomed so much during this century that in 2017 it was reported that there were more indexes than there were public stocks outstanding.[xiii] In this desire to measure things using, benchmarks, investor may get performance or risks that they do not want. If an investment firm is hired because the client thinks they have a great investment system, a focus on benchmarking can neuter that. Sometimes investors should step away from indexes and really decide what they want from their investment portfolio.

There is no perfect investment for everyone. People have different time horizons for their investments, different return goals, and different risk tolerances. This sounds simple, but it is important to remember when investing. Does the investor want the fastest growth and appreciation in value, regardless of risk, or do they want to preserve capital and generate a healthy stream of income on which to live? The goals of investors and institutions are extremely varied and just chasing an index may not be the best way to achieve these, often complex goals.

Market indexes are used to describe and analyze broad movements in security valuations. Performance of stock and bond indexes can sometimes be viewed as a barometer for the overall economy. The analysis of subsectors within an index can give insights into which industries and types of companies can attract new capital. Indexes can also be used to compare returns of one type of security market to another. The proliferation of investment strategies that look to copy index performance is changing the quality and meaning of the data within indexes. When new money comes into index hugging strategies it is typically now being allocated based on market capitalization, not any relative value criteria. This is distorting the value of current index data. These factors must be considered today in any analysis that uses current index and stock price information relative to historical data.

---

i Goodhart, C.A.E. (1975), *Problems of Monetary Management: The U.K. Experience. Papers in Monetary Economics Reserve Bank of Australia. I.*

ii Chrystal, K.A., and Mizen, P.D. (2001, November), Goodhart's Law: Its Origins, Meaning and Implications for Monetary Policy. Retrieved from Cyberlibris.typepad.com/blog/files/Goodharts_Law.pdf

iii Janoski, S. (2018, January 25), Leonia's Ban on Commuter Traffic Along Local Roads: Is it legal? *Northjersey.com*

iv Authers, J. (2015, August 16), Investing: The Index Factor. *Financial Times*. Retrieved from FT.com

v Ibid.

vi Vayanos, D., and Woolley P. (2017, December 20) Why Investors Should Be Weaned off Tight Tracking to Market Indices. *Financial Times*. Retrieved from FT.com

vii Authers, J. (2015 August 16). Op. cit.

viii Yen-Chang,Y. Hong, and H. Liskovich, I. (2103 October), Regression Discontinuity and the Price Effects of Stock Market Indexing. *NBER Digest*. Retrieved from www.nber.org

ix Elliot, W. Van Ness, B. Walker, and M. Warr, R. (2008 October 27), What Drives the S&P 500 Inclusion Effect; An Analytical Survey. *Financial Management*. Financial Management Association.

x Nakamura,Y. (2015 July 7), The Hugely Profitable, Totally Legal Way to Game the Stock Market. *Bloomberg News*.

xi Ibid.

xii Authers, J. (2015 August 16). Op. cit.

xiii *Bloomberg News* (2017, May 12), There are Now More Indexes than Stocks.

Part 3: **Math Moves—Remembering That
Everything Changes**

Chapter 6
Means Move—Analyze the Averages

Calculating an average is probably the most widely used statistical tool. You can look at average goals per game, grade point average, the average amount of time spent on a website. Averages pop up everywhere. There are several different types of averages that are appropriate for different types of situations, which are worth reviewing. It is also important to discuss how averages are misused. The simple fact that averages are dynamic and change often gets ignored. When there is more change, averages may become a less valuable reference point.

The most common types of calculations referred to as averages are the mode, the median, and the mean. The mode is the figure that appears most often in a data set; there can be more than one mode. The median is the figure in a data set that separates the upper half of the data set from the lower half. The mean is by far the most commonly used of these calculations. The mean is the sum of the numbers in a data set divided by the number of figures in the data set. When the word average is used in this book (and generally in conversation) it is assumed to be referring to the mean. Examples are shown in Figure 6.1.

The mode for this data set is 4	(2,3,4,4,4,4,5,5,10,11,12,12)	
The median for this data set is 4	(1,1,2,4,6,6,7)	
The mean for this data set is 4	(1,1,2,6,6,8)	(1+1+2+6+6+8)/6=4

Figure 6.1: Three Common Types of Averages

While the mean is the most common to use there are instances where the mode and the median can be more helpful. For example, if you want to find out the most common salary in a group of workers you would use the mode, as the foreman's salary might skew the mean. The median can be good when most numbers in the data set are clustered close together but there are one or two extreme outliers that really skew the mean.

Some other averages are quite common when running investment analysis. These include the geometric mean, a weighted average and a moving average.

Geometric means are good when each figure in the data set is dependent on the others. An example of this would be if you were tracking a company's revenue growth from one year to another. The geometric mean multiplies all of the numbers in the data set and then takes that product to the "n" root, "n" standing for the number of figures in the data set. This type of mean is often used to

DOI 10.1515/9781547400751-006

examine investment returns. Typically, when using a geometric mean all of the numbers in the data set need to be positive, but you can manage around this by adding one to each figure in the data set. If the data set included annual investment returns (0.2, 0.1, 0.2, -0.1, 0.1), you could add one to each data point (1.2, 1.1, 1.2, 0.9, 1.1) then take the product of these figures to the 1/5 power and subtract one to get the geometric mean (the other option is to just never have any negative returns).

Weighted averages are commonly used in indexes, portfolio, analysis and probability theory to develop expected values. Investors often use indexes that use weighted averages. For example, an index may track the stock prices of the 100 largest public companies. The index could weight each stock the same and calculate the average price of the index. Getting this figure at the end of the day on a percentage basis would show you how much the average stock in the index moved. However, it would not show you how the value of the overall index moved. A common way of showing you the move in the value of the index is to "weight" each stock in the index based on what the equity market capitalization is (equity market capitalization = (number of shares outstanding * stock price).

In mid-2017 on a market weighted basis just four companies accounted for 10.6% of the S&P 500 U.S. stock index; these top four accounted for more of the index than the bottom 200 companies in the index combined.[i] It is pretty easy to see how in this scenario the market weighted performance of the S&P 500 can look very different than the performance for the majority of the companies in the index. With the incredible proliferation of the use of indexes these types of distortions in indexes are important to understand. It is not a bad idea to occasionally look at an even weighted version of these indexes to get a different understanding of what is happening within the indexes.

Moving averages are typically used with time series studies. In a time series an investor may want to look at how an index or a stock has performed over time. Perhaps they want to look at how two different investments performed during a recession or a period of rising interest rates. Part of the value in using a moving average is that it can eliminate the impact of a one-day aberration in the price of a security.

Moving averages are often used when examining stock price performance. To calculate a moving average, you could take the trading history of the stock price of company A, and calculate a 200-day moving average. If the most recent date that you had stock price data for was November 25, the data set would consist of the average price of stock A for the 200 days prior, so from November 25 to May 9.[ii] On November 26, to do the same calculation the oldest day of the series would move to May 10 and May 9 data would be dropped so that there would still be 200 data points.

You might argue that deciding on 200-day old data is not as valuable as the most recent day's data, and you would be right. However, looking at the most recent day's data in isolation is not as valuable as looking at a long-term trend. Therefore, you might want to give more weight to the most recent data and use a weighted moving average.

One way of calculating a weighted moving average would be to use the price of the stock for each day of the period you are measuring and apply a weight to that day (usually in percentage terms). More recent days would get a larger weighting. If there are 5 days of data you are measuring the weighting of the first period could be $(5/(5+4+3+2+1)) = 0.33$ and then you would multiply the stock price from that first day by 0.33. The second period weighting would be $4/15$ or 0.27 and so on. The weighted moving average can be customized as well, you could choose to make the weightings more subjective (e.g., maybe 10 for the most recent data and then 7 for the second oldest, etc.) or even overweight older data points rather than newer ones if you can come up with a logical reason to do so.

A more common way of increasing the weighting of the most recent data points versus older trading points is to use an exponential moving average. This formula makes the most recent price more heavily weighted than in the simple weighted average, sometimes this is called "reducing the lag." This weighting bias will be greater in small data sets. The formula for this calculation using daily stock prices would be:

(Closing price – previous days exponential moving average (EMA) price) x $(2/(N+1))$ + the previous days exponential moving average price.

N is equal to the number of periods in the data set, for a 200-day moving average N would be equal to 200. To start the series the first data point can either be a simple moving average price or just the price on that date.

Investors will often use these types of moving averages as part of technical analysis to find entry and exit points for investments that are liquidly traded. They will often compare short-term trends to long-term trends. As an example, if a 50-day moving average price of a stock crosses above a 200-day moving average it may be a buy signal to a trader, as shown in Figure 6.2. This is a signal that there is a divergence in more recent trading patterns than long-term trading patterns. Technical traders may also look at the angle of the moving average, if it has minimal slope it may imply the stock is range-bound and is not showing an upward or downward trend. There are many other technical analysis tools and a large body of research in the field.

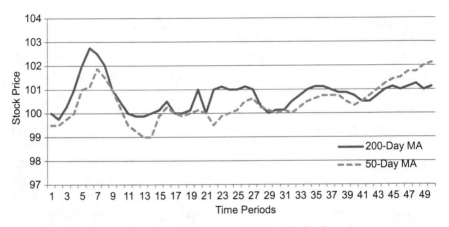

Figure 6.2: Hypothetical Cross-Over of a 50-Day and 200-Day Moving Average

If you are looking at investments in stocks or currencies, there are several programs that prepare charts with various types of moving averages and data on volumes and more. Many stock brokerage firms offer technical analysis software on their websites for clients. Additionally, while technical analysis can be utilized when investing in many asset classes, it is most useful for highly liquid assets that have good disclosure about prices and trading volumes such as stocks and currencies.

Averages are made up of old data points. Comparing the trend lines of moving averages over different time periods can be a valuable tool to identify a divergence in newer data versus older data. However, there are problems with using averages and mistakes are constantly made because investors do not realize that an average may not be telling them the same thing today as it was 200 days ago.

One commonly used investment refrain is that, "returns tend toward the mean." This is also known as "mean reversion." This implies that if the price of an asset is either well above its historical average or well below it you can make a profit by assuming that the price will return to its historical average.

It is always an interesting phenomenon to explore when asset valuation is very different from its historical average and it should not be ignored. Mean reversion has worked as a strategy in many cases, especially when there is a temporary aberration in valuations. It is important to recognize when it is not going to work. This might be when the components in the "average" are going through considerable change. There are frequently times when the components (or the characteristics) of some average that is being used in a time series has changed so much that historical data that is driving the mean is just not applicable to the present. This will often make mean reversion somewhat irrelevant. Consider the earlier example of the S&P 500 Index. The types of companies that dominate the index have changed. The four largest companies in the S&P 500 Index in 2017 were Google, Amazon, Netflix, and Facebook. All internet-based companies, two of which are clearly pure service providers. Ten years earlier the top four components of this same index were Exxon Mobil, General Electric, Microsoft, and AT&T,[iii] all but AT&T sells products. The profit profile is very different between the top companies in 2017 and 2007. Google in 2017 converted about 33% of its revenue into cash flow, while in 2010 Exxon converted only 9%.[iv] If you are comparing the historical averages of the S&P 500 stocks over the last ten years, you are looking at an index that has had a significant change in its largest components, it is logical that certain data in the current index will look very different than the ten year average data. When people wave mean reversion in your face, think of the underlying components that make up that mean and apply some common sense.

Too much blind acceptance of an average as a static target will result in bad decisions. You must do some analysis of the data to understand if it is still meaningful to the current environment and apply some logic.

---

i Domm, P. (2017, July 28), Fang Tech Market Concern Volatility. www.cnbc.com

ii This includes weekends and holidays for this example; in a real analysis you would just include trading days.

iii Johnston, M. (2012, December 2014), Visual History of the S&P 500. ETF Database. Retrieved from Etfdb.com

iv SEC Filings 10Ks. Retrieved from Bloomberg.com

Chapter 7
Rethink Regressions and Resist Correlations

Bill Gates and his team at Microsoft are to blame for some very bad statistical analysis. Their Excel program has made regression and correlation analysis way too easy to do and too many people use it without any understanding of the process or logic in designing the analysis. Despite this creation of a potential monster from Microsoft, regression and correlation are two very helpful analytical tools. However, they do not provide all the answers in any situation and need to be used with careful thought about the data being input, the structure of the analysis, logic, and a healthy dose of cynicism about any analytical conclusions. Both regression and correlation analysis are based on historical data. Therefore, when major changes occur in how different factors interact, this data can be misleading. Even when these tools are applied to the physical sciences they are notorious for creating false positive and negatives, this logically would increase when applied to the less consistent social sciences like economics.

Simple regression attempts to use statistics to determine if the movement in one variable(s) (the independent variable) impacts how another variable (the dependent variable) moves. You can think of the independent variable as the cause and the dependent variable as the effect. Correlation is an output generated from regression analysis that measures the strength of a relationship between two variables. More advanced regression models can use multiple variables.

If a regression shows that a 1% growth rate in a country's gross domestic product (GDP) (independent variable) usually causes a 2% increase in the price of the stock of the Sunshine Corp. (the dependent variable), this could be a powerful predictive tool for investing. This relationship could be positively or negatively correlated (e.g., a negative relationship would show a rise in GDP causes a decline in the stock price). This is a simple and unrealistic example of how regression can be used for investment decisions.

Regression uses a method known as "ordinary least squares" that generates a formula for a predicted line. The line will be made up of data points of what the regression analysis "predicts" the value of the dependent variable will be (plotted on the y axis) for each data point of the independent variable (plotted on the x axis). The dots around the line show the actual data points. The closer the dots cluster around the predicted line, the stronger the quality of the relationship between the two variables and then this would imply that the independent variable is a strong predictor of the dependent variable.

Figures 7.1 and 7.2 show two regressions. The outcome that the regression predicts is represented by the squares along the line. The diamonds show the actual

DOI 10.1515/9781547400751-007

results. Figure 7.1 shows a hypothetical relationship between the number of sales people and the level of sales, if the diamond is below the square for the same level of salespeople it implies that the salespeople should have produced more in sales according to the regression. The difference between the two is called a residual. Figure 7.1 shows a strong evidence of dependence on the independent variable. You could make the case that you could use the formula of the line to predict what the sales level would be for a given number of salespeople. Figure 7.2 shows a regression of the relationship between the commute time of employees and the sales per employee, this regression shows a much weaker relationship as there is little clustering around the predicted line.

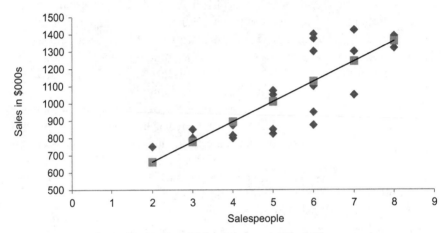

Figure 7.1: A Hypothetical Regression of Sales/Salespeople ($R^2 = 0.65$)

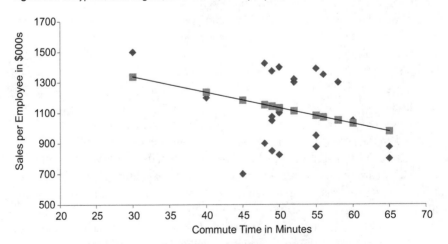

Figure 7.2: A Hypothetical Regression of Sales per Employee/Commute Time ($R^2 = 0.10$)

Regression analysis kicks out lots of other data. Perhaps the most widely used is the coefficient of determination which helps to show how closely a regression fits or how well the independent variable explains the outcome of the dependent variable. This is also known as the R^2 and is a measure of variance of the data from the mean.

R^2 will be between 0–1. You can see in Figure 7.1 the R^2 of the data is high and is 0.65 while in Figure 7.2 it is low and is only 0.10. The R is the correlation coefficient and measures the correlation of the independent and dependent variable. R measures the strength and direction of the relationship between the two variables, going left to right the upward sloping relationship in Figure 7.1 shows that it is a positive relationship (i.e., more salespeople results in more sales), Figure 7.2 has a downward sloping negative correlation, in this case the implication is that longer the commute the lower the sales per employee.

These measures of correlation are often used separately from a regression analysis. For example, you may be thinking of launching a new product, like an electric fork, before you do this you may want to see if in the past there was a correlation between new product launches and total sales revenue increases, or if new products just took revenue away from existing products.

These tools can be hugely valuable in analyzing relationships and trying to develop predictive tools. However, they need to be used with common sense. The number of times your golden retriever sniffs a bush on a morning walk may have a high correlation with the performance of the U.S. Treasury futures on that day. Even if the correlation is very high, it is hard to develop a theory that your dog is causing some change in the futures market. The famous saying on this topic is that, correlation is not causation.

With Excel's regression so easy to run, sometimes there is not enough thought put into how you are going to run the regression and what variables you are going to use. Let us assume you are interested to see if the number of customer service people that you employee impacts your sales. Before you run a regression, you should think through some of the potential pitfalls of analyzing the relationship.

Potential problem 1:
Think about your choices of variables. The employees are not salespeople, these are employees servicing customers. Should there be a relationship? Are the customer service people cross-selling or up-selling products in addition to supplying service?

Potential problem 2:
Is the predictive model set up wrong? Is the increase in customer service employees dependent on how much revenue is being generated?

Potential problem 3:
Does this relationship work well to a certain level of sales but then at some point adding more customer service people results in sales going down, implying it is a nonlinear relationship where regression does not work well?

Potential problem 4:
Is the relationship between the two variables caused by something else?

There is always the possibility you have the relationship between the dependent and independent variables wrong. In this example, it could be that as sales grow customer problems increase and this results in requiring more customer service support. In this case it might be that customer service people are being added because the company has an increasingly unhappy customer base and the revenue growth is unsustainable. Anytime you see a regression the logic of the relationship needs to be questioned. Even if the output from the regression looks good, be cynical.

There are numerous other potential problems with using regression and correlation techniques that are often ignored because of how easy Excel has made it to run. Excel can run many of the tests you can use to check for these problems. A common problem in casual regression analysis is when the sample size being used is too small to develop a statistically meaningful relationship, but unfortunately these small sometimes meaningless sample sizes do not stop people from throwing data into a regression analysis and talking about the relationships. Another common problem is autocorrelation, when the independent and dependent variable are not truly independent of each other, or more specifically their "residuals" are not independent. There is a statistical test for autocorrelation called the Durbin-Watson test and there are adjustments to the data that can be undertaken to remove autocorrelation. Heteroscedasticity is a problem when residuals of a regression model have very unequal variances. This is usually detected by plotting the residuals. Multicollinearity is a problem in multiple regressions when you are using more than one independent variable to try to predict the dependent variable and the independent variables are highly correlated with each other. There is also the potential to use hypothesis testing within set confidence levels that is quite common to use. These are just a few examples of some of the issues to consider in undertaking regression and these need to be explored if a regression analysis is really going to be helpful at all. It is also important to remember that regression analysis has issues when a relationship is not linear.

Residuals for Relative Value

Earlier in the chapter residuals were discussed. Residuals can be an interesting tool in creating a framework to compare relative value of various potential investments. Let us assume that you run a regression on annual revenue growth (independent variable) versus the annual move in the stock price for twenty companies. For any company you chose the residuals will be the difference between the predicted value on the fitted line and the dot representing the actual data for the company. A hypothetical example is shown in Figure 7.3. Each diamond represents the growth rate in revenue and the stock move for each company, the fitted line represented by the squares shows what the regression is predicting the gain in the stock price should have been for each company, given its revenue growth. Theoretically any company dot above the line appears to have seen too large a stock price move, and arguably should trade down to its fair value, shown on the fitted line, the opposite is true of any company dot below the line. The numerical residuals (the difference between the fitted line and the dot) are shown in Figure 7.4. The table shows that the model predicts that based on its revenue growth Alpha stock should have been up 14%, but increased by about 2% more than that, implying it is overvalued by this methodology. This methodology could be used to develop a list of buys and sells, but it is very simplistic and can be easily manipulated by the companies and data you choose to use. Typically, it would require much more analysis to determine if there are other factors that explain these residuals.

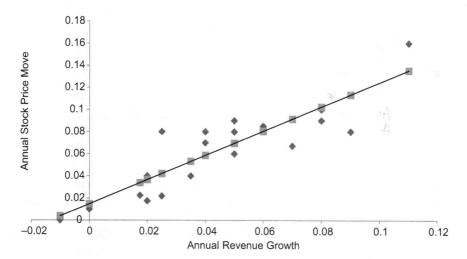

Figure 7.3: Regression of Hypothetical Stock Price Move to Revenue Growth ($R^2 = 0.76$)

Company	Predicted Stock Move	Residuals
Alpha	0.14	0.02
Bravo	0.07	(0.01)
Charlie	0.04	0.04
Delta	0.06	0.01
Echo	0.10	(0.00)
Foxtrot	0.11	(0.03)
Golf	0.10	(0.01)
Hotel	0.09	(0.02)
India	0.07	0.02
Juliet	0.00	(0.00)
Lima	0.01	(0.00)
Kilo	0.04	0.00
Mike	0.06	0.02
November	0.07	0.01
Oscar	0.08	0.00
Papa	0.07	0.02
Quebec	0.05	(0.01)
Romeo	0.04	(0.02)
Sierra	0.04	(0.02)
Tango	0.03	(0.01)

Figure 7.4: Residual Output

All kinds of investments strategies focus on correlations. Some hedge funds and multi-asset strategies charge high fees and base their strategies on owning negatively correlated assets assuming that one asset will hedge the other if there is a dislocation. There may also be trading strategies put in place to take advantage of leading or lagging correlations between an index and derivatives on that index. However, there are hellacious tales of these supposed correlations looking brilliant until a period of stress happens and then the correlations break down. The infamous Asian currency crisis in 1997, the Russian default crisis in 1998 and the financial crisis of 2008 all led to changes in correlations that hurt some supposedly hedged trades. Economics does not follow the laws of physical science and regressions and correlations that look good can change quickly when just a few factors change the data. There is a myriad of reasons correlations breakdown. Sometimes the correlation calculations may have been based on a time that does not properly cover enough varied types of environments and sometimes there are changes in the make-up of the data. As an example, it appears that the development of fracking technology that increased product of oil in the United States caused a change in the relationship between the price of oil based on the European Brent Crude Oil Index and the U.S. dollar. There was a negative correlation between Brent crude oil prices and the U.S. dollar for a long time but then from 2015 through 2018 the correlations collapsed, money could have been lost if you assumed these negative correlations would be in place indefinitely. The correlations are shown in Figure 7-5. Correlations can show some powerful relationships that are well worth monitoring but they should never be viewed as irrefutable facts on which to base 100% of your investing decision; relationships in economics, as in secondary school, can be fleeting.

Correlation of trade weighted U.S.$ to Brent crude oil prices in U.S.$	
January 2009–December 2014	January 2015–May 2018
(0.77)	(0.39)

Source: U.S. Energy Information Administration Board of Governors of the Federal Reserve System

Figure 7.5: Correlation of the Trade Weighted U.S.$ and the Price of Brent Crude Oil

Let Us Not Forget Standard Deviation

Averages, regressions, and correlations are some of the most common tools used in investment and business analysis, another one is standard deviation. This measures how the data points in a data set spread out from the mean. A lower standard deviation occurs when the data points are all closer to the mean. If you assume that the data is in a normal distribution the standard deviation can be very valuable tool in developing a confidence level in the data you are analyzing. A normal distribution means that the data is equally distributed around the mean, or it can be thought of as the median and the mean being equal. When a data set is normally distributed 68.3% of the values will fall within one standard deviation of the mean and 95.5% within two standard deviations of the mean. If you are measuring the number of tires manufactured in a factory per day and the average is 100 and the standard deviation is 20, that means on 68.3% of the days the factory will produce between 80–120 tires per day (either the mean + the standard deviation or the mean—the standard deviation).

When investors examine the volatility of an investment over time they typically use standard deviation. Investors will look at a times series of return data for an investment. The standard deviation of these returns will be viewed as the level of volatility in the returns of this investment. Traditional portfolio theory associated volatility of returns with the risk of the investment. A common goal is to maximize return and minimize risk. Though volatility measures a level of unpredictability, it does not actually measure loss and loss is the true risk when you are investing. Other ways to measure risk should be considered such as analysis of average drawdowns or value at risk calculations. Using standard deviation of returns as a measure of risk also assumes that you are looking at a market that operates efficiently, meaning there are very frequent and regular transactions from which you get regular price data, such as stock and currency markets. In less liquid investments standard deviation may be a much less valuable measure of risk. This also can make comparisons of the volatility of different asset classes a bit difficult if they have different levels of trading liquidity.

Regression and correlation analysis are incredibly helpful tools in understanding investment relationships, but they are tools, not the answer. Given the huge amounts of data that are available now and the ease of running a regression and correlation, there are more possibilities of doing poorly constructed analysis and making bad investment decisions. This can lead to developing and overweighting casual relationships between variables that are not truly meaningful. However, there are things you can do to limit the risk of being misled.

- Understand what the data is that you are using as well as possible. Try to analyze how the data was gathered, is it an estimate, is it based on a survey, has it been recently impacted by a major technological or sociological change?
- Remember all of the data used in regression and correlation is from the past. For example, think about how meaningless historical data on the relationship between job growth and public transportation may be, if the region you are studying is growing rapidly in telecommuting jobs.
- Be clear about what the question is you are actually looking to answer. Do not try to do too much just because there is so much data available. You may have 100 years of inflation data on 100 different products, but if you are trying to see if rising oil prices in Europe impact the cost of manufactured goods you will want to be selective on which periods and which data you utilize.
- Try not to try to force the data to a conclusion you want. Look at other relationships than the one you are trying to prove. Do not add complexity to get the answer you want.
- Do not just rely on R^2 alone look at other tests, there may be other factors that are skewing the data, check for things like autocorrelation.
- Always look at the data visually as well as numerically. Sometimes it is helpful to sort the data in other visual ways than just a scatter diagram, use histograms and other layouts.
- Share all the data and the visual representations with other people that can question your work and look at it from different angles.
- Develop your own checklist to avoid misusing these statistical techniques.

Selected Ideas from Parts 1, 2, and 3

Topic	Concepts	Investment Impact
Data Changes	Rapid broad reaching technology innovation devalues the use of much historical economic data.	The components of economic data changes over time, today it is changing more quickly. Analysis of historical data may not be relevant to where assets are valued today.
Data Changes II	Greater computing power can drive people to more complex models, each data point's value changes rapidly.	Data relationships are more fluid, it is easier to inadvertently use data incorrectly, a smaller relevant data set is better than a bigger one that may have too much noise.
Trends	Historically, positive economic trends have lasted longer than corrections. Shocks are infrequent.	Technology increases economic flexibility and can make positive macro trends last longer and corrections shorter and shallower. Historical definitions of cycles are changing. Investment trends are more important.
Innovation Impact	Innovation is not always smooth, it has many positives, but disrupts and displaces existing frameworks. causing creation and destruction.	Macro trends will benefit from innovation, but middle (medi) and microeconomic levels will face disruption and "pocket" recessions in select industries and business. The value of investment and sector selection will increase.
Government Policies	A predictable, fair rules-based economy is positive, but government may be the biggest risk to technology benefits.	Some of the biggest risks to reaping the macro-economic benefits from technological efficiencies is in the form of over-regulation and excessive monetary and fiscal activity by governments.

Topic	Concepts	Investment Impact
Economic View	Economics is driven by personal choices. What people choose to buy or do is not a constant it is dynamic.	People make economic decisions. At different times even the same person can make different choices. Sociological changes impact economic reactions.
Disruptors	Disruption is not new. Economies are in constant change, especially in a free market system.	Do not confuse a good idea with a good business. Consider the potential lifespan of the disruptor and derivative impacts.
Culture	Societal and cultural changes impact economics.	Popular trends and generational habits have a huge impact on economics and how economic data can be used.
Goodhart's Law	Once you target something as a goal, the reasons you sought that target may get distorted as people aim for it.	Over emphasis on investment benchmarks distorts markets and valuations and can cause people to lose sight of their actual investment goals.
Averages	Averages change over time so they do not always *mean* the same thing.	Be wary of investment conclusions that are overly dependent on averages, unless you are certain the data is "currently" meaningful.
Regression	Regression is a useful but overused tool to see if some factor, or factors, influenced the result of another data point.	Regressions need to use relevant data, be set up right and employ logic to analyze the results. It does not predict, it is a tool not an answer.
Correlation	Correlations between various data and asset values can be powerful investment drivers.	Correlations work until they do not. Shocks or even minor redirections of a long term trend can throw off correlations. Disconnections are always happening.

Part 4: **Big Economic Data Points**

Chapter 8
GDP—Overrated

Gross domestic product (GDP) is probably the most universally followed economic data point. It is old and lumbering and frequently wrong. There have always been many shortcomings in the measurement and use of GDP, but it is widely used to measure economic growth and the size of an economy. However, as an economy goes through periods of innovation and rapid changes, its use as a tool to measure actual economic activity gets even weaker. Despite its flaws the securities markets still react when the GDP news release comes out, understanding GDP's weaknesses and the value of other measurements of economic activity can give an investor an advantage.

GDP is the total market value of goods and services produced in a country. It measures personal consumption (C) plus business investment (I) plus government spending (G) plus net exports (NX) to total GDP, or:

$$C+I+G+NX=GDP$$

GDP is not supposed to be a measure of the welfare of a country. It is a reasonable measure of the overall size of an economy and the broad trends of economic activity in a country. The GDP report is given in nominal and real terms, the real terms adjusts for inflation and shows it in "constant dollars." Real GDP is usually what is used, as it separates improvements in the production of the economy from price increases. The seasonally adjusted rate of quarter-to-quarter growth is typically what is focused on. This is supposed to be a measure of the expansion or contraction in the economy and the rate of growth is often factored into the analysis and financial models when examining an individual industry, company, or investment project. Often you would want to compare the growth rate you expect for a company or industry to the overall economy to see if it is performing in line or not and if it seems your expectations are realistic. GDP results and expectations are also obviously an important influence on the policy being set by the government, including central banks.

GDP is also a good tool to use when analyzing the differences between countries if you are making cross-border investments. You can compare the overall size of economies as well as their growth rates using GDP. It is common when comparing data by country to put the data in ratios relative to the size of each country's GDP. For example, you might compare countries' level of deficits to GDP ratios or government debt outstanding to GDP. Segment reporting within GDP releases can give insights into the drivers of one country's economy versus another. For

DOI 10.1515/9781547400751-008

example, reports on exports and imports can be most helpful in examining these exposures in an economy. The degree to which a country's economy is global can be a good thing in some environments and a bad thing in others, but it is worth understanding each economy's dependence on these markets

GDP in the United States is part of the National Income and Product Account. The government collects data from multiple sources both private and public using reports and surveys. The Bureau of Economic Analysis releases three batches of data on quarterly GDP, the first is an advanced report about four weeks after the end of the quarter, and then it releases two revisions each about a month later as more data comes in. The first release is the least accurate but seems to get the most attention from the media, politicians, and the markets. Many European countries have only two releases.

The full GDP report in the United States, and most other developed countries, breaks out several sub-categories, and the trends in these categories can be more interesting than the major headline numbers. In the United States one of the most watched pieces of the GDP report is the section on personal consumption expenditures (PCE) as the United States is a very consumer driven economy right now. There are other important categories, for example, there are breakouts for durable and nondurable goods and services. There is also a breakout for fixed investments and private inventories. The inventory number can be a major swing factor and sometimes an indication of slacking demand or the expectation by corporations that demand will increase. GDP includes what is produced in the country and if an item is made but not sold it is assumed to go into inventory.

Examining the subsectors of GDP reports can show important long-term trends and give you a sense of a country's drivers. For example, if one country is more dependent on service industries than another or one is more manufacturing based it will be evident when comparing subsectors. There are some major items that often skew comparisons between countries. Some examples include dependence on foreign exchange, defense spending by the government, and in some emerging markets remittances can be important and not always captured properly in the data. One factor to consider closely is how rapidly, and in what ways, technological advances are happening in the different countries and how each country is evolving economically from these changes (e.g., new businesses, faster growing business segments).

There are all types of decisions about what gets measured in GDP. It does not count the value of unpaid services, the value of a parent that takes care of a child at home and transports them to school would not be captured in GDP but theoretically a baby sitter that is hired to do the same service would be included in the GDP calculation. Similarly, illegal or gray market activities are not included in GDP so that items like undeclared tips, off the books' employees, and significantly more dodgy activities are not captured (this is a larger factor in some countries than others). GDP does not include the benefits of a domestic company owning a plant in another country and selling products there. There are many imperfections in GDP. It is very much a lagging indicator. In the United States it is only measured quarterly. The first reported number is released about a month after the quarter ends and the final revised report three months after the quarter ends. Therefore, these reports include data that is as much as six months old. Long-term the agencies may make revisions years later but they often have no noticeable impact on asset valuations. The revisions in GDP can be very meaningful from the initial advanced report to the final release on both an absolute and a percentage basis. Figure 8.1 shows some recent United States GDP reports and revisions with some larger revisions highlighted as well as the expectations of the survey of economists as prepared by Bloomberg L.P. The market usually reacts the most to the first release. In one study on the United Kingdom's GDP report in *The Blue Book* it was found that the 1959 GDP was revised eighteen times and went from being reported in 1960 as 2.7% and eventually was revised over time to where in 2012 the revised 1959 GDP was reported at 4.7%.[i] A report by the Organization for Economic Cooperation and Development (OECD) found that developed countries tended to have very large revisions to GDP. In the clear majority of countries, revisions increased the initial estimate of GDP; interestingly the notable exception was the United States where the first estimated GDP figures were commonly too high.[ii]

Date of Release	Period	Survey	Actual
1/27/2017	4Q A	2.20%	1.90%
2/28/2017	4Q S	2.10%	1.90%
3/30/2017	4Q T	2.00%	2.10%
4/28/2017	1Q A	1.00%	0.70%
5/26/2017	1Q S	0.90%	1.20%
6/29/2017	1Q T	1.20%	1.40%
7/28/2017	2Q A	2.70%	2.60%
8/30/2017	2Q S	2.70%	3.00%
9/28/2017	2Q T	3.00%	3.10%
10/27/2017	3Q A	2.60%	3.00%
11/29/2017	3Q S	3.20%	3.30%
12/21/2017	3Q T	3.30%	3.20%
1/26/2018	4Q A	3.00%	2.60%
2/28/2018	4Q S	2.50%	2.50%
3/28/2018	4Q T	2.70%	2.90%

Source: Department of Commerce and Bloomberg.
Figure 8.1: Examples of Revisions in U.S. GDP Annualized Q-o-Q

GDP is also often a critical measure of determining when a country is in expansion, recession, or depression. When you think about some of the relatively short recessions in the United States and the lag in getting the final GDP data this measurement does not seem to be very helpful. The 2000–2001 recession in the United States took place from the fourth quarter of 2000 through the fourth quarter of 2001. However, with a three-month lag in reporting final GDP numbers, the country was almost half way through the entire recession before it could officially be declared by these measures.

A Bit of GDP Background

In the early 1930s the United States and Europe were going through a major depression. Congress in the United States decided it needed a good measurement of the economy. It enlisted a Russian immigrant Simon Kuznets and organized a team of economists to estimate the national income. Similar work was being undertaken in Great Britain. Mr. Kuznets treated government spending as a cost to the private sector (it is after all typically funded by private citizens and corporations). However, on the other side of the ocean the very formidable Noble laureate economist John Maynard Keynes argued that it should be included as an addition to GDP. Mr. Keynes used the example that during wartime purchases by the government had to be treated as demand or GDP would fall even though the economy was growing and the crisis of war simply redeployed people's spending. As GDP reporting become more systematized Mr. Keynes's model won out. When the United States began its aid program after World War II, countries that received funds under the Marshall Plan were required to develop an estimate of GDP. Then in the 1950s the United Nations drew up a plan for GDP accounting and this plan also followed the Keynes model on government spending.[iii] It is worth noting that economic theory might have evolved differently and looked at government spending as an expense to the economy rather than an addition to economic activity.

A major concern in the current transitioning economic environment is how much business activity GDP reports may actually miss due to its methodologies in measurement. GDP reports in most countries breakout industry data. One concern is that in the United States the services segment of the economy is more than two times the size of the "goods" segment. However, the services segment is broken into slightly fewer categories (eight vs. seven); this is similar in many other developed countries' reports as well. In the U.K. it is five categories versus four (but to be different they list them horizontally rather than vertically, or maybe the United States is different). You would think if services were so much larger there might be more nuanced categorizations, or perhaps it highlights how the service economy is harder to track than manufacturing. Another fact that may indicate new industries are not all being captured properly is the relative growth and sheer size of line items in the report that are labeled "other." In a corporate financial report when anything is labeled "other" (e.g., "other revenue," "other expenses") and is a very large or growing line item, you need to question it. Therefore, it comes up as a red flag in these GDP reports when the figures for "other" categories are large and growing.

When the economy and businesses are transitioning rapidly, GDP becomes a weaker measure of the economy. GDP captures and records if one product is being produced and sold more and another is produced and sold less, it does not capture if there are massive improvements in the product that are being made. Consider that at one point a person may have bought a computer, a camera, a device to play portable music on, and a mobile phone. A few years later the sales of all those products are probably down significantly and that same person is simply buying a new mobile smartphone that can do all of the same things on one device—this will, at least initially, cause some noise in GDP unless the prices of the replacement products and the displaced products are exactly equal and all the surveys are properly capturing this change.

The modern economy sees all kinds of changes that distort old measuring tools. In some cases what was once a product has become a service. The likes of Elton John, Paul McCartney, and Robert Plant have been producing music that is ranked in the top of industry sales for decades. However, while they keep making music, what is being bought by the consumer has changed dramatically during that time. Initially when fans of these artists bought their music it was on flat discs made of vinyl. For many people it transitioned to a taped product—cassettes, or the terribly designed, eight-track tape. These products were all linear, but then music switched to digital formats and people bought music on compact discs, more music could be put on this product so in some cases people were getting more for their money (though liner notes became harder to read). Sales were also boosted as people upgraded their libraries to this new enhanced technology (the multigenerational upgrades has probably helped The Eagles Greatest Hits, be the top selling album of all time). Up to that point there probably was not much change in how GDP captured this data. However, then MP3 players and Apple's iPod were introduced and things really began to change. You could download individual songs or entire albums from the computer, but these were still sales of individual items that could be recorded on the GDP ledgers. Individual sales of music have become more complicated to measure now as much of the industry has transitioned to more of a subscription model where for a few dollars you can get regular streams of, what seems like, an endless selection of songs. This has changed the economics of the music industry tremendously and it is hard to believe there has not been significant leakage in the GDP figures as revenue went from buying a physical product to buying a digital file to paying a subscription. The music industry may be one of the most fascinating cases of adaptation to technology, both on the creative side as well as the business side. In music, even the organizational structures have changed over time from ensemble to orchestras to rock bands driven by technology and financing.[iv] Similar changes in sales from a product to a stream of service has occurred in other industries such as in mobile telecommunications when plans went from minutes to unlimited plans and usage and revenue shifts have occurred due to the introduction of texting. All these factors cause disruptions between actual economic activity and how GDP measures it.

There are numerous data points available that can be used as a predictor of GDP, or more importantly, as a better gauge of real time economic activity in the economy. Many of these measures can give more insight into trends that can impact business decisions and investments, especially as the world moves faster. Some reports are better about trends and some are good about factors impacting specific economic segments, other reports are good gut checks on GDP. Below are comments on some other reports, but it is far from exhaustive.

One very good report to monitor is a monthly release from the Federal Reserve Bank of Chicago, cleverly titled The Chicago Fed National Activity Index (CFNAI). The index is a weighted average of 85 indicators focused on economic activity and growth. It is divided into four categories: (1) production and income; (2) employment, unemployment, and hours; (3) personal consumption and housing; and (4) sales, orders, and inventories. Monthly data can swing around but the report includes a three-month moving average, even more cleverly named, CFNAI-MA3, this is a more valuable tool to track. Some of the data that is used is lagging and some leading, but the report and its segments can be very helpful trend indicators.

The Federal Reserve Bank of New York puts out a monthly report titled U.S. Economy in a Snapshot. It gives a brief overview and then has break out sections on economic activity, business activity, households, and inflation, and so on. It also usually includes a special focus section. Both this report and the CFNAI are heavily dependent on government data, much of which is not very timely. However, both reports try to incorporate more real-time data and are helpful as they incorporate so many different key aspects of the economy in one place.

Two of the most widely followed, nongovernment issued, indexes are the Institute for Supply Management's (ISM) manufacturing and nonmanufacturing (i.e., services) purchasing managers index (PMI). The releases come out monthly and are both timely and highly responsive to changes in expectations of economic conditions. The PMI is a single figure based on a diffusion index. More details of data at the medi-level of the economy are in the Report on Business, which accompanies both releases. IHS Markit is a commercial entity that prepares PMIs for manufacturing and service segments for the United States and economies around the globe. This can be very helpful in having comparably prepared data across various national markets. Securities markets tend to react to major moves in the PMI figures or a major change in the direction of the numbers.

Diffusion Indexes

Many survey-based indexes that fall into the category of "soft data" utilize diffusion indexes; these are often misused by the media and politicians. It is important to understand them. Diffusion indexes show the dispersion of change. A simple calculation would be to take a survey of a group of sales people on their expectations for the next year's sale. Any one that expects sales growth above +0.3% would be given a value of one and any one that expects sales growth to be between +0.3% and zero would be given a value of 0.5 and any that expects sales to decline would be given a value of zero. You then would average the results and multiply by 100. If the number is above 50, more people surveyed are expecting growth above 0.3%.

If a survey asks a 100 snake oil salesman if they are selling the same, more or less snake oil each month and the data is put into a diffusion index, the index will show if those sales people think sales are going up or not. It will not necessarily capture if a sales person is selling three times the amount they sold last month or just barely more than they sold last month. It may also not capture if the salesperson that says they are selling more makes up 20% of all snake oil sales or 1%. More sophisticated diffusion indexes can capture some of these nuances. The important thing is to realize that a diffusion index moving up does not automatically say there is more snake oil being sold it simply says more salespeople are expecting an increase in sales. One of the popular uses of diffusion indexes is also to analyze trends in gainers and losers in the stock market for technical analysts, this type of index, of course, is just based on numbers not a survey question, but can be skewed by which stocks are included or excluded.

A key to a good diffusion index is that any survey question is constructed well with little room for ambiguity; even a slight amount of ambiguity can change the results. As with all surveys the sample size and the composition of who is surveyed can make a huge difference.

There are also surveys and overview pieces about economic growth that are published and readily available, often these are less statistical but give good color. In the United States there is a publication by the Federal Reserve eight times a year known as the Beige Book that is based on regional surveys. In Japan there is the Tankan Survey published by the Bank of Japan quarterly that is broad reaching in its scope. Similarly, in Germany the Bundesbank puts out a monthly report that gives both commentary and statistics. The list can go on from the Reserve Bank of India to the Bank of England. As much of the global economy is dependent on energy sources, it is not surprisingly that one of the best sources for global economic trends is the OPEC Monthly Oil Market Report, which focuses on energy but includes good sections on the broader world economy.

Of course, stock markets, earnings reports, and interest rates can be hugely helpful indicators of what is happening in the economy. However, the reactionary, short-sightedness of daily or hourly focused market traders and technical flows must be considered when using this data. Market action and earnings over a short period of time are notorious for giving false positives and negative indications, looking at short-term trends can be more valuable than single intra-day data points. Stock markets are notoriously focused on near-term growth results.

Trying to compile detailed data on a massive complex economy, like GDP attempts to do, will always result in data that is flawed. The methodologies need to be based on samples and surveys that will be imperfect and by the time they are tabulated they will often be dated too. You can build baskets of corporate financial data that can give a clearer picture of the private sector of an economy. For example, you can build a model that tracks the revenue, cash flow and capital spending trends of the five largest public software companies and use it as a monitor for that industry, this can be repeated for each major industry sector. Corporate financial data on an individual company basis, or aggregated, can be a valuable tool in analyzing economic trends, this data will be more accurate than the broad economic information, but much narrower in scope. Growth helps drive returns for many types of investments and GDP is typically used as a measure of broad economic growth. While previous parts of this chapter have raised concerns about GDP as an effective tool to measure near-term economic activity, it can still be very valuable to use, especially when examining long-term growth trends. However, you must understand what it might be missing. Not all growth is created equal and where growth is coming from must be considered. If a considerable amount of growth is coming from government spending it can raise many concerns. Most government's primary source of funding is debt or taxes—though some own means of production (e.g., a nationalized airline or toll roads). If a country is seeing growth but it is driven by government spending, you must investigate how it is being funded and how sustainable it might be. You will also want to look at where the growth in an economy is coming from in the private sector. If an economy is getting all its growth from a few narrow industry segments it would be weaker than if an economy was seeing growth from a more diversified basket of sectors. Also, be cautious if government subsidies are driving an industry's growth, this is an insidious way for the people's taxes to be directed to benefit a sector that cannot attract enough business in the market place to support itself.

It is Not All about Growth

There is a bit of an obsession in the investing community, and in the media, about growth. It is worth remembering that there are investments that are much less dependent on growth. This is particularly true for income driven investments, bonds, preferred shares and higher dividend stocks can all post quite reasonable and relatively predictable returns during periods of slow growth. It is not that these types of investments benefit from declining economies, but in a slow growth environment their returns can shine on a relative basis.

As an investor you need to decide what GDP means for you. It is a number that is not timely but over several years can give a reasonable indication of trends. It is not a strong tool to capture near term trends that are driving economic activity, markets, and businesses. The release of GDP numbers often does move financial markets, shifts political policy, and influences consumer expectations. Therefore, it can not be ignored. However, it is such a lagging indicator to the real economy that any surprise in the figures that cause an initial reaction in asset valuations can create opportunities to enter and exit investments especially if it is an aberration from what the long-term trends are indicating.

It is no easy task to measure an entire economy. The economists that measure GDP have obligations to manage changes to the measurement tools in a very thoughtful, rules-based regimented fashion. This is an important job and data integrity is critical given how broadly this data is used. This makes it difficult to keep up with the level of innovation in the economy. The same is true for many other key economic figures that do not try to capture nearly as broad a spectrum of the economy. The faster an economy is developing new and different businesses the less likely GDP is going to be an accurate measure of the economy, therefore, GDP may be the weakest at giving insight into the newest segments of an economy.

---

i *The Economist* (2016, April 30) GDP revisions Rewriting History, The Nation's Income is a Constantly Moving Target. *The Economist.*
ii Zwijnenburg, J. (2015, July) Revisions of quarterly GDP in selected OECD countries. *OECD Statistics Brief #22*, OECD.
iii *The Economist* (2016, April 30) Measuring Economies, the Trouble with GDP. *The Economist.*
iv Cowen, T. (2018 April 21) The Symphony Orchestra and The Industrial Revolution. *MarginalRevolution.com*

Chapter 9
Unemployment versus New Employment

Employment figures may be one of the most important economic data points. It is not only an incredibly valuable indicator of the economy but employment levels can be vitally critical to the sociology and political stability of a country. Two famous economists that wrote about revolutionary economic change, Karl Marx and Joseph Schumpeter, focused on prognostications of how labor markets would change over time and would eventually result in the collapse of the capitalistic structure. How and where people work has changed dramatically over time and it appears that the freedom of most capitalistic societies has created more prosperity and allowed for more flexibility and choice for labor than those economic theories anticipated. Technology and changing attitudes and approaches of many millennials are changing work trends and the types of employment more than in the early twentieth century when Marx and Schumpeter were writing. However, the methodologies to measure labor have not changed that much over time and may be missing many of the changes that are occurring in the labor markets, understanding this can help you decide how to best use the abundance of employment data that gets released. This data often drives near-term trading in securities markets in part because of how regularly it is released and in part because the data can have far reaching effects on political and central bank actions.

The "big" report in employment in the United States is the Employment Situation. It is put out by the Bureau of Labor Statistics, which was established in 1915.[i] Even though it is a report that appears to be increasingly flawed, as the constructs of employment change, it has an incredible amount of data worth looking at. The focal point is often on the payroll figure that shows the number of people employed and how many were hired in the latest period. The full report beyond the headline numbers should be looked at. Subsectors include significant data on wages and segments like unemployed persons and reasons, as well as a similar report by duration of unemployment and employment data by industry.

There is a seemingly endless list of other employment related releases, beyond the Employment Situation and comparable reports in most countries. In the United States there is a Weekly Claims for Unemployment that is widely followed. This is an attractive data point to use as it is a relatively factual data set (as opposed to a survey or sentiment report) and it is released weekly. However, this should not be looked at in a vacuum and at the very least it should be compared to the labor participation figures. There is also a monthly report from a company known as Automatic Data Processing (ADP) that releases the ADP National

DOI 10.1515/9781547400751-009

Employment Report, which can be a harbinger for payroll figures. Another report in the United States, made popular by former Federal Reserve chair Janet Yellen, is the Job Openings and Labor Turnover report (JOLT). All of this data should be looked at relative to the labor participation rates and reports on income.

The data in these reports may have some weaknesses relative to the actual economy as the population has changed their communication and work habits. The key parts of the report are based on a household survey and an establishment survey. The household survey gets a very high response rate. The concern is whether it is reaching the right people, as younger people have different levels of usage of landline communication, cohabitating and appear to be generally living more mobile lifestyles. The establishment survey focuses on businesses with more than 1,000 employees.[ii] If employment growth is being driven by demand for traditional workers that have homes, phones, etc., this data may be reasonable. However, if the employment factors are being driven by an independent operator with an Amazon store or Airbnb properties, or even, by six young people working at a start-up and sharing an apartment, this type of survey is likely to miss much of the actual employment activity. As these types of "jobs" become a larger part of the economy, traditional data can become more flawed until methodologies are adopted to address these changes.

How companies employ people and how people choose to work changes over time. There are points in history where these changes are more dramatic and can cause seismic shifts in the labor market. When major changes occur, whatever data was being used in the previous employment paradigm is probably not measuring employment correctly. For these reasons trends in labor data, while important, may not be the best ways to examine shifts in major economic trends. Anecdotal information is helpful in understanding how some changes are occurring, but be cautious when too many anecdotes are used it probably means there are not enough facts or data.

Understanding how much employment has changed over time can be helpful. In many countries that underwent rapid industrial development, corporations become the dominate employers (corporations were a relatively new concept back then). This occurred as societies tended to move away from agrarian economies and corporations became repositories of capital, starting to replace the construct where capital was almost solely stored in land. In early corporations there were many cases where workers were forced to endure dangerous and excruciating work environments in order to earn just a subsistence wage. Over time unions were formed, in many places, as a means of consolidating the value of human capital and bringing a more even balance of power between employers and employees. Any casual reading of economic or social history will show how dramatically the labor movement changed how people work and the employer–

employee relationship in countries like the United States and the United Kingdom. In a truly free market economy the formation of corporations and of unions make perfect sense and is another way market forces can solve problems, as long as regulators and lawmakers maintain a consistent and level playing field for all groups involved.

For many years in Japan when an employee was hired by a company there was almost an implicit contract stating the employee would be loyal to the company and never want to leave for a better opportunity and in return the company would have the employee as part of the company for his working life (because it almost exclusively was a "he" in most cases at that time). Economic struggles and a more global economy forced this to change. This has affected social attitudes and some have theorized that the move to a more uncertain employment market has caused the birth rate to drop and the population demographics to age more rapidly. Generally, economic history has taught corporate leadership that it is beneficial to keep the best employees and not have constant employee turnover. The result has been that greater employee–employer interaction and employee ownership has occurred. In Germany, as an example, many companies have governing boards on which employee representatives have a right to sit. All these cases highlight how employment relationships can vary and how the labor market evolves over time, it is not a static economic constant. In many cases technology has been a key force in changing employment constructs.

In developed countries there are new types of "blue collar" factory workers. These are the computer coders. They toil a way usually as part of a large team working on large projects or maintaining systems and their work structure often resembles modern assembly lines. This is not a statement on their skill level or value, they are certainly skilled and specialized labor, just like a high quality machinist. However, they are also not always given the fairest treatment. They are frequently given a temporary contract, as opposed to being hired as full time employees. This limits any benefits and many employee protections they would get and certainly limits their job security. These workers are also under constant threat of their skill set being rendered obsolete as new languages and skills are developed, and younger coders coming out of school may know these systems better and will work for lower wages. This uncertainty can change spending and savings habits, though these types of changes are not easily gleaned from macroeconomic data points released about the employment market.

Economic Data Is Not Gathered for Your Benefit

You can argue that much of the headline economic news that is released by governments is not ideally designed to help make investment decisions or plan your career. You might come up with several ways that could make it more valuable. Before you get too frustrated by the data's shortcomings remember what was behind the creation of this data and its reason for existing. Most of it was designed to help drive policy decisions by the government and to help guide public perception of the economy. This has not changed.

These factors are likely to subtly influence how the methodologies behind the data get tweaked over time and why these changes may not be 100% aligned to make it more accurate. Keep in mind the true goal and purpose of any data you utilize and the motivations behind its creation, it may help you understand its biases and flaws. As the saying goes, if you know where a man comes from you will understand better what he is actually saying when he speaks.

We can use international trade as an example of how the data that government policy makers may want is very different than what someone making an investment decision may desire. International trade data is often calculated primarily on the transfer of goods and services between countries; this can actually differ meaningfully from profits of an international corporation that you may invest in. If the Great American Hammer Company of America is a United States corporation and has a plant in China where it sells hammers in China, Thailand, Vietnam, and Japan, this will not show up in many of the most common United States economic releases and it is not likely to add as many jobs for United States citizens as a United States plant would. Understandably this is a concern of United States politicians who probably care more about the jobs than the company profits. Even though the Chinese factory helps the profits of the Great American Hammer Company of America and may support United States-based operations leading to a few more United States jobs, the policy makers do not necessarily care about capturing that data.

Employment is going through another major change in the technological age and it is devaluing the value of analytical work using historical employment data. In areas like Silicon Valley the increased flow of information, the competition for specific skill sets, and a relative abundance of a certain type of "venture" capital have led to changes in employment. Wages are less of a factor. Lifestyle is often more important. Flexibility for telecommuters or allowing people to bring dogs to work is part of employment compensation. There is more of an emphasis on giving equity ownership in the firm than wages this creates an opportunity for employees to capture the upside if the company is sold. Employees in this environment often have less company loyalty because they know the corporations may be more fleeting, and in some cases companies are being formed just to be sold. Workers may also work several jobs part time. This may be particularly true for the digital world's blue color factory worker, the computer coder. This is all changing the value of data on wages and hours worked.

There is also a new type of self-employment that is harder to capture in labor data, this can include internet businesses run from someone's home on a full or part-time basis or other part-time peer-to-peer employment. Think of a car owner in Los Angeles that has chosen to utilize their "excess capital" to drive for an on-line car service like Uber or Lyft (the excess capital would be their car sitting parked and unused). Think of an entrepreneur mother of three young children in North Liberty Indiana who buys used baby clothes at flea markets and swap meets, repurposes them, and resells them in her "store" on eBay. These examples indicate that the potential for gaps in employment data is large.

Part of the attraction of labor data to investors is that it theoretically gives indications into several other key areas that can impact the economy in many ways and over several years. The reach and impact of employment data includes (a) insight into what major corporations and the government are doing (more employees implies growth in corporations and costs in the government); (b) it is a major influence on central banks decisions about interest rates as it would be politically tenuous to raise rates dramatically with increasing unemployment, and in the United States full employment is part of the central banks mandate, and; (c) it can be a huge political barometer as employment levels can have an impact on elections and economic policy.

Leading, Coincident, and Lagging Indicators

Employment figures garner significant market reactions because they are considered a "leading" indicator. Certain economic data points are considered leading indicators, as people believe they are more predictive of future economic trends than other data. There are also factors that are considered coincident and lagging. Among some of the economic data points that are often considered to be leading indicators are: employment figures, wage data, new orders data and expectation surveys. Coincident indicators are considered data points that give a good view of the current economy such as: payrolls, personal income, production figures, and recent sales. Lagging indicators are considered to be factors that show where the economy has been, these might include inventories, labor costs, data on the level of private sector loans, and consumer credit.

During certain economic environments some of these types of data points have been good indicators of where the economy is going, where it is, and where it has been. However, at times there is a disconnect. Indicators that are reputedly leading sometimes are not a great predictor of things to come. Often some key data points work as a great indicator of future growth for a period of time, and then the environment changes and it no longer has the same predictive strength. As the Co-CIO of Shenkman Capital, Justin Slatky, is fond of saying about trendy investment themes and market indicators, "It works, until it doesn't." Blindly assuming that because some factor once predicted a big move in valuations, that it always will have strong predictive powers is an easy way to lose money.

While employment data is somewhat flawed it may be the most important economic factor in political and policy decision making. Healthy levels of employment bring untold societal good, such as lower crime, higher levels of citizen's sense of self-worth, more household and business formation, more consumer spending, and a lower need for transfer payments. It is an incredible hot button for politicians, and good employment numbers should favor incumbents. When comparing cross-border investments the employment environment can be a factor in trying to handicap political stability.

There is the constant fear that technology will always replace labor, this has been in society since at least the Luddites, who destroyed factory machinery in protest in the early nineteenth century. Technology is more likely to change labor than replace it. Think about a cycle where employee headcounts rise for a period of time, labor costs start to rise and instead of hiring more people or raising wages, employers choose to invest in cheaper labor-saving technology, thereby driving the employee headcount down as a substitution effect occurs. This type of rotation keeps employees off balance about job security and likely limits job growth. However, at the same time, technology is creating new jobs and allowing employees to have multiple careers as they can telecommute to a job and "face-time" in the office may be less important than it was.

Employment data can be an indicator of economic growth rates and inflation. Employment gains within a business sector may be a harbinger of growth and success in that industry, but just as easily could be a signal of over hiring and inefficiencies leading to pressures on profits. Recognize that markets react heavily to employment data; however, technology and societal changes are leading to an increasing disconnect between traditional data points on employment and the reality of the employment market. Therefore, employment figures may increasingly move along their own trend lines and not have the same correlations with other economic data points as they once had.

---

i www.bls.gov/opub/hom/pdf/homch2.pdf
ii Ibid.

Chapter 10
Wages Are Different Now

The fact that wages and employment are linked should not be shocking news. Wages are the market price for employees. There are many factors that prevent the supply demand relationship between labor and wages to function like a typical free market. Employers want to avoid employee turnover costs and there are usually regulations about wages and terminations. Employees may consider benefits of employment other than just wages, that may not be captured in pay data and also often want a level of predictability in their incomes. Many of these factors tend to make the price of labor less volatile than some other economic figures.

Much of the wage data that is used in economic analysis comes from the same surveys used for employment figures described earlier. The wage data primarily uses information coming from the establishment surveys. In the European Union (EU) similar data appears in the quarterly and annual EU Labor Force Survey, based on household samples. There are similar reports for other countries and regions as well. There are also measures, such as personal income, that include broader definitions of wages and there is data that is less dependent on surveys that often is derived from tax records. Although tax data tends to be made available on an annual basis rather than monthly, therefore usually has a longer lag.

Much of the data used in the widely followed reports is based on pure hourly wages; it is clearly more focused on traditional businesses and manufacturing style companies. Much of the data released on wages does not factor in bonuses or deferred pay or those that take equity in a company in lieu of wages. The apparent increased use of these various payment methods has weakened the value of utilizing traditional wage data, especially in countries with a high proportion of younger people in the workforce. Personal income, which is a broader definition of earnings, is a better measure than many of the hourly earnings and wage data, especially as compensation methods shift. While personal income reports are typically available monthly and do not come out as frequently as some other wage data, reports include nonwage compensation, personal income on rental properties, government transfers, and other breakdowns. When looking at wage and income data across various countries averages can be misleading; dispersion of income can vary greatly and be a sign of income class stratification, which can increase a countries potential instability.

Wages and income data do not always capture the whole cost of labor, or the whole benefit to the laborer. There is usually training costs and facility costs for the employer. For the employee, they may get the benefits of training, or the employee may have paid for themselves to get a considerable amount of training from

DOI 10.1515/9781547400751-010

which the employer benefits. In the United States it is typical for the employer to offer health care, but there may be other family benefits or perks like child care, savings plans, or Friday keg parties. More critical than keg parties, there are increasing differences in the way people are paid. There appears to be greater use of bonuses, profit sharing, or payment in equity in younger entrepreneurial companies. All these shifts in pay can distort the data that is being used to measure wages.

Traditional theories involve a high linkage between employment, wages, and inflation. One of the impacts of structural and technological innovation appears to be that this linkage is breaking down, or at the very least the reaction time between employment increases, wage hikes, and inflation is slowing down meaningfully.

How the interaction of specific factors in the employment, wages and inflation connection transmits through an economy is one of the more exciting concepts in economics. Below is a simple outline of a classic economic cycle influenced by employment and wages in the economy:

a) Employment increases as capital is readily available and companies expand.
b) The supply of available workers shrinks.
c) Companies raise pay to win workers from competitors or get workers to reenter the workforce.
d) Companies need to raise prices to pay for higher wages.
e) With more people employed, there is more demand for product.
f) Higher prices and more demand increases inflation.
g) Central banks raise interest rates to hold down inflation.
h) Higher interest rates slow down the economy, easing the demand for workers.

If you let technology disrupt this cycle you can play a game of "what if." In step c), what if companies decide wages are already too high and it is cheaper for them to invest in new technology that can substitute for workers than hire anymore? Will that shift the timing and limit the level of inflation? Will the threat of such substitution cause workers to avoid asking for raises? Now ignore the change to step c) and look at potential technology changes to step d) in the cycle. What if technology and the internet of things has increased pricing information for consumers and made global products available for the consumer to purchase? Companies will have much less pricing power in this environment. Every time a company looks to increase prices potential, customers look on the internet or scan the bar code with an app that tells them where they can get the item cheaper. This lack of pricing power may squeeze corporate profits. A final example could be "what if" in step d). Instead of substituting technology, the companies shift employment to lower wage regions using improved communication and logistics technology to either outsource work or relocate a facility to locations where labor is cheaper. It is constantly surprising to hear policy makers and investors talk in the media about technology displacing workers, but still think the employment, wage, inflation cycle works the same as it always, supposedly, did.

Trendy Until it Ages

It appears that in every age younger people do things differently, from rock 'n' roll to punk rock to rap to hip-hop to dubstep. Many changes that are currently being highlighted as new economic trends are most prevalent among younger people. Current examples might include working multiple part-time jobs instead of one full-time job, working independently using technology such as Uber, or telecommuting. Similarly, some of the shifts in compensation are primarily associated with younger workers too—most notably greater focus on lifestyle over a wage and a greater willingness to take an equity stake to participate in the potential upside of a firm and have a lower wage.

These factors cause distortions in the traditional labor and wage data, especially as millennials are such a large part of the population in many countries. However, it may take years to see if all of these current trends will actually change long-term economic patterns or not. Some of these trends may not hold as the current younger portion of the workforce ages. For example, living with six roommates may be fun at 21, but be less appealing at 35. Working independently or multiple part-time jobs may remain a popular lifestyle as people age or it may not. As people get married and have children their focus may turn toward current income versus equity in a start-up or they may find it harder to telecommute when the home they are working from is full of three kids under the age of eight that need to get ready for school. Some of these trends may subsist as a younger generation ages, but others will subside. Investors can make a mistake if they expect a youthful fad to be a long-term trend and they are wrong, if a fad can have appeal to multiple generations it may have a longer lifespan and impact long term economic trends.

Like other employment data, wage trends are an important factor in consumer confidence and can influence savings rates, which impacts capital formation. Rising or falling wages can have a major impact on the decision for people to enter or leave the work force shifting the participation rate and the potential growth of an economy, which then impacts tax revenues used to support governments. Even with flawed data, it can be valuable to explore wage trends within industries and across countries. Wages, even more so than some other statistics, can not be looked at it in a vacuum. Training, education, health, and other factors all impact an economy's employment and wage levels. Wage data can vary greatly by the type of worker and job that is being created and by the amount of technology investment being put into a business. There is a large difference if wage declines are occurring because the economy is firing software coders and hiring stock room employees or if wages are just being cut across the board for everyone. Technology is changing the value of labor and wages.

Chapter 11
Inflation—Just a Little Bit

Inflation is a symptom, not the root cause of an illness. Various economic factors interact and then inflation can crop up and have a huge influence on interest and currency exchange rates, consumer spending, savings, and corporate profits. Inflation is also very similar to plumbing in an old house. If it starts to leak it is not always easy to tell where it is coming from or how to fix it. If you can not stop it, it may get out of control and cause significant damage. A country also does not want inflation to run too hot or too cold. Just like trying to adjust the temperature in a tricky shower—if it runs too hot you can get burned and if too cold, things shrivel up.

All investible countries have some measures of inflation and like all big numbers taken from multiple surveys they are both valuable and problematic. There are many different measures of prices and inflation. The one that has historically received the most attention is the consumer price index (CPI); almost every country has a version of it. In the United States the personal consumption expenditure deflator (PCE) and the producer price index (PPI) are also widely followed. Different countries have variations. In the United Kingdom. the retail price index (RPI) and its variations are popular; some versions include mortgage and interest payments. Also, in countries where there is value-added taxes (VAT), measures are adjusted for these taxes.

The most widely followed version of the CPI is the core consumer price index (core CPI). In most countries this type of inflation measures a basket of goods that the government believes represents a cross-section of regularly purchased items by the consumer and price changes are tracked. The reason it is considered "core" is that it takes out items related to energy and food. These segments are considered too volatile and can distort short-term trends. In the United States the Federal Reserve over the last few years has preferred the PCE as a tool for monitoring inflation. The PCE is considered to cover a broader set of goods and focuses on what is consumed by households rather than a basket of goods, like the CPI. The PPI is often viewed as a leading indicator for the CPI as it measures a fixed set of goods and services like the CPI, but the focus is on the cost of the output of United States based producers (so no imports). The PPI measures the cost of goods by the revenue received by producers rather than the amount spent as in most consumer-oriented inflation reports.

The rationale for using "core" is that these "commodity" items fluctuate too much and do not give a good picture of inflation's near-term trends for the policy makers. However, food and energy are a huge factor in a person's budget

DOI 10.1515/9781547400751-011

and frequently for companies as well. The cost of food, and especially, energy, transmit through the economy over time and show up in the core numbers, but their impact on spending habits has already been felt strongly by that time. As an example of the dangers of only focusing on core inflation, the 50% rise in energy prices in the United States in 2008 was a major contributor to the recession that followed but would not have been captured in the core number. Recognize that policy makers may use core inflation measures and it is often what the media talks about, but the full CPI is a vital reflection of how inflation is impacting the economy in the short term.

There are many theories on the causes of inflation, and when inflation occurs it is generally not just due to one factor:

Cost Push Inflation: This is usually associated with a rising cost of the inputs to production. This traditionally has included raw materials, like oil or cotton, and labor. When it is heavily related to the cost of labor it may be called "wage push inflation." A major factor that can deflect this type of inflation is the ability to substitute cheaper or more efficient inputs into production. In some cases technology is lowering the cost of inputs or the amount of inputs needed. Logistics technology is decreasing the cost of developing lower cost inputs from alternative geographies.

Demand Pull Inflation: This is driven by increasing consumption, or by too small an amount of supply of a product. Either way, purchasers of products are buying more and willing to pay more so producers and retailers raise their prices. Sociology may be having some effect on this form of inflation, as the great recession has appeared to cause more cultural frugality making people more likely to defer purchases or find substitutes when prices move up. It is also easier today to find substitutes because of global supply chains and access of information about alternative products over the internet.

Money Supply: This is often linked with demand pull inflation. The theory focuses on a country putting too much money in circulation, which increases demand and drives prices up, in part because the value of the currency has declined due to its increased availability. Sometimes this has occurred in a country that has created a large debt burden and is using the increased money supply to help address it, instead of cutting expenditures or increasing taxes, the country effectively prints money.

Currency Devaluation: For many reasons currencies can become devalued (e.g., political instability, trade imbalances, gross domestic product [GDP] declines). When there is a significant devaluation in a country that is particularly dependent on imports it can result in a spike in inflation as imported goods cost more. If the country has a reasonable export economy its lower currency could help to sell more goods abroad.

Inflation Expectations: Interacting with all of these theories above is the population's inflation expectation. When people's expectations are more extreme it can be self-fulfilling. In other words, if people expect prices to go up by a significant amount they may buy more goods because they expect products to be more expensive causing demand pull inflation. Thus far millennials have not really seen a major inflation shock, as this age group gets older inflation expectations may be set in a very tight band and reactions to even a mild inflationary move could spiral.

A certain level of inflation is usually desired in an economy. Prices historically go up with an expanding economy, asset values increase and this helps to encourage economic activity. However, when it gets out of hand it erodes the value of a currency, reduces savings, and stretches consumers' budgets, and especially hurts those on fixed incomes. It can create shortages of goods as the reduced value of the currency makes it more expensive to buy materials from overseas. Also, deflation is not good. It means the value of people's wealth is declining. For example, the value of their home may be worth less each year. It also means they are seeing prices of goods going down each day, so if their expectations are for continuing deflation they will defer purchases, further hurting the economy as consumption drops. You can see that too much inflation or deflation are both particularly damaging to people on a fixed income and those that may have a significant amount of their net worth tied up in a hard asset like a house. So countries with an aging population have to be particularly sensitive to balancing inflation levels.

Economies seem to thrive when there is modest inflation and relative price stability. In the developed countries, and many lesser developed countries, the central bank's primary mandate is to try to maintain price stability. It is typical to have a target rate of inflation in the low single digits. Central banks try to manage inflation through shifting short-term borrowing rates. Investors around the world and within each country may adjust their expectations for inflation in a given country depending how convinced they are that the central bank of that country has the tools and the fortitude to properly manage inflation.

Technological innovation has an impact on inflation in a multitude of ways. New technological products can have a deflationary pricing trend as they get adopted and this has had an impact on inflation, especially as technology adoption has accelerated. Some of this decline in the prices of technology products is due to scale, as a technology gets more widely accepted, some of the price decline is due to competition entering the market after a new technology is introduced and some is due to other efficiencies that are developed over time. As an example of technology pricing trends, in 1983 when the Motorola DynaTAC mobile phone was put on the commercial market it sold for approximately $3,995. By 1996 the Motorola Startec was introduced and it was selling for approximately $1,000.[i] Mobile phone prices did not rise again until smartphones were introduced by Apple, and they do the job of multiple products (e.g., cameras, music players, planners, etc.). During the same time the average price of an automobile in the United States went from $10,607 to $18,525.[ii]

Technology-driven improvements in logistics, efficiency, through energy savings, communication, and modern financing tools, has allowed companies to expand their supply chains to source the most cost-efficient supplies around the world. This has also had a major deflationary impact, but has introduced risks that can shock inflation. Shocks could come from a spike in transportation costs, civil unrest within the supply chain, or natural disasters far away from where the final product is sold.

Since the great recession many central banks have struggled to get inflation to their target rate, but the problem has generally been that inflation has been below the target rate, not above it. Many central bankers and investors continue to look at old models to factor in the drivers for inflation. It is not that factors, such as employment levels, do not matter anymore, they just do not matter as much as they once did, in part because of the impact of technology. While almost everything else in the world is moving faster, it may appear that inflation is moving slower. It is not necessarily slower, it is just that people can react much quicker to address the causes of inflation. While most people still look at traditional models of inflation, understanding the changes from technology in inflation can give you an advantage in picking investments. Inflation is increasingly likely to simply move in a narrower band. One of the dangers to the economy can be if regulators and policy makers do not acknowledge and adjust for the impact of technological changes.

---

i Ooma.com/blog/cell-phone-cost-comparison
ii Blog.chron.com/carsandtrucks/2016/04/cost-of-a-car-in-the-year-you-were-born

Chapter 12
Interest Rates and Falsehoods

Interest rates, like London fog in a Victorian era movie, are ubiquitous and seep into almost every aspect of people's economic life while still maintaining a certain air of mystery. To carry on the simile, even when the characters in the movie are all sitting inside by the fire, interest rates are out there impacting inflation, currency rates, car and home sales, and the decisions by companies to invest in new projects or not. Rates impact stock valuations as fixed income assets become relatively more or less attractive versus equities and funding costs for trading desks, hedge funds, and other margin loans move. Interest rates creep into every aspect of the economic and investment decision process.

Keep in mind that interest is the price of money. Specifically, it is the price to lend and borrow money. Your bank deposit on which you are paid interest is effectively a short-term loan to a bank. Most loans however have an interest rate and a payback date. The longer the date of payback, theoretically, the higher the interest rate. The reason for this is that money in your hands a month from now is more valuable than money in your hands ten years from now. If you are lending somebody money for ten years you are going to want to be paid more than if you lend it to them for a month. This is the main reason why there is a yield curve, in which, for example, a two-year bond typically pays lower rates than a ten-year bond. The interest someone is paid when they loan money along with any anticipated changes in the principle of the loan is the yield on the investment.

Yield Curve Steepness

The yield curve is sometimes measured by how steep it is. This is typically done by comparing the yield on a three-month government bill to a ten-year bond, or sometimes a two-year government bond to a ten year (sometimes a thirty-year note is used), but theoretically you could use any period with a different maturity on the bonds. There are theories about the steepness of the yield curve being predictive of the outlook for economic growth; this typically assumes a steeper yield curve implies higher growth, a flatter yield curve implies a weaker economy, and an inverted yield curve (longer dated bonds yielding less than shorter dated) implies a recession. This theory does generate a fair number of false positives and particularly the theory on an inverted yield curve has some timing issues as a predictor of a recession. For example, the yield curve in the United States inverted in late 2005 but a recession did not happen for over two years,[i] if you had held any of the major United States stock indexes and sold it when the yield curve inverted you would have left significant returns on the table for the next 24 months.

DOI 10.1515/9781547400751-012

There are probably as many theories and ideas on why interest rates move as there are traders and economists. There is a theory that interest represents the time preference for money, where a person prefers cash now than later. There is a theory that interest rate levels are based on a liquidity preference instead of a time preference. There are also theories tied into inflation such as interest rates are compensation for inflation expectations. All these theories seem to be right some of the time, which means they are also wrong some of the time, because at different times rates move based on different reasons and combinations of reasons. Focusing on just one structural theory is bound to make you miss some of the changes that can help your investing.

However, interest rates are never left to their own devices. Central banks and fiscal policies are constantly influencing how interest rates move. Most central banks have price stability as their core mandate and their major tool to control inflation is interest rates. However, even if a central bank could use interest rates perfectly to control prices, there is no assurance that it would pick the right level of inflation to target. In the United States the central bank has a dual mandate that also includes employment. Having the dual mandate is more honest politically as no central bank can just focus on price stability without an eye on growth, employment, and other critical economic factors. But the major tool they must do all this with is various adjustments that focus on impacting interest rates. Specifically, central banks influence rates through regulatory control over the traditional banking system and certain short-term borrowing rates for banks as well as purchases of securities in the open market. Often when central banks assert themselves to try to change interest rates the yield curve gets distorted. This can be seen in Figure 12.1, which shows the United States yield curve often flattening during periods when the Federal Reserve was raising their key lending rate. However, it is unusual for central banks to raise rates if the economy is not doing well and there is always the fear that they will go too far and crush the economy by making the cost of capital too high.

With increased global capital flows, rapidly available digital data on global government bond rates and more financial innovation, interest rates appear to be more influenced by investors and speculators than at any time in the past. One sign of this is that the trading volume in United States Treasury futures has surpassed the volume in actual Treasury bonds, implying more speculative trading.[ii] This weakens central banks' control and can change the patterns of interest rate movements. It appears that with more capital sources and information available rapidly on borrowing sources, the economic system can add leverage quicker than in the past and rate moves can impact more aspects of the economy.

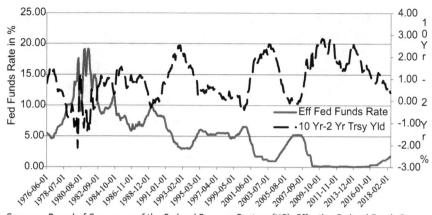

Sources: Board of Governors of the Federal Reserve System (US), Effective Federal Funds Rate
[FEDFUNDS], retrieved from FRED, Federal Reserve Bank of St. Louis; https://fred.stlouisfed.org/
series/FEDFUNDS, September 2018.
Federal Reserve Bank of St. Louis, 10-Year Treasury Constant Maturity Minus 2-Year Treasury
Constant Maturity [T10Y2Y], retrieved from FRED, Federal Reserve Bank of St. Louis; https://fred.
stlouisfed.org/series/T10Y2Y, September 16, 2018.

Figure 12.1: The Effective Federal Funds Rate versus the 10-2 Year Treasury Curve

Since the financial crisis, central banks have used more tools to influence the
markets and theoretically add more stability. One of these techniques has been
called quantitative easing (QE), which involves using the central bank's balance
sheet to buy a large amount of fixed income securities, such as mortgages, corporate bonds, etc. This takes bonds out of circulation and puts more cash into the
economy, hopefully encouraging more lending. They have also influenced banks
activities with regulatory and reserve requirements. The central banks need to be
careful about political and legal backlash. They may overstep their mandate by
pursuing some of the regulatory efforts, especially if they look beyond the traditional banking system to impose a regulatory agenda.

Some key points about central banks include: (a) their action generally only
influence short-term rates and they assume the markets will transmit this to longer
term rates; (b) their primary mechanism to exert pressure on rates is through the
banking system, if banking becomes less central to the monetary system they
might have less control; and (c) they have little control over fiscal policy and debt
issuance by the government, theoretically the two can work at cross-purposes.
When investing you want to watch what the central bank is doing, but do not kid
yourself and think that they are completely controlling the rates or that their economic predictions are an indicator of where financial conditions truly are.

People watch central banks, perhaps too carefully, to try to figure out their future actions on interest rates. People analyze everything they do, looking for some signaling to see what direction they may go. The central banks keep a significant amount of controls around information. In the United States the central bankers have set cycles of press releases and their speeches are generally announced ahead of time and prereleased. The media and analysts use algorithms to do word searches on these speeches and press releases so they can rapidly "interpret" each announcement. Sometimes the markets will convince themselves that the change of one word in a meeting is a major interest rate signal and this will trigger a market reaction. On May 9, 2013, Chairman of the Federal Reserve Ben Bernanke utilized the word "taper" about the U.S. Federal Reserve's bond buying program and triggered a "Taper Tantrum" causing the yield on the United States 10-year Treasury bond to go up by 65% over the next five months without any significant actions being undertaken by the Fed during that time, and well before there was any tapering.

Central banks do not always act the same, they may have certain rules and regularities around how they act, but stylistically the central banks can change. Central banks are made up of people and their personalities can influence the bank's actions. The head of the bank usually defines the personality of the it and their terms are usually long. The banks are supposed to be politically independent, but virtually nothing in the world of human interaction is completely free of politics, especially if it is based in places like Washington, D.C. The change in the U.S. Federal Reserve leadership that occurred in 2018 may prove to be an interesting personality study. Both Ben Bernanke and Janet Yellen headed the Fed for about 12 years combined. Both were academically trained economists and had spent their entire careers in academics or the public sector. Their replacement was Jerome Powell. He was trained as a lawyer and spent many years in the private sector. It will be interesting to see what changes occur in how the bank acts and communicates with this new leadership. Economists from academia and the public sector are often very wed to their models. While they are aware that these are just models, they may be less likely to change policy if it does not fit this construct and they can sit patiently and wait for reality to conform to the model over time; this may make them less reactive to signals from the market. Lawyers tend to be advocates and very pragmatic and willing to change more quickly. This leadership transition may lead to differences in how quickly the Fed responds to moves in the markets and investors may take time to realize that there may be new developments in the central bank paradigm with a new person in charge. It is not the central bank but usually a treasury department that issues government bonds. In the countries of the highest credit quality the interest rate on government debt is often referred to as the "risk-free rate." This is the case for countries like Germany, Switzerland, Japan, the United States, and a hand full of others. This does not mean that these notes do not bear risk from changes in interest rates; it means they do not have a risk of defaulting on their obligations. The difference between the government "risk-free" interest rate and the yield, or interest rate required on other types of loans of the same maturity is called *the spread*. This spread can be looked at as a measure of risk that a lender is requiring to get paid. If the five-year government bond is offered for sale at 2% and an investor is lending money to a company by buying its bond that matures in five years at 5%; the spread is 3. Usually, this spread is quoted in basis points[iii] (bp) so it would be +300bp. If that spread (i.e., credit spread) moves out to +375bp it implies that the perceived risk of that bond failing to pay back its obligations has increased. Obviously, many other things can influence that spread, such as supply and demand of bonds and the relative attractiveness of other investments as well as general economic and market volatility. However, spread is often viewed a measure of credit risk. These same factors are true with mortgage loans and other types of fixed income instruments. Examining the direction of the spread of different groups of bonds can give a good picture of how markets are perceiving risks in the economy or select parts of the economy.

Historically credit spreads on the debt issued by banks has been an interesting measure of perceived financial conditions. As financial markets evolve, banks are still an important part of the financial system, even though alternative financial entities are increasingly important. Bank credit spreads can be a valuable tool when comparing financial risks of various countries. Bank credit spreads are helpful to watch, but the value of this measure may diminish over time as other financial institutions evolve.

The Magic of Fixed Income Investing

Investors often focus on growth and price appreciation, which lead them to concentrate on equities. Investors do not always focus on interest income as a tool for return in their portfolio. In most fixed income investing, the bulk of the return stream comes from the interest income. Price appreciation can be a bonus in fixed income investments, but it is usually not the driving force behind the returns.

In fixed income investments you do not need to care what other people think. When you make a bond investment it has a maturity, at which time the borrower pays you back; it has a contractual interest payment, which the borrower will pay you while the loan is outstanding. If you have at least a five-year investment horizon and you buy a bond that has a yield of 10%, with a maturity in five years. You bought it because you thought the rate of 10% was a good return for the risk. To be right in this investment, all you must do is hold onto that bond and when the company pays you back your investment goal was achieved; it does not really matter what anyone else thinks. If you buy a stock at $25 and think it should be worth $30 in two years, it is not going to get to that price unless several other people are also convinced it is worth $30 and keep buying it until it gets to that price. Then you will have to sell your stock to one of them to achieve the return. Now the bond investor may have given up some better investment opportunities by holding onto the bond for five years, rather than trading the stock for a 20% gain, but, despite this opportunity cost, their expected and predicted return was achieved.

The return on the stock is dependent on the behavior of other actors in the market. The return on the bond is dependent on you just being right in your investment decision. Many people view fixed income investing as more conservative and in many ways it is given its higher level of predictability.

With huge amounts of capital some investors borrow money and use leverage to buy stocks so do not think that interest rate movements are a phenomenon impacting fixed income investments only. A small rise in rates impacts the return on leveraged stock holdings. The same goes for business investments. A project that can be funded with low interest rates may be less attractive if rates are higher. Having a view on the direction and level of volatility of rates is important and is part of the reason a company's capital structure matters. A view on interest rates can cause shifts between where in the world of fixed income investments you might want to concentrate and whether you want to be in fixed income or equities.

Credit spreads can be a valuable tool for understanding the markets' view on risk and a very good item to monitor. The increased access to capital from multiple sources other than banks and the increased trading volumes in government issued assets has changed the control that central banks have over interest rates. While it has not appeared in the economy recently, these dynamic non-bank flows of capital could lead to more volatility in interest rates over time. While many interest rate watchers focus on central banks, it is equally more important to be watching how long-term interest rates and credit spreads are acting in the markets as well as to monitor how much and what type of borrowing at the government, corporate, and household level is occurring.

---

i Federal Reserve Bank of St. Louis, 10-Year Treasury constant maturity minus 3-month Treasury constant maturity, *Federal Reserve Bank of St. Louis*.
ii Brettell, K. (28 March 2018), Rate futures volumes surpasses Treasuries as market evolves, Reuters. https://uk.reuters.com/article/us-usa-bonds-futures-analysis/rate-futures-volumes-surpass-treasuries-as-market-evolves.
iii 100 basis points = 1 percentage point.

Chapter 13
Currencies—Chicken and Egg

Currencies are the largest trading market in the world, markets are open 24 hours a day, and there is estimated to be more than $5 trillion of trading volume per day.[i] Currency markets are often where you see the quickest reaction to macroeconomic and political news. Exchange rates influence inflation, the ability for companies to sell products internationally and drive the cost of production materials. Analyzing all the potential interactions that currency valuations have in the economy can feel a bit like having to peel off all the layers of an onion with tweezers, especially as both can bring tears to your eyes.

Even if you are an experienced investor the foreign exchange markets (Forex) can be tricky to understand; it is not that it is difficult, it is just different. You typically see a stock or a bond quoted in a price. For example, perhaps the Pelham Pallet Company stock can be bought at $25 per share. You do not typically quote it in the price of another stock. For example, if Sunshine Casino Corp. stock was trading at $100 per share you would not say Pelham Pallets can be bought for 0.25 Sunshine Casino shares or a Sunshine Casinos share is worth 4 Pelham Pallet shares (i.e., $25/$100=0.25 or $100/$25=4, respectively). However, in currencies that is how it is done.

Currencies are typically quoted in pairs. As an example, EUR|USD is telling you how many U.S. dollars can be bought with one Euro. So when someone says, "The U.S. dollar is up today" what does that mean? First, the person may not know what they are talking about, or perhaps they are just not clearly explaining what they are saying. Is the U.S. dollar up against all currencies or just one currency in particular? While trades in currency are usually done in pairs, like the EUR|USD, there are indexes that can be traded that compare a single currency to a basket of other currencies. So that person that told you the U.S. dollar was up, may be quoting the price movement relative to a basket of other currencies. This is quite common. These baskets are usually done using just the largest liquid currencies—and each country's currency is typically weighted in the index based on how much they trade with the base country—in this case the base currency is the U.S dollar so the weighting of each major currency in the basket would be based on the volume of trade with the United States. The other thing to note in how currencies trade is that what seems like small percentage movements can be big factors in profits and losses because the trades are usually very large in size and often are leveraged.

Corporations, investors, and individuals that have significant overseas operations or investments often use hedges on currencies. This allows them to lock in

DOI 10.1515/9781547400751-013

an exchange rate for a period using futures or forward contracts for delivery of a currency. These simple option markets are enormous, too. Investors and specula-tors will often just trade in these futures and forwards markets and that will effec-tively add to the volume in trades related to Forex and speculation has had some distorting effects on exchange rates at times, technology has made it possible for all of this trading to happen almost instantly around the world.

Currencies are not just trading vehicles they impact the economy broadly. If an exporting economy sees a decline in the value of their home currency relative to their trading partners, that makes their products cheaper to those countries where they sell. That might lead their economy to grow dramatically and lead to inflation as more money is coming into the economy and imported goods are more expensive. That may cause the central bank to raise interest rates, which could cause the currency of the exporting country to increase in value as more capital moves into that country to take advantage of the higher rates, hurting the country's exports. You can see how this cycle can go and how many aspects in an economy get involved. This description assumes that the exchange rates are operating in a free-floating regime. Do not think that these regimes are truly free floating because governments get involved too. In addition to the natural flow of trade and speculation by investors impacting currency levels, central banks and treasury departments get involved in trading currencies all the time for various reasons. Sometimes they do this to manipulate the exchange rate to benefit their policies and sometimes to build up or wind down reserve currencies they are holding as a safety buffer.

Do not believe that the current floating exchange rate mechanisms and environment are a forever thing. For many years the major countries managed their exchange rates on a gold standard. There have been many periods where exchange rate mechanisms have been very different and there are many regions where exchange rates are fixed, or pegged. There are also partial fixes where a range is set and a currency only floats in that range. There have also been regional currency groups that manage their exchange rates in unison. There, of course, is also the great ongoing monetary union experiment known as the Euro. This has several countries sharing one currency and has only been in place since 1999. Currency arrangements change and currency regimes change. The current inter-action of exchange rates is unlikely to be in place forever.

It is worth reviewing some of the traditional theories on why currency pairs trade as they do. Currencies do not trade directly in line with these theories, as many factors play into the actual value of a currency, including speculation and future expectations, but they are valuable to understand.

Since money is generally used to purchase things, one theory focuses on purchasing power parity (PPP). This implies that if you built a basket of goods in the United States and it cost you $5,000 if that same basket cost you CHF6,000 Swiss francs the exchange rate between the USD|CHF should be 1.20 (USD|CHF = 6,000/5,000). This of course does not factor in taxes, import, restrictions on goods, etc. This relationship does not appear to hold true over many cycles, but many economists have believed that the relationship holds well over a very long period.

Interest rate parity is another theory of how currency trades over time. If one country has a higher interest rate than another the exchange rate compensates for this, otherwise there would be an arbitrage. Meaning if a United States citizen could get 5% annual interest rates but saw that in Mexico they could get 7.5% in annual interest, they would want to do that for a year. However, if the exchange rate right now is USD|MXN = 10 at the time you want to do this transaction, it will take you a year to get the interest and by that time the exchange rate should have adjusted 10(1.075/1.05) = 9.77. Therefore, the United States citizen will get back fewer pesos than they got in the original exchange and this will wipe out the gain on the higher interest rate. The rationale is that the difference in the exchange rates is due to differences in the countries' inflation rates, and the related monetary policy. Therefore, the country with the higher inflation is creating more supply and its money is worth less. Forex forwards do trade at levels based on anticipated future interest rates.

The level of confidence in a strong economy and political stability can drive currency exchange rates as can demand and supply of that currency. International trade is a huge market and technology and globalization have increased international supply chains and the volume of transactions. Trade balances can greatly influence currency exchange rates. The demand for a country's goods often leads to demand for that countries currency as others need to pay for those goods. However, this theory does get impacted by the fact that not all international transactions take place in local currencies. Many types of transactions are contracted to take place in the largest most stable currencies in the world, most commonly the U.S. dollar. About 64% of global central bank reserves are also held in the U.S. dollar and about 39% of all debt is issued in U.S. dollars.[ii] This position of the U.S. dollar led, Francois Mitterrand, former president of France, to declare that the dollar had exorbitant privilege.[iii]

The scenarios of what drives currency exchange rates can get very convoluted and one must play through numerous actions and reactions to try to track where the valuations might move to in various scenarios. Think about some reactions in the market. If the U.S. Federal Reserve Bank announces a rate hike and the European Central Bank (ECB) does not, the U.S. dollar should rise in value, unless the expectation is that the ECB will raise rates soon. If the economic results in Europe are much stronger than the trends in the United States, this might counterbalance the move upward in the U.S. dollar. However, if oil prices rise, that usually increases expenses in Europe more than in the United States, which could put downward pressure on the Euro. These iterations can go on and on. Other factors can include the level of trade, speculative actions, and currency purchases by central banks. Additionally, keep in mind in the example above that there was only one currency pair being examined, in reality traders are comparing a multitude of exchange rates.

Watching how currencies move in response to an economic news item or a change in the language of a central bank commentary can quickly give you some color on how the markets are viewing the news. However, you must remember that there is a plethora of items that can move currencies around in value. When using currency movements as a gauge for market reactions there must be an awareness of all the day's economic headlines. It is always helpful to also try to get a sense of what the perception is outside of your home market. One tool to do this can be online subscriptions to the *Wall Street Journal* and the *Financial Times* that allow you to pull up United States, Asian and European versions of their papers, as well as some other regional versions. It is a healthy exercise to periodically review what the differences are in the top stories in various markets to get a better view on what the rest of the globe outside your home market is focused on.

If you are looking to monitor market reactions in currency on a global scale, sometimes following individual currencies may give you too narrow a picture. One tool is to build thematic currency baskets to monitor. For example, you could build a basket of "safe-haven" currencies that might include the United States dollar, the Japanese Yen, and the Swiss Franc. You could pair them all against another currency like the Euro or use their trade weighted baskets. When this basket goes up it could imply that global capital flows are looking for safer markets and de-risking, or just heavily favoring developed countries. Another theme could be commodities. Many large economies are heavily dependent on commodity prices. For a commodity currency basket you could include both developed and emerging currencies and include the Canadian and Australian dollar, the Brazilian real, and perhaps the Russian ruble. You can build out other themes such as monitoring the view on global trade by building currency baskets of major exporters or importers or countries dependent on supply chains. These baskets can be an interesting tool in developing investment themes or if you are monitoring currency for a global business.

The increased flows in international trade are increasingly causing factors other than just interest rates and inflation expectations to drive exchange rates. Short-term moves in currency markets are interesting gauges of market reactions, while longer-term moves in currencies can be a sign of a trend. Just because currency markets are a bit different, they should not be relegated in importance when undertaking economic and specifically investment analysis; they influence everything and at the same time are influenced by everything.

---

i World Bank.

ii https://www.thebalance.com/world-currency-3305931

iii Eichengreen, B. (2012, September 1), *Exorbitant Privilege: The Rise and Fall of the Dollar and the Future of the International Monetary System.* Oxford, England: Oxford University Press.

Chapter 14
Expectations Theories—Always Changing, Always Relevant

Expectations drive markets. Immediately after economic data is released traders and media outlets are comparing them to "expectations." Intuitively it feels odd that there could be an announcement of gross domestic product (GDP) being down –2% and the stock markets trade up because expectations had been for –2.8%. However, this is the power of expectations and why expectations are often as important as the data itself. As discussed earlier, expectations about inflation can theoretically be more important than what the inflation numbers are. This is because this expectation is what impacts the consumers' decision to spend or to save. The same can be said about expectations for interest rates and economic growth.

Where do expectations come from and have they changed over time? Typically published expectations for company or economic releases are set by a survey of analysts or economists at major banks and brokerage houses. It is worth noting that these composite expectations are not weighted by the size of the institution making the estimate, the resources they have dedicated to the task, or the historical success of those making the forecast. Importantly, the same source may be used over time (e.g., Bank A's research department estimates) even though the actual forecaster or analyst team has changed. A factor that is sometimes ignored has been how many of these organizations that hire analysts and forecasters have changed the resources they have dedicated to pay and staff research departments that make these forecasts primarily because of government regulation. Additionally, whoever is preparing the estimates that get rolled into composite expectations all will have conscious or subconscious biases that are driving their expectations. As John Silvia, former chief economist at Wells Fargo wrote in one of his books on forecasting, "Unfortunately, analysis often starts with a view and then tortures the data until it reaches the proper result."[i]

Banks are not the only source of expectations. Companies often put out their own guidance for earnings and other key performance indicators (KPIs). There are also several organizations, including government agencies, that put out economic outlooks and forecasts. These sources include central banks like the Fed and the Bundesbank in Germany as well as specific agencies like the U.S. Department of Agriculture. There are also regional federal reserve banks in the United States that publish forecasts and international agencies like the International Monetary Fund (IMF), the World Bank, and the Organization of the Petroleum Exporting Countries (OPEC) that publish macroeconomic expectations.

DOI 10.1515/9781547400751-014

The reaction in markets to a "beat" or a "miss" on expectations is not often long lasting, unless it is viewed to be a change in trend. It is still the longer overall trend that ends up driving asset valuations. When there is a reaction in the short term to a result that is an outlier, if it disagrees with your long-term view it may create an opportunity for an entrance or exit into an investment. The expectations of individuals and how these expectations make them act is a fascinating field of economics. While this has been an area of inquiry for centuries, it recently had been getting labeled behavioral economics. One of the aspects of human nature is that it is hard to predict what will change someone's view of the future. When you look at some of the major surveys about consumer confidence or inflation there are periods where it may surprise you how small or large the changes were even though the current events seemed extreme. For example, in the United States, in one survey, shown in Figure 14.1, consumer confidence dropped more during the tech stock collapse in the early 2000s than after the 9-11 terrorist attacks.

Source: University of Michigan, University of Michigan: Consumer Sentiment [UMCSENT], retrieved from FRED, Federal Reserve Bank of St. Louis; https://fred.stlouisfed.org/series/UMCSENT, September 17, 2018.

Figure 14.1: Michigan Consumer Confidence Survey

Most of the surveys about economic expectations revolve around consumer sentiment and consumer and business expectations for inflation. The Organization for Economic Cooperation and Development (OECD) releases surveys about consumer sentiment on their member countries, in the United States several regional Federal Reserve banks release surveys on expectations. There are numerous other surveys as well that can be very valuable. Surveys about confidence, economic expectations, and sentiment change rapidly. How quickly expectations change can be important. It is difficult to isolate if the proliferation of newer and faster sources of information are causing more shifts in expectations or if it is actual events that occur that cause the speed at which expectations change to accelerate or decelerate. Surveys may show changes, but in reality economic view may not change that rapidly. As Neal Soss, the vice chairman and former chief economist of Credit Suisse has said, "You don't usually have one outlook for inflation in the morning and then after lunch completely change your view, inflation expectations take time to change."

Sometimes expectations are heavily influenced by recent trends. When economic factors stay consistent for a long enough period of time, people tend to fall into a pattern of expecting these factors to remain in place. For example, they get used to ultra-low interest rates, or rising oil or a relationship between unemployment and inflation because it has been that way for an extended period of time, just like when people adjust to an odd smell in their home and do not even notice it, given enough time. This does not mean the environment, or the smell, is normal, people have just come to expect it. When the economic environment starts to change, people have varied reactions. For example, some people will assume it will revert to the recent patterns and others will become more uncertain about the future and move to safer havens being more willing to pay more for risk aversion. Rapid adoption of technology can cause these patterns to change quickly and investors have to try to calculate if new technology agents that have been introduced to the economy are destroying an old trend or not.

Sampling Techniques Can Skew Data

Many of the key economic data points that are followed by the market are based on surveys. Surveys are based on taking a sample of a total population. The sample that is chosen can be a critical factor in the results. There are two broad types of sampling, probability sampling, in which every person or institution has a chance of being selected in the sample, and nonprobability sampling in which a subjective decision is made as to what people or institutions are included in the sample. Probability sampling can take different forms. One methodology used in large surveys is stratified samples where the population may be divided into various categories, such as geography or age, and then the population in each stratum has an equal chance of getting selected, but a cross-section of the population is also reached. Nonprobability sampling is often undertaken out of convenience, such as a poll taken of people walking past a street corner or coming out of a voting location.

Most of the agencies and organizations that provide this data try to do a good job at updating contact methods and often pride themselves on the high level of responses they get. One of the realistic dangers of surveys in the current world is how much communication is changing. This could come from people cutting the cord on wireline phones, screening calls, telecommuting, and so on. This increases the risk that what may seem like a probability sample is becoming a nonprobability sample and subtly skewing the data.

It is worth reviewing some of the historical discussion on expectation theories: One of the simplest expectation theories focuses on interest rates and forward interest rates. The pure expectation theory states that forward interest rates and the term structure of rates represent the combination of everyone's expected future short-term rates. Therefore, if the aggregate view is that the short-term rates will be higher in the future the term structure of interest rates should rise over time.

The widely discussed rational expectations theory can claim many parents. The legendary John Maynard Keynes expressed the idea that profit expectations and the level of confidence that corporate management had in those expectations impacted the level of business investment. These views were also expressed by economists John Hicks and A.C. Pigou. John Muth outlined a more formal aspect of the rational expectations theory. This more carefully explains how producers and suppliers use past events to predict future business operations; this could also be applied to consumers. There has been significant research on the rational expectations theory since the 1960s. Some of the works done by Keynesian's argued that people were very reactive to changes in their income or other facets of their economic well-being. This implied a drop in income for one year would increase a person's expectations of volatility and would transmit to a drop in consumption. From this the economist Milton Friedman responded with the permanent income theory. Mr. Friedman suggested people make assumptions about their long-term income and smooth their consumption over time and for these reasons are not as reactive. Another theory has focused on adaptive expectations, which implies, among other things, that a piece of material new information, such as a drop in income, will not cause an immediate drop in consumption, nor will it be ignored and completely smoothed into a lifetime average. This information will cause a person to shift their expectations over time.

Rational expectations theory has been the basis from which much of the modern investment theory has evolved. Most notable is the efficient market theory. This theory outlines that the best guide to future asset values is present asset values. This is because all investors should look at all the available data, which will move everyone toward the same valuation for an asset and profit seeking investors will buy that asset until it reaches the correct price. A "strong" version of efficient market theory assumes equal amounts of information are available to all. A "weak" version assumes that some people do not have all the information or may not have the time to access all the information but they make rational decisions given limited information. The theory holds that when there are random disruptive events, valuations can change. Efficient markets theory is also tied to modern portfolio theories that incorporate concepts like the efficient frontier and measures of alpha and beta. Criticisms of rational expectations focus on the fact that people are often irrational and subject to biases. They may act in line with others or get excited about recent performance and develop irrational exuberance. Critics also cite that people don't necessarily learn from past mistakes and tell themselves, "that it is different this time." Ultimately much of the research on expectations theory has shown that, at the very least, people react differently to anticipated and unanticipated inflation, this may translate to other economic expectations as well.

The world today, of course, is changing how you must think about expectations. Much of the research done on expectations and modern investment theory is based on everyone in the market having equal access to all available information. There is a significant amount of work on the impact of market participants having symmetrical or asymmetrical information. The field is viewed as important enough that the 2001 Noble Prize in Economics was awarded to George Akerlof and Joseph Stiglitz for their work on the impact of asymmetrical information, even though Mr. Akerlof's original paper on the topic was rejected by three academic journals.[ii] Today there may very well be a new kind of information asymmetry occurring in which there is so much information available that it is difficult to process it and those who can process more or select the right information to focus on have an advantage over those who can not. If this information processing asymmetry proves to produce different results, you could get more divergent market views and more variance in expectations and thus different reactions when results deviate from trend. Regulators (except for the MiFID II rules) have done a very good job at increasingly leveling the playing field for access to information for all investors, but with so much information, knowing how to prioritize it is increasingly important.

How the population changes will trigger different responses in expectations and reactions. A changing population will have experiences and biases that vary from the existing core of the population, these human variances can be more difficult to analyze in algorithms, especially as they evolve real time. The biggest example of this might be the large millennial population that will start to increasingly shift economic expectations. Their experiences with technology and the great recession will increasingly change the aggregate expectations in the economy.

Part of the theoretical work on expectations certainly veers into the areas of neuroscience and psychology. Much of the research in the area has focused on how much people's views are determined by their experience and by their goal to maximize their utility, whether that utility is profit, happiness, or time sleeping off a drinking binge. If the outcomes do not differ too often from what people expect, many theories hypothesize that people will continue to trust their expectations and not revise their outlook considerably, therefore, changes in behavior will be minimal. There are occasional failings in this theory, but they are either outliers or people adjust to these changes and realign their expectations. When there is a big enough change to alter long-term expectations, asset valuations get reset. This reset factor may be interesting in the current environment, given the millennial population bubble consists of many people that for most of their investing life have been experiencing an economy impacted by post-great recession central bank policies that have created an extended period of low interest rates and inflation. If this environment changes dramatically it will be a new experience for a large portion of the population and they will need to reset expectations.

Expectations are massively important when making investments. Investors do not like uncertainty and when results vary from expectations, uncertainty increases. It is quite possible the composite expectations being used now are much weaker than in the past, primarily because of cut backs at banks and given that models may not be adapting as quickly as they should, given all the rapid changes in the economy. Surveys are an increasingly valuable tool to monitor the economy, given how quickly they can reflect new developments compared to some traditional economic reports. Consumer and business survey data can have numerous shortcomings, but this "soft" data may be more valuable in catching rapidly changing subtle shifts in consumer spending, business investment, and inflation trends than the much delayed "harder" government releases.

---

i Silvia, J. (2011), *Dynamic Economic Decision Making*. United Kingdom: John Wiley & Sons.
ii Frangsmyr, T. ed. (2002), *Les Prix Nobel. The Nobel Prizes 2001, George A. Akerlof Biographical*. Nobel Foundation. Retrieved from www.nobelprize.org/prizes/economics/2001/akerlof/auto-biography

Selected Ideas from Part 4

Topic	Concepts	Investment Impact
GDP	It is a measure of growth and size. It has a long lag.	There are more timely measures of economic activity. The fastest growing new dynamic businesses are likely underrepresented.
Unemployment	Changes in work habits, like multiple part-time jobs and self-employment distort the real economy from reported figures.	Employment is critical to political stability, and consumer driven themes. The value of this data may deteriorate as work habits change.
Inflation	Technology, globalization, and sociology have changed buying habits and inflation drivers.	Pricing power has eroded and if costs rise it could hurt corporate margins. Supply chain shocks are a bigger inflation risk.
Interest Rates	Major factors impacting rates are more complex and diverse now than just banks and central banks.	Central banks have less control over rates and capital. System can add leverage quicker, so a move in rates impacts more aspects of the economy.
Currency	It is the most active trading market, it has major technical components. Currency moves are felt everywhere.	It frequently shows the quickest reaction to macro and political news. Hedging costs are an increasing factor in capital flows. Select currencies move on certain types of news, for example, instability or commodity spikes.
Expectations	Markets value assets based on future expectations. In some cases quality of the expectations has weakened.	Values move if results differ from expectations; if expectations are poorly managed there may be opportunities to exploit a market bias. Information is more symmetrically available, but the ability to process it may be more asymmetrical.

Part 5: **Old Capital, New Capital**

Chapter 15
The New Role of Capital and Capital Formation

In the hit musical *Hamilton,* the second act has a song entitled the "Room Where It Happens." Along with introducing the use of a banjo into hip-hop style music, the song covers a famous compromise in United States history. Alexander Hamilton agrees to move the capital of the new country from New York City to the Maryland–Virginia area in exchange for Virginians James Madison and Thomas Jefferson approving Mr. Hamilton's financial plan. The plan called for the federal government to become responsible for the Revolutionary war debt of the states. It also effectively allowed for the formation of a central bank. Mr. Hamilton saw the need of the newly independent United States to have access to capital to grow and diversify its economy. He saw that the best way for the new country to have credibility in the capital markets of that time was to repay all the debt from the war and not allow some states to default and others to stay solvent. Mr. Hamilton traded location of the capital for control of the nation's financial capital, highlighting what capital he viewed as being more valuable.

The little pun at the end of the first paragraph shows how the word capital can be used in different ways. Even within the world of economics it is used in many ways. In its simplest form, capital is wealth. It can be in the form of physical capital, such as a house, a factory, or a copyright. It can also be in a financially liquid form like cash, stocks, a bank account, or even a line of credit has value.

Capital formation brings benefits to companies, individuals, and nations and is a common economic goal. Capital can be used as a tool to improve the quality of life, as a storage mechanism of wealth, as a means of production, or consumption. Capital flows are critical to companies and countries, they use it to pay for maintenance and expansion and use it as a safety net in weaker times. Monitoring the general access to capital as well as the amount and type of capital available and what type of capital is being used is critical in understanding micro and macro investment themes.

Capital is often thought of in its more liquid forms, like cash or securities investments. This type of capital formation is viewed as being initiated by savings and is one of the reasons savings rates are monitored by investors. A simple example of how savings helps access to capital would be a person deposits money into a bank, the bank uses the money to loan it to others to capitalize a new business or borrow money to buy a new car. Another example could be when a person puts money into a mutual fund that buys the stock of a company either giving that company more money to expand or increasing the value of its stock.

DOI 10.1515/9781547400751-015

There is a significant amount of capital in less liquid forms, such as a manufacturing plant or a brand name. Home equity loans tap into the excess capital of a home and transform it into liquid capital. Capital exists in all types of less liquid assets from a car to a Picasso painting. There are increasingly new ways of tapping into some of this capital. If a person wants to use a room in their house and rent it out over the internet they are tapping into a previously underutilized part of their capital to generate income. Underutilized or untapped capital has great potential. A Peruvian economist, Hernando DeSoto, has written extensively on how developing countries must utilize their less liquid forms of capital and government institutions need to improve how they monitor ownership so people can use this illiquid capital as surety to gain access to more liquid capital and grow their businesses.

Today flows of international capital and global supply chains link together corporations from diverse countries so that various nations' economies are more intertwined than before. Some writers have felt that this has reduced international conflicts and some of this fluid capital has helped development in some poorer countries. Digital information, improved communications, greater institutional consistency, as well as the growth in assets of nonbank financial institutions have all helped capital to be more mobile than in the past.

Market systems generally allow capital to go where it will get the best return. This usually results in capital going where there is growth and to companies that are seeing demand for their products and services. This differs from systems where a third party decides where capital should go, even if there is no demand for it. Like a government program that decides to use capital to send milk to dairy farmers or a copy of *Das Kapital* to a Kindergarten.

This does not mean that market systems always have the fairest flows of capital or the fairest access to capital, but market systems do allow for capital to generally flow toward people's freely selected choices. Technology is increasing the accessibility and therefore fairness of capital flows. In Indonesia they have had some of the highest proportion of unbanked adults of any nation, however it has incredibly high mobile phone penetration and firms are seeing rapid and massive take up in e-banking offerings through mobile phones helping make access to capital more broadly available, some of this is being driven by an internet-based ride hailing company that has offered a mobile wallet service to its drivers.[i]

Corporate capital typically comes from a combination of three sources. The first is cash generation at the company. Second is from equity capital that is created by selling an ownership stake in the company. Third is from borrowings. The amount of capital that a company can raise from third parties is usually based on their perception of the value of the assets of the business on the open market. The value is typically based on the ability of those assets to generate cash flow.

The amount of liquid capital available to people, businesses, and nations can impact the ability to grow the economy or weather an unexpected crisis. Understanding capital availability can help you make investment decisions. At one point most capital for companies came from banks and equity offerings, but there has been significant innovation in finance and it is getting increasingly harder to accurately trace availability. In some countries there are good surveys that can help gauge capital availability. These might include measures of business and individual confidence as well as surveys of bank lenders. There are also databases of public equity and debt financings as well as syndicated bank loans. When optimism is high, capital is usually more readily available.

Whichever sources you choose to monitor, try to notice changes in the direction of capital availability and the mix of the capital being raised. Too much debt or equity issuance can be troublesome signs. Debt is often considered to add more risks into an economy, though if too much equity capital is being raised it may mean company managements' see valuations near a top or investors are too willing to invest indiscriminately.

Keep track of the type of sectors of the economy that look like they can raise capital and those that can not, it can be an important differentiator. If a sound industry can not attract capital it may face major problems, keep in mind that in many cases bank lenders are getting monthly financial reports. Changes in what the bank lenders are doing may be early signals about a company's or an industry's health.

Equity sources of capital have become more varied than in the past. At one point in history this was almost exclusively private, sort of a friends and family circle of investors. With the help of the development of the limited liability company capital, in the form of public stock, became more readily available. More recent innovations have been private equity, venture capital, crowd funding, and even the television show *Shark Tank*, where entrepreneurs compete to win equity capital for their early stage companies.

Debt capital has been available for centuries. However, debt capital has taken on many forms over time. In the modern system, banks can process more loans because they often take the fees and sell off the bulk of the loan to other investment pools, such as mutual funds (increasing the danger of moral hazard.)[ii] Bond structures have become increasingly creative. In addition, there are mezzanine loans, microfinance lending, and direct lending sources available. There are also a variety of securitizations that can raise capital on any number of assets that offer a relatively predictable stream of cash flows, from communications towers to credit card debt. Securitized debt was even issued backed by anticipated music royalty streams, the first bond securitized by music rights was done using David Bowie's first twenty-five albums, and these bonds were dubbed Bowie Bonds.[iii]

Much of this financing is being done without traditional banking through investment firms, family wealth offices, major pension funds, and government's sovereign wealth funds. Creative financing has come from many areas. There are also online sources now to raise equity and/or debt. The increasingly varied sources of capital and increased speed at which capital can be raised is becoming more important to the economy but all of these developments make it more difficult to find meaningful statistics on capital raising and renders some of the older data, which is mainly based on bank borrowing and public equity raises, less valuable.

Short-Term Capital

Businesses are often in need of short-term capital for operations. This can be because of seasonality in their business, a sudden surge in demand, or perhaps shocks to their supply chain or logistics. The world of short-term finance can be critical to a company and make a meaningful difference in their financing costs.

There are many options to fund short-term working capital from commercial paper to factoring receivables. Short-term loans are quite common and are often secured. A common form of working capital loan is secured by the receivables owed to the company by its clients. All these short-term finances tend to have lower costs than long-term capital and, if managed right, can lower financing costs.

Trade credit is another typical form of short-term capital. In this instance a supplier may extend credit to a customer for a period, effectively financing their customers purchase for a short period. For example, an aluminum company, Alpha Corp., may deliver its raw product to a company that makes fenders for cars, Beta Inc. Instead of demanding payment immediately, Alpha Corp. may give Beta Inc. terms that state they have thirty days to pay them for the aluminum and if they pay within ten days they get a 3% discount on the price. This is known as 3/10 net 30. In many ways this was some of the original peer-to-peer lending, without all the technology. The internet has obviously opened many more avenues of short-term financing for companies in need of capital.

Government regulators are facing challenges in trying to keep up with all the new sources of financing, some of which they may not actually have jurisdiction over. They need to be careful not to choke off access to capital for newer business entrants just because they are getting capital from innovative sources. They do not want to create an uneven field benefitting incumbent companies over new ones. However, they do need to maintain order and fairness and prevent fraud from both those raising money and those offering to invest money.

From an investor point of capital can be an important tool to be used in measuring performance. Perhaps the first and most important rule for many investors is to preserve the initial invested capital. However, capital does not have a constant value. Some places that you invest capital you would expect to stay relatively constant, such as a savings account. Most other places you would put capital you would expect some greater level of asset value appreciation, like in buying a government bond or investing in a stock or even in a less liquid asset like buying a house. With a house you are hoping to get two forms of reward, you are getting utility from the use of the house and hopefully experiencing asset value appreciation.

Sometimes when you invest capital the expectation is the value will go down. For example, a common statement is that the value of a new car drops 10% the minute you drive it out of the lot. It is generally recognized that physical capital investments often decline through usage. In the case of a business that builds a new plant, it anticipates getting a return on the investment from the cash flow the plant generates. Studying how well a company deploys its capital and the type of returns it can get on this capital is an incredibly valuable tool to utilize in analyzing an investment and comparing the relative value of different investment possibilities. Unfortunately, while these return on capital calculations are valuable the methodologies tend to allow for a significant amount of subjectivity so when making comparisons it is key to strive for consistency.

When a company invests in a physical plant it is an asset and accounting rules will depreciate this asset over the expected useful life of the investment. Increasingly rapid innovation may cause the actual resale value of this invested capital to depreciate much more quickly than the accounting methodology, which means the stated book equity value of the company will not properly reflect the value of that asset. This is one of the reasons why, when it is possible, using the market value of a company is more valuable than the accounting "book" equity value. Many of the fastest growing and more innovative companies in the world are investing less in physical plant and in many cases are investing in less tangible assets (e.g., customized software, supply chain specs), which may have strong potential for cash flow generation for a specific company, but if a company was forced to sell its assets the specialization of these "soft" assets may limit the value they could fetch from other buyers. This could hurt the returns for investors if a company goes into distress.

Return on Capital—A Subjective Tool

Return on capital (ROC) measurements are a valuable tool to help measure how efficient a company is at making a profit from the capital they have raised or invested. In principal it is a simple concept. It is a measure of earnings divided by some measure of the company's capital. A basic formula is:

$$(\text{Net income} - \text{Dividends}) / (\text{Debt} + \text{Equity})$$

It is a particularly good tool to use in examining capital intense companies, like oil and gas companies or utilities. However, the performance of this ratio should be analyzed over time, not just as a snapshot, especially when comparing companies.

Economic formulas often look complex but the concepts are simple; in finance the ratios often look very simple but the potential complexities are quite difficult. The ROC measure is such a case because as you try to make the formula more relevant for today's world more subjectivity enters the equation and can bias comparisons and outcomes. We can examine some of the potential complexities of the ROC formula by looking at the possible issues with the numerator and do the same with the denominator.

On the numerator side of the formula, net income may not be the best measure. There could have been significant acquisitions or some other change in their assets, so depreciation does not match capital expenditures, or there may be certain one-time benefits or charges that make comparisons between companies difficult. As an alternative you may choose a measure that is more cash flow oriented such as earnings before interest, taxes, depreciation, and amortization (EBITDA) or just EBIT. You also may want to consider how to factor in decisions to deduct dividends or stock buybacks. All of these are nuances that can affect the analysis when you compare ROC ratios overtime for the same company or between various companies or projects.

On the denominator it may seem straight ahead, but there is the question of the value of using -book equity, especially in situations when new technologies may have reduced the value of the balance sheet assets. One option may be to use market value of equity or another measure like assets net of current liabilities. Another question to consider is how to account for any large portions of cash that is not being deployed in to the business.

Sometimes the ROC is compared to the weighted average cost of capital (WACC). This ratio uses the cost of a company's debt and the cost of its equity on a weighted average basis. This ratio has its own very large issues of subjectivity. While the cost of any debt is easy to calculate, the cost of equity is very subjective as it technically has no explicit value. Typically, some form of expected return is usually used to value the cost of the equity and this then can incorporate a whole variety of methods and opinion.

Factoring in all these issues can take a fairly simple ratio and make it quite complex.

There are new, diverse and more rapidly available capital sources than in the past, but they may not be available to all companies. New industries are often deploying capital into less tangible assets and many of these companies have easy access to capital relative to incumbent businesses. If an industry experiences a new competitive threat and the threat is getting strong capital flows and the incumbent can not raise capital, the capital flows may prove to be a self-fulfilling prophecy of which will succeed and fail.

---

i Maulia, E. (2018 September 5), Go-Jek sparks an Indonesian banking revolution. *Nikkei Asian Review*. Retrieved from FT.com

ii Moral hazard is generally considered to occur when an entity takes on risk, with the understanding that another entity will actually be responsible for any loss, such as an insurance company. In this case the danger is that a bank does not do a thorough job of underwriting because, while a failure of a loan represents a reputational risk, the bank expects the actual financial risk of any loss to be borne by the entities to which it sells the loans.

iii Wolff-Mann, E. (2016 January 11), Bowie Bonds: How David Bowie Securitized His Royalties and Predicted the Future. *Time*. Retrieved from Time.com

Chapter 16
International Capital Flows—Increasingly Critical

The digital transmission of communication across borders has given investors much greater confidence to invest out of their home markets and allowed companies to use global value supply chains with greater confidence. International capital flows have often been from investors chasing returns but increasingly have been driven by the globalization of business operations and international supply chains.

When balancing the decisions to invest in your home market or in international markets following capital flows can be critical when monitoring the health of a country, you can often see the interdependence of various countries' economies and get a sense of what is driving a country's economy. The ability of a country to attract foreign capital as well as retain its own capital for investment is a considerable strength. The ability to attract foreign capital can lead to dependence on foreign capital which is a classic economic double-edged sword. Many types of foreign investment can be quite fickle.

Foreign capital flight is an issue for concern but so is flight of domestic capital. For example, if it becomes obvious a country is moving to devalue its currency agents in the economy that can shift to foreign currencies will move out of a country as quickly as foreign capital might, assuming there are limited or no capital constraints. If a country's capital is leaving to go invest in foreign markets, you must ask why it is leaving too.

Traditionally international capital flows fall into three categories; foreign direct investment (FDI), foreign portfolio investment (FPI), and debt. A fourth form of increasingly common capital is foreign bank or liquidity deposits related to supply chains.

FDI is generally considered the stickiest of the forms of investment. It is usually defined as a foreign entity (usually a company) taking a meaningful, relatively illiquid, ownership stake in an asset overseas. For example, this might be a large ownership stake in a gold mine or a fish farm company. Some papers have defined this stake as having to be over a 10% ownership stake up to 100%.

FPI is when a foreign entity takes a smaller ownership stake in an asset. This usually is in the stock of a company. It frequently is in publicly traded stock markets and therefore is liquid and tradable. It may be for a trade in the security or a long-term investment, but it is usually below a 10% stake in a company and liquid.

Debt investments are exactly as they sound, a contractual loan of some kind. Note, that debt can be in the lender's currency or the borrower's currency or even

DOI 10.1515/9781547400751-016

a third nation's currency. It can also take the form of bank loans or bonds or some other form of securitized or unsecured instrument. As bonds are often more tradable than loans, some people differentiate between the two and refer to the more liquid bond debt investments as foreign portfolio debt.

With the increase in global supply chains, many companies have opened bank accounts in foreign countries and store cash there, or invest locally in other short-term instruments. Some might include this in FDI, but it has separate dynamics as the companies are not always making any form of equity investment but simply putting liquid working capital into the market. If this money sits in banks or elsewhere it can then be recirculated as capital through bank loans, it increases available capital in that country. Additionally, some of the supply chain relationships are creating capital sources. A company's local supply chain partner may be able to access capital because it has a contract from a large foreign business. Companies may also extend trade credit to their international supply chain partners.

Some of the theories behind the drivers of foreign capital investments focus on push attraction and pull attraction. Push factors are generally driven by the environment in the country where the capital is coming from, usually wealthier countries. These push factors are typically driven by central bank actions or other actions that are causing a domestic environment of low returns or increased risks that push investors to look elsewhere for returns or safety. This leads them to invest in foreign markets. Pull factors are specific to the country that is attracting the capital. These might be levels of economic stability, the quality of the rule of law and its institutions. Of course, a major attractor of capital is growth potential and opportunity for asset value appreciation that is greater than in the investors' home market.

Investors tend to be cautious about making cross-border investments. Reasons for this can include variations in rules and laws, capital flow restrictions, as well as concerns about currency fluctuations. There are also major concerns about asymmetrical information, meaning that local investors and operators will have more access to better information than foreign investors, sort of a home field information advantage. This will allow home market investors to trade or invest better than the foreigner. Real-time communications and news have helped reduce this concern, but not completely. Because of this you will often see greater capital flows between countries with similar cultures, rules of law, proximity, and/or language.

As international capital flows have increased the interaction and interdependence between nations has increased. This leads to greater linkages, when things go bad the can spread across numerous markets quickly, this is called contagion. Because of these increased linkages capital outflows or large international capital losses can more easily end up not just being an isolated regional problem but a global one. Capital outflows can be triggered by a problem in the country that is being invested in and/or from the country that is doing the investing. Diversification by region and the types of economies can help minimize the impact of such events. For example, if your international exposure is all coming from commodity dependent countries or tech service-oriented countries you are more exposed to a specific global industry rout. It is also important to keep in mind that every time there are issues in a country, or even a region, it does not trigger contagion; an infected toenail does not always spread all the way up your leg.

When looking at a country's risks you want to see if there is a high concentration of international credit. If one country is heavily invested in another or a country is heavily dependent on the capital of another, risks are high of contagion between the two nations. Similarly, if foreign capital is heavily concentrated in one industry it presents risks for that sector and the investors. This has occurred in the past as there was too much foreign capital supporting the Korean banking industry at one point and the Indonesian natural resources businesses.

In trying to monitor that accessibility of capital and the types of capital being utilized there is data, but it is often far from complete and seems to have significant gaps in measuring the new sources of capital rising. There are data sources on public capital raises and there is data on international capital flows, these include balance of payments reports and the U.S. Treasury's Treasury International Capital (TIC) report.

Data on international capital flows can be found in the databases of several organizations, some of the most accessible are the International Monetary Fund (IMF), the Bank of International Settlements (BIS), the Organization for Economic Cooperation and Development (OECD). Numerous government reports and agencies also have data on these flows. Much of the information is dated by the time it becomes available. The development of softer, faster data in this arena has not really evolved as much as other areas of economic reporting.

Much of the research in this area is focused on flows from developed countries to lesser developed countries. In many cases foreign capital is more important to these advancing countries and it is a larger portion of their overall capital. However, monitoring international capital flows factors can highlight important signals for developed countries as well and can impact growth, currencies, inflation, and other key data.

The greater use of global supply chains has caused a somewhat surreptitious increase in foreign capital investments. At times this "investment" is simply not coming from a company's balance sheet, but from its expense line, simply by buying products overseas it is sending capital to that country and that industry even if it is not an investment. This growth has been driven by technology improving logistics and information flow. Local capital commitments to infrastructure in exporting countries, especially in Asia, have also fueled this expansion. Supply chains have increased capital in many countries with large exports of intermediate goods. This increase in global supply chains is also distorting current capital flow data from historical information.

When decision making about international investments, foreign capital flows and data on a nation's balance of payments is an important part of analyzing a country's political and economic stability, infrastructure and growth. However, recognize the data tend to have a long lag, especially compared to the increase in the speed at which capital can move today. It is also quite likely that globalization and supply chains have distorted some of this current data relative to historical statistics. Foreign capital flows do not happen in isolation. When capital flows out of a country and into another, something is triggering an investor to make that decision, even if it is as benign as a wish to diversify.

Chapter 17
Human Capital—The Real Data to Watch

While Michael Milken is best known for his pioneering work as a financier and philanthropist, he has also been a longtime proponent of recognizing the value of human capital. Early in Mr. Milken's career he formed a lasting friendship with Gary Becker, the University of Chicago economist and Nobel laureate, who is credited with bringing the term "human capital" into the academic mainstream. Mr. Becker estimated that at least three-quarters of a nation's wealth was in the knowledge and skills of its people. Mr. Milken emphasized that you can invest in human capital and advocates for three major ways a nation can build human capital: through education, health (extending the length and quality of lives), and immigration.[i]

Mr. Milken's prosperity theory formula was originally written during his time as a student at Berkeley and Wharton:

$$\text{Prosperity} = \text{Ft}(\text{HC+SC+RA})$$

The formula states that prosperity is equal to financial technology (Ft) multiplied by the sum of human capital (HC), social capital (SC), and real assets (RA). This recognizes that human capital is as important to a country's, or a company's, success as physical and financial assets, and that financial technology has a multiplier effect on these assets.

Through his charitable organizations Mr. Milken emphasizes the long-term returns on investments in human capital, which he refers to as "the world's largest, most important asset class." Through the Milken Institute[ii] he has also tried to affect change with projects including a joint venture with the International Finance Corporation[iii] supporting finance professionals from developing regions, and the Milken Scholars program supporting high school graduates who have overcome significant personal hardships.

The quality of human capital in an organization and its ability to develop this asset can be critical to the success of an investment. This is true at the corporate level and all the way up to the national level. It is a major factor in how well the infrastructure of governments and markets operate. Tools to measure the quality of human capital have been evolving but tend to focus on a national basis not as much on a corporate basis.

Analysis of a company will include studying the quality of the physical plants, brand value, or the software code. However, there is not as much emphasis on

DOI 10.1515/9781547400751-017

analyzing the quality of management and employees—the human capital. There is some analysis of ratios such as a company's revenue per employee or employee turn-over, but typically there is not a more complete assessment of human capital in the investment selection process, even though it is critical to an investment's success. Human capital may be less scrutinized at the corporate level because of the higher level of subjectivity that needs to be involved in the analysis and the more qualitative than quantitative characteristics of this type of analysis. It can lend itself more to checklists and matrixes than financial ratios. Examining human capital also requires in-person visits rather than computer screens and financial statement analysis.

A pragmatic analysis of human capital is an important part of an investment decision. At Shenkman Capital, Mr. Shenkman established (mentioned in Chapter 2) a credit approval process that has been in place for over 30 years. It requires that credit analysts meet with managements and must continuously reevaluate management. The credit report contains a management assessment checklist and credit score. When you make a decision to invest in a company, management is the caretaker of your invested capital; hence, a prudent manager must judge, rate, and monitor that caretaker.

It is also not just the management and the track record that is important; it is the institutional and structural factors that are in place that allow an organization to get the best out of human capital. This includes corporate governance, organizational structures, education, training, recruitment, and retention of quality employees. Despite developments of analytical tools, much analysis in this area remains soft and needs to be done with company visits, conversations, and observations in a hands-on process. Turning around the culture of how human capital is managed in a corporate structure can take time just like rebuilding a plant. Any turn-around in which you are investing is not likely to happen rapidly and needs to be monitored.

The development of human capital at a national level is more widely followed. When making investments across-borders you will want to analyze the differences in the ability of nations to get the best from their human capital, it is a much more far ranging analysis than for a corporation. Even a well-managed company in a difficult national or regional environment will have problems.

Mr. Milken often cites Abraham Maslow's hierarchy of needs,[iv] which turns out is a good framework for considering a nation's ability to develop human capital. This hierarchy outlines that in priority order people need (1) to meet their most basic needs, such as food and security; (2) safety, employment, and health; (3) friends, family, and intimacy; (4) self-esteem, achievement, and respect, and (5) self-fulfillment through achieving their fullest potential. The simple point is that a nation must be able to provide the basic needs first before it can truly tap into its human capital potential.

In assessing the ability to maximize returns on human capital in a country metrics can include health, access to nutrition and shelter, education, and general safety. Political stability and institutions that allow for transactions to occur without exorbitant costs also help tap into human capital. Increasingly the communications and transportation infrastructure is critical as well. Finally, cultural issues can make a difference, how people treat each other and how much of the population has access to tools with which they can enhance their human capital. Under the leadership of World Bank Group President Jim Yong Kim, a former medical doctor that redirected his career to finance as a way to help countries, the World Bank has developed a Human Capital Index and has undertaken a Human Capital Project that helps countries emphasize these types of investments rather than just physical plant investments.[v]

In all of these matters there is the tendency to look at averages and as always averages are dangerous because they are too easy. Averages on measures of human capital do not often capture levels of inequality. Levels of inequality and the percentage of the population actively involved and engaged in productive endeavors can make a large difference in the stability of a country and poor numbers in this area indicate a nation is not probably maximizing the return on human capital.

Alan Krueger has written about the Great Gatsby Curve that shows that when a country has high inequality in one generation financial mobility on an intergenerational level is lower in the next.[vi] He argues that if the return on education increases over time, and higher income parents invest more in their children's education than at other income levels, inequalities can grow. This can get exasperated if networking and family connections are a major factor in career success and the Great Gatsby effect could be more severe.

The focus on human capital goes back at least to the writings of Adam Smith, the father of modern economics. In the 1776 classic *Wealth of Nations* he writes about, "... a man's skills being his fortune." and "... the value to a person's fortunes in honing skills and education."[vii] There is also a proverb that appears in many cultures that predates Mr. Milken and Mr. Smith and sums up all the scientific research on the topic, "Give a man a fish and feed him for a day, teach a man to fish and feed him for a lifetime."

Inclusion is a vital ingredient in how well a company or a country uses human capital. If any groups are excluded from being able to contribute then the maximum potential of an organization is not close to being reached. It makes sense that if someone had an incredible set of tools everyone should want to see them get used not just left on a shelf.

Productive workers in this modern era appear to be requiring more varied benefits than in the past in developed countries. Certain softer aspects of attracting employees get a fair amount of publicity because they are so different than traditional methods, these newer benefits might include being able to bring your dogs to work or a free Friday beer keg to share with coworkers. While some of these may seem extreme, they are indications of organizations trying to improve their human capital and should not be ignored in any assessment of a company. However, when looking at a company's approach to human capital flexibility can be the key. Corporations need to remember there are excellent team-oriented employees that would prefer to go and have a pint somewhere other than the office or perhaps they would prefer to get some extra training on new software.

Improvements in human capital can skew more recent data from historical statistics in categories like employment, wages and productivity. These changes have to be considered when running historical time-series on this type of data, especially in more developing countries and industries where changes might be more rapid and extreme.

In assessing human capital, it is important to examine that a company or a nation is focused on creating the support and infrastructure to allow human capital to flourish. The environment that is created can be critical to be able to maximize this form of capital. As company formation happens more quickly assessing the management of human capital prior to investing is important. In the rush to get started, it is all too common to focus on gaining revenue and market share and not realize how important human capital is to sustain and succeed in a business.

---

i Milken, M. (2014 July 8), To Renew Prosperity, Focus on Human Capital, *The Wall Street Journal*.

ii The Milken Institute is a nonprofit, nonpartisan economic think tank.

iii Part of the World Bank.

iv Maslow, A. (1943), A Theory of Human Motivation. *Classics in the History of Psychology*. Retrieved from psychclassics.yorku.ca/Maslow/motivation.htm

v World Bank (2018 August 3), Investing in People to Build Human Capital. *World Bank*. Retrieved from www.worldbank.org/en/news/immersive-story/2018/08/03/investing-in-people-to-build-human-capital

vi Krueger, A. (2015 January 20), Human Capital in the 21st Century. *Milken Institute Review*. Retrieved from Milkenreview.com

vii Smith, A. (2003), *The Wealth of Nations*. Bantam Classic.

Chapter 18
Aristotle, Infrastructure, and Capital

Aristotle had some very non-capitalistic views on money and wealth; however, he was also a big believer in private property and the market system and won praise from Austrian economist and libertarian leaning writer Murray Rothbard. In Mr. Rothbard's essay[i] on Aristotle he points out that the philosopher understood the importance of having market systems and believed they are extremely important for the proper functioning of society as they allow people to get what they want and need. Aristotle also strongly favored private property as a critical tenant in running a society's legal and economic system and he recognized that laws and institutions are critical to the functioning of markets and prosperity.

The ability to raise capital is based on investors trusting they will have recourse to get paid back. Therefore to attract capital and to have a fluid capital market, the legal and financial infrastructure is as important as any physical infrastructure in a country. Rules-based capitalism and institutions that support it are keys to success.

Economic theories on comparative financial systems often contrast market-centric systems to nonmarket or bank-centric economies. The United States and United Kingdom. are often cited as market-oriented economies. Countries like France and Japan are often cited as more bank-centric systems. Market-based economies have more varied sources of capital, such as established and diverse markets for stocks and bonds. The markets can take on somewhat more exotic structures, like converts, warrants, and securitizations. Bank-centric economies tend to primarily have much less diversified capital markets and the bulk of funding comes from banks. In some cases there is an intricate network of national and regional banks and sometimes banks with industry specialization. This latter system typically allows for more regulatory control over capital and more standardization of the types of financing available. That can result in only certain types of companies and projects getting capital, stifling innovation. It also means that if the bank system faces problems, there are limited alternative financing resources to access.

In reality the lines are increasingly blurred between market and bank-centric systems. The more market centric, the more flexible and innovative the market is. Increased communication technology helps market systems react quicker and have more data on which to make decisions. Technology is changing traditional barriers and allowing new entrants to force their way into all markets. It can not just be the access and sourcing of capital that improves, it also must be improvements in information for the investors. Better information will allow the lenders to more appropriately asses the level of risk worth taking and let them price the

DOI 10.1515/9781547400751-018

risk appropriately. This should allow quicker response times to financial needs and can help avoid liquidity crunches from ballooning into a financial crisis.

Mortgage Lending and Fintech—Changing Things Up

In some countries, homeownership is very high, for example, in Romania[ii] it was 97% in 2018. In the United States it is estimated to be about 64%.[iii] It is one of the biggest investments and stores of capital for many people around the globe. Financial technology is changing how and who finances home loans.

The ability to borrow and refinance homes in many countries is a major part of capital flow and profitability to banks. In the United States there is a massive amount of federal and state regulation around mortgage lending that increased after the 2008 crisis. Despite the incredible myriad of regulations, which typically benefits incumbent operators, companies like Quicken Loans are changing the process for home loans. If you want to fully understand the difference between the legacy real estate lenders and how they are being challenged walk into a bank and say you want to get a mortgage and see how it progresses and the time it takes. Then go on to a site such as Quicken Loans and go through the process. The latter is faster, less cumbersome, and more pleasant. Supporting documents can be downloaded and the lender can verify by accessing records, which can be done in a centralized location that creates the ability to be scalable and have more control than some bank branch structures.

A study undertaken by the Federal Reserve Bank of New York[iv] found some exceptional results for "fintech" (financial technologies) lenders, in part defined as non-deposit taking institutions. The market share of these lenders grew from 2% in 2010 to 8% in 2016. The mortgages typically closed about 20% faster than traditional banks and closing times did not increase as much during busy periods as they do with bank lenders. Additionally, default rates were lower. It is critical that newer fintech lenders also use technology to maintain credit information on the borrowers to keep these default rates low.

As more homeowners become comfortable using these types of lenders the speed and ease of the system may lead to a meaningful increase in refinancing. There are already fintech companies in other areas of lending that are increasing the access to capital for consumers, small businesses and students as well. One of the dangers is that this may all make getting loans too easy and too much leverages creeps into the system.

As newer forms of capital raising increase it will disrupt some of the organizations that regulators have the most control over. These developments will put pressure on traditional bank systems to attract both sides of their balance sheets, deposits and loans. This may also weaken central banks' and treasury departments' control over capital flows and factors that impact the velocity of money. Of course, traders like to trade, salesmen like to sell, and regulators like to regulate, therefore, they will likely find ways to regulate new capital sources and transaction methods. While there is a constant struggle between the benefits and the detriments of regulation on the financial industry, one benefit is that when an industry is regulated there is more data available to analyze, but that is definitely not worth the price of heavy-handed innovation stifling regulation.

The more choices in capital structures and the access to varied capital the better. Different companies need specific types of capital structures and even the same company needs different types of capital structures during its lifetime. Mr. Milken wrote in an article that he used to debate his late friend Nobel laureate Merton Miller about whether capital structure was an important part of management's job and if it impacted the valuation of a company. Mr. Milken was right in the view that the capital structure has a huge influence on valuation and risk. Just as importantly, he points out that capital structures have to evolve and be dynamic.[v] This means that the ideal capital structure for a company will vary depending on many factors including where the company and industry are in their life-cycle and numerous macroeconomic factors.[vi]

Sometimes capital is considered a competitive advantage. Uber, Airbnb, and WeWork are all innovative companies with first mover advantages that have touted their access to capital as an advantage over other start-ups that might compete with them. If capital access continues to increase more quickly and it is readily available, it will become less of a competitive advantage. It was not that long ago that some of the incumbents that these innovative new economy companies were threatening, thought they had a capital advantage. Frequently, incumbents have an opportunity to move quickly against competitors, but often may fear undermining their existing invested capital. Imagine a retailer that did not want to undermine all of the investment in retail locations, so it chose to avoid diluting the value of its stores and chose not to sell products on the internet, this would have resulted in falling way behind the competition.

There are cases where incumbents have tried to suppress innovation in what appears to have been an effort to protect invested capital, and it has led to failure. Kodak is a great example of this. Kodak was founded in 1888 and became one of the largest makers of film and cameras. At its peak Kodak was estimated to control 70% of the photographic film industry. Eventually digital cameras crushed the market for physical film and cameras. By 2012 the damage caused by the development of digital photography and bad corporate decisions forced Kodak to file for bankruptcy. Ironically, in 1975 an engineering team at the company actually invented the first digital camera. Management was likely trying to protect its existing market and the investment in it rather than looking ahead; they could not suppress a major innovation.[vii,viii]

The ability of technology to improve access to capital and quickly supply more information for investors to monitor and check on their investments is changing the economic landscape. Capital movement is faster. It can rapidly get repriced and moved to where it is needed. This can smooth out market disruptions. Nations' infrastructures can help facilitate it and regulators need to monitor and set rules for newer forms of capital access without suppressing innovation.

All of these changes make it more difficult for analysts to monitor where capital is flowing. Capital will likely move much more quickly than the data.

———

i Rothbard, M. (2006 February 1), *Economic Thought Before Adam Smith – An Austrian Perspective on Economic Thought.* Ludwig von Mises Institute.
ii tradingeconomics.com/romania/home-ownership-rate
iii U.S. Bureau of the Census, Homeownership Rate for the United States [RHORUSQ156N], retrieved from FRED, Federal Reserve Bank of St. Louis; fred.stlouisfed.org/series/RHORUSQ156N, July 2018.
iv Fuster, A., Plosser, M., and Vickery, J. (25 June 2018), How is Technology Chasing the Mortgage Market. *Liberty Street Economics.* Federal Reserve Bank of New York.
v Milken 2012 piece.
vi Milken, M. (2002 4th Quarter), The Corporate Financing Cube: Matching Capital Structure to Business Risk. *Milken Institute Review. Milkeninstitute.org.*
vii *The Economist* (2012, January 24), The Last Kodak Moment?
viii Photosecrets.com, The Rise and Fall of Kodak.

Selected Ideas from Part 5

Topic	Concepts	Investment Impact
Capital Source	Financial capital is now more rapidly available in varied forms and sources.	This should be good for long-term positive trends in the economy as capital can go where needed more rapidly.
Cost of Capital	It is critical that information flow keeps up with capital flow, risks can be assessed and priced correctly.	If money becomes too easy and at too low a cost, it may be too easy for bad investments to destroy capital.
Capital Flows	In long periods of growth, capital may be more available to high growth start-ups than incumbents.	Although more flexible capital flows will help the broad economy, it may increase winners and losers at a more microlevel.
Capital Investment	Technology and innovation are changing how to look at capital investment.	Rapid innovation is accelerating declines in value of physical plants. More investment is being made in nontangible capital. These factors make typical balance sheet book value a less valuable data point.
More Capital	Capital is generally more available for more market participants.	This is likely to weaken the concept that capital is a competitive advantage, as anyone with a lead can easily be caught.
International Capital	International capital flows have increased with trade.	Capital flows info gives insights into drivers of economies. If capital goes somewhere, it has to leave somewhere.
Human Capital	Human capital is as critical in an investment as physical and financial capital.	Human capital should not just be a factor in country investing but must be analyzed when corporate investing, too.
Human Capital Investment	Do not just examine current statistics, but also the structure supporting employees.	You want to examine the flexibility and thoughtfulness in the structures put in place to support the human capital when investing.
Capital Infrastructure	Laws, enforcement, stability, and transaction structures allow for the best returns on capital.	New technologies should allow lower and more secure transaction costs, which may increase volatility but allows for more flexibility.
Capital Regulation	New capital sources are making it more difficult for regulators.	Regulators are challenged to manage new technologies and capital sources that are more global, but they risk hurting innovation.

Part 6: Tonight the Role of Government Will Be Played By...

Chapter 19
Government's Role: Past and Future

Earlier writers on economics often referred to the topic as political economy. That phrase captures the intertwined relationship of how government polices impact the performance of the economy and vice versa. Economic models do not typically have a factor in their models for politics, as it does not fit well into quantitative analysis. However, big changes in policies can have a huge impact on the economy and specific investments. Investors have to remember that policies can change valuations.

Social media is diversifying and accelerating the communication of political ideas and causes. It may change where the influence on policy comes from and may disrupt the major political parties. There is also a large demographic bubble of the millennials that are impacting the politics in many countries that are more likely to be influenced by digital media than older age groups. All of this may lead to more dramatic changes than in the past. Even in more totalitarian undemocratic regimes the access to information from the internet is forcing some of these countries to open up and liberalize some policies giving more choices to their citizens. All of this means that economic policy can take paths that diverge from the historical trends and can change more suddenly due to rapid real, or manufactured, public reaction. It is too easy to assume the policy stays status quo when planning investments and that is not prudent.

When the U.S. Government Took the Gold—Executive Order 6102
Assuming economic policies do not impact your investments is foolish. Particularly when the political environment is tough or major disruptions occur government policies have a tendency to be more extreme. Crisis is always a time for increases in governmental powers and this was certainly the case during the administration of President Franklin Roosevelt and how he came into office in the United States in the midst of the Great Depression. Some aspects of his New Deal platform may not have seemed as fair as others.

In 1933 President Franklin Roosevelt signed Executive Order 6102 shortly after gaining office. The order required all individual and corporate gold holdings to be given to the government for $20.67 per troy ounce. At that time U.S. dollars were redeemable into gold. Over the next year the president moved the official gold price to $35 per troy ounce,[i] which immediately devalued the dollars that had been given to the gold holders, thus the government booked a gain and the citizens a loss. There were exceptions to the gold rules, such as, for use in manufacturing, jewelry production, or if the gold was in coins that had value as collectibles and there was carve-out for five try ounces per household.

There is no question 1933 was a scary time with an incredible crisis in the United States. However, it should not be forgotten that the government can step in and dramatically change the economy or the rules by which the economy is governed. Valuations can change rapidly, due to actions that may not seem "fair" or constitutional.[ii] There is a generation of voters that have

DOI 10.1515/9781547400751-019

different views on many social issues, have seen, and probably believe in the incredible power of innovation, have experiences and biases from the great recession, and are technologically attuned. They may be anxious to have a different set of rules in the economy and investors have to be aware that the changes can be dramatic.

There are different views of what the government's role in the economy should be. They tend to vary around three major questions:

1. How much should government control the economy?
2. What methods should the government use to influence the economy?
3. Can these policies work within the political system and maintain support from the citizens?

Politics and economic policies are intertwined and increasingly economic ideologies are being mixed. No one system is right for every economy. It can depend on the size, diversity, institutions, and stages of economic development. Certain systems may be better for one country than another and countries may shift between systems over time.

New blueprints for economic systems are always evolving. Both China and India have shifted more toward market-based systems over the past decades and it has coincided with much greater economic growth, however, these have been evolutions not revolutions and each have evolved their own styles. You can see dramatic changes in China over the last few decades. While not a democracy by Western standards, China has shifted their economic structure and growth has accelerated as market forces have been introduced into their system, which had previously been very centralized. Manufacturing has been a major feature of this expansion. You could argue that manufacturing and infrastructure are more easily run in a somewhat centralized system like China's, but a transition to a more consumer-based system may be more difficult in such a structure. Meanwhile, India is a democracy, and a very different country culturally than China. India for many years had a government steeped in social democracy, protectionism, public ownership of key asset, and heavy regulation. It has rapidly shifted toward a market economy beginning in the early 1990s. Its economy has grown exceptionally fast, but unlike China its growth has been heavily driven by service industries. While markets are pretty free much of the government interference is still in the form of bureaucracy.

Below is a list of some systems of political economy. It is brief and incomplete. It also mixes some ideas from economics with the world of politics. The goal is to give a flavor of the varied approaches to "political economy."

- Capitalism is characterized by private property, competition, and noncentralized market mechanisms to determine supply, demand, and prices. This typically is associated with a limited role of government.
- Socialism is most strongly characterized by the doctrine that ownership and control of property should be owned publicly. The view is that everything that is produced is part of the social fabric and everyone is entitled to a share in it. Pricing, supply, and demand are not set in free markets because it can lead to exploitation and only help the rich, centralized governments make most of these decisions (even though they may be made up of rich people that benefit from its decisions).
- Social democracy, while originally focused on a peaceful shift to a fully socialist society, has evolved into a system that generally allows for private ownership but in a very highly regulated environment with extensive limitations on business. As it has evolved it has generally been accompanied by a high level of social welfare programs, which has led to more public ownership of certain industries and high tax regimes.
- Laissez-faire policies espouse as little government involvement in the market place and peoples' lives as possible. Libertarians tend to favor this approach. Believers in a laissez-faire approach to the economy usually prefer a more monetarist approach to economic intervention, but generally prefer to defer to market forces to move the economy, no matter what level of instability is introduced.
- Monetarism is based on the belief that the amount of money in an economy is the best way to manage growth. This favors influencing the economy through interest rates rather than fiscal policies, preferring to minimize government interference. Monetarism is also closely linked to the view that inflation is a key factor in economic stability.
- Keynesian economics (for the record, much of this theory evolved after Mr. Keynes's death) favors governments having an activist approach to the economy using fiscal spending to smooth out business cycles. This approach is quite comfortable using taxation as a policy tool and with temporary deficit spending. Managing unemployment tends to be a critical factor of focus in trying to limit capitalism's inherent instability.[iii]
- United States liberalism tends to favor more Keynesian philosophies.[iv] This is often based on the belief that capitalism can lead to economic extremes and societal evils. It favors interventionist centralized policies that it believes can smooth out these inefficiencies. This often leads to favoring wealth transfers and higher taxes.
- A socialist market economy is what has evolved in China. Under this evolving model many aspects of capitalism and a fair amount of private ownership

is allowed, but all of this is heavily controlled by the government. Markets operate and can drive a certain level of decisions and choices, but this occurs with significant government intervention. The government has exceptional power to claim property and still controls huge parts of the economy through direct ownership or regulation.

Broad-based market systems with a strong sense of private property and competition allow economies to run efficiently and historically have produced the most for their people. They also allow for people to have the most freedom in what they do and what they want to buy as businesses need to react to the consumer, or perish. However, these market-based economies need infrastructure including good information requirements and strong rules of law to work successfully and fairly, this is usually the responsibility of government to put in place, adjust, and enforce.

Market-based economic structures allow for a high level of innovation and change. To be successful a market structure requires competition. Any system that allows for competition, change, and innovation will cause some disruption to incumbent operators and systems. Therefore, market systems produce great good but also have periods of instability often resulting in taking some steps backward.

Sometimes a country's leadership decides it is willing to trade off prosperity and innovation in order to offer more stability. Certainly growth at any cost is not a good goal. These trade-offs however, usually seem to work better in smaller economies that often have a reasonable amount of wealth. There are also some societies that have varied priorities, such as a religious agenda, and may decide to sacrifice freedom and/or prosperity for other goals. Much of the world is experiencing a long reaching growth trend thanks to developments in technology, this may prove historic as it could last longer than any in recent memory, even though it is likely to have some dips. There are always risks to such a scenario and government actions might be the biggest ones. Over (or under) regulation, aggressive or misguided use of interest rates, or profligate deficit spending and its consequences all could derail the potential for a historic period of growth. The lines between the different approaches to government and economics are not always clear. Shifts from one ideology toward another are not uncommon and can lead to major changes in policies such as taxation or competition. The increased use of social media combined with demographics may cause political changes and more rapid policy changes over the next few years. This can disrupt business models and change the competitive playing field so investors can not be complacent about policy.

i Ash, A. (2015 April 5), Governments Still Heavy-Handed 80 Years After FDR's Gold Confiscation. Forbes.com

ii Woods, T. (2008 August 13), The Great Gold Robbery of 1933. *Mises Institute*. Retrieved from Mises.org

iii It is interesting that much of the period in which Mr. Keynes was doing his work in the United Kingdom, the nation was racked with unemployment and many of the policies derived from his work focused on trying to improve this aspect of the economy with fiscal policy. Meanwhile, one of the leading proponents of a more monetary approach, Fredrich von Hayek was studying in Austria where hyper-inflation was destroying the economy, and the Austrian school of economics and monetarist-related economists tend to focus on inflation as critical to improving economic conditions. This highlights that understanding people's experiences often explains their biases.

iv Though United States liberalism does not actually fit with how liberals were initially defined, originally liberals would have leaned more toward a libertarian approach.

Chapter 20
Government's Job

A job is usually easier when the duties are defined; the same is true with the government. However, there are many different views on what the job description for government should be and in democracies it can change after each election.

The government needs to set the laws of the land and oversee their enforcement. Safety is usually top on the list. Governments almost always manage a nation's national defense though there can be debates on how to handle local police and other public safety services. Education is another major task of government. Availability of schooling through secondary school is fairly universal. After these few categories the debates can get quite loud and nasty over what the government should or should not do. These topics can include university education, health care, food programs, physical infrastructure, and beyond.

Policy changes on what the govenment will and will not do can impact how willing the private sector may be to commit capital. If a government is regularly changing policy in a sector and affecting changes in value then there may be less capital that is willing to invest in a sector, think of health care in the United States or in a more extreme case the oil industry in Venezuela. This has also been seen at the local level as well. Imagine if a company had a cable television franchise in a city and part of the agreement to retain the contract was that they would build out a 100% coverage of high-speed data service in the region, even if much of the coverage was not-economic for them. Now after the company invested that capital how does the value of that network change if five years later a new set of elected officials decides to use government money to build a free high-speed Wi-Fi system to cover the whole city? The answer is the value of the private network changes massively. Policy changes can wipe out or enhance asset valuations. This is more vital to factor into investment analysis as social media can increase the speed at which an issue gets addressed by public policy.

President Reagan was quoted as saying, "Government's view of the economy can be summed up in a few short phrases: If it moves, tax it. If it keeps moving regulate it. And if it stops moving, subsidize it." In the current environment with so much innovation ongoing, overregulation or bad regulation may be one of the biggest risks to burgeoning flexibility and strength in many developed economies. In a system like the United States, rules are made by administrative regulators and they must be aligned with the laws and bills passed by the legislature. Regulatory rules are subordinate to laws, but both are enforceable by law. Regulatory rules definitely proliferate more than laws. For example, in the United States 2016 was a record year for regulatory rules. At the national level there were

DOI 10.1515/9781547400751-020

eighteen regulations passed for every law and as a measure of complexity the *National Register*, which includes regulations and regulatory notices, totaled approximately 97,110 pages.[i]

Regulation is a massive force on the economy. Bureaucracy can kill business projects or add to their cost. The level of rationality in regulations can run the gamut from sensible to absurd and mind-boggling. Occupational licensing is one area where regulation has often gotten out of control and can limit labor options for people. In Tennessee you needed a high school diploma to cut hair; shampoo professionals were required to have 300 hours of training. In some area permits are needed for lemonade stands run by children. In the United States each state requires their own licenses for many professions like nursing and teaching, especially disadvantaging a military family's ability to have a spouse working in these fields as they move frequently. Understanding what the motivation is behind regulation is important; frequently it is a form of incumbent protection that prevents innovation. Noble laureate Milton Friedman wrote, "The pressure on the legislature to license an occupation rarely comes from the members of the public...On the contrary, the pressure invariably comes from members of the occupation itself."[ii]

Regulation also has multi-faceted costs. There is a cost to the tax payers to pay for regulators. Then there is the cost to the private sector to meet the regulations as well as legal costs should anyone want to challenge a regulation. Redundancy can add to the costs of regulation, for example a typical bank may have to answer to at least six regulatory agencies. Then there is the potential cost to the public should a regulation not be in place that could have prevented some kind of damage.

To challenge a regulation a person or business has to be willing to take on an extensive commitment of time and legal costs. However, it may become increasingly common to see the use of social media to try to create groundswells against, or in favor, of certain regulations, which could accelerate change. Of course, those who are under the regulatory scrutiny may fear real or imagined retaliation and this may limit the use of the media by those being regulated.

One of the problems with regulation is that there is significant leeway written into legislation and this gives an inordinate amount of power to regulators. Some of this is by design as the legislature may build a law to purposely allow for more flexibility and let the structure of the rules be made by those "closer to the process." However, in other cases the legislature may just be abdicating its job and avoiding taking the responsibility of carefully designing the language in a new bill. When laws are written weakly regulators have a greater influence on the economy and changes can happen more quickly, but it may not always follow the full intent or letter of the legislation. Recourse for the public to be able to challenge regulations or regulators is not as easy as pulling a voting lever, because they are not elected officials.

One of the concerns about regulation is the lack of accountability and transparency in the process of rule setting. Regulators are not typically elected officials but they have a huge impact on how the government runs. Many are so far away from the public eye that an elected administrator or legislator may not effectively monitor them. Additionally, the sheer size of some of these organizations and the plethora of regulations in place make any form of monitoring quite difficult.

It is logical that regulators will lean toward increased regulation and favor studies that support their interpretation of legislation. Not because the regulators are malicious, but because of natural human biases. Most of the time they are doing what they deem to be best. However, it is natural that a regulator's default position is to keep any regulation in place. From their seat, they are not rewarded for economic gains or streamlining of any rules, but only blamed if something goes wrong because a regulation was removed. Regulatory trends can be very important to watch as they change the cost structures in industries. They can also have secondary and tertiary impacts economically. For example, why do carmakers make unprofitable fuel-efficient cars that sell poorly? Many believe it is to meet "fleet" emission targets. Therefore, an economy's resources are being redirected to make products people do not want under regulations in place to help lower pollutants. Additionally, if the cleaner energy cars are not selling, the regulations are not actually meeting the goal of lowering pollutants.[iii] More recently some states have gone after banning plastic bags and possibly plastic straws. Plastic appears to be the current "tobacco." Any time there is a new series of regulation think about what it might impact, in this case the dynamics for the plastic industry and also demand for feedstocks used in making plastic, there are always derivative impacts from regulations.

It is not easy to find centralized or consistent data on regulations. In the United States the George Washington University Regulatory Studies Center does some excellent statistical compilations and regularly publishes on regulation. There are think tanks and lobbyist groups in the United States, such as the Competitive Enterprise Institute, Brookings Institute, and the American Enterprise Institute, that do a very good job of watching the trends in regulation. On a more global basis the World Economic Forum releases a competitiveness report on most countries that includes a good section on the burden of government. All of these reports can give you a good sense of trends and information on specific data points.

Government regulatory policies appear to be impacting the economy more than legislative policy. Through digital social media, public opinion can apply political pressure and cause regulatory policies to shift much more quickly than in the past. Shifts in government involvement can cause massive disruption to businesses and any regulatory change will always trigger a multitude of consequences. Regulation can change bank lending rules, block a merger, or change how stocks can be traded all with no change in legislation. The style and reach of regulatory entities should be included in any analysis of an industry or a company.

Digital media allows for greater scrutiny of regulators. Logic would dictate that they would increasingly err on the side of caution, because social media exists to get noticed and rarely draws much attention if it says, "Golly these people are doing a good job," it gets noticed when it finds a mistake and it goes on the attack. Therefore, regulators do not benefit by being more laissez-faire in their policies.

Many of the innovations driven by technological advancements should allow the economies of the world greater flexibility and result in much greater insulation from instability, but inappropriate poorly designed regulation may pose the greatest risk to this being achieved.

---

i Crews, C. (2016 December 30), Obama's Legacy: 2016 Ends With A Record-Shattering Regulatory Rulebook. Forbes.com

ii Friedman, M. (2002), *Capitalism and Freedom*. The University of Chicago Press.

iii Sneed, A. (2016 December 1), Why Automaker Keep Beating Government Standards. *Scientific American*. Retrieved from Scientificamerican.com

Chapter 21
Funding the Government: Taxes and Debt—Good, Bad, and Completely Lost

Whatever extent the government is involved in the economy, it needs money to operate, even if it is operating in the most limited manner. Governments only have a few sources from which to get money: (1) taxes, (2) debt, or (3) monetizing its assets (e.g., leasing out oil drilling rights on land it owns). Most large countries tap into all three resources to fund themselves. The mix of revenue generation a government chooses can impact how investments act. As technology gives more voice to more of the citizenry policies on revenue generation will likely shift and it will impact asset valuations.

Taxes are supposed to be used to raise revenue, but they have become an instrument of policy and in some cases have been used as a weapon. The complexity of the tax code in most developed countries has led the private sector to undertake financial and legal structures to avoid taxes. This is a massive waste of economic resources and implies poor revenue generation design. Scott Hodge the president of the Tax Foundation wrote that in 1955 the U.S. Internal Revenue Code stood at 409,000 words, by 2016 it was 2.4 million words. Additionally there are roughly 7.7 million words of tax regulations to go along with it. He has also cited that it takes 8.9 billion hours to comply with the United States tax code.[i] Taxes are a common source of revenue for the government, but they annoy everyone and redirect resources inefficiently.

There is also an incredible amount of duplicate taxation. In the United States it is often taught that part of the rallying cry in the War of Independence was, "No taxation without representation." Yet several hundred years after the revolt, if you commute from New Jersey or Connecticut in to New York City you get taxed by New York City and New York State and have no vote on their policies or elected officials. Sounds significantly like taxation without representation. You also are probably taxed by your hometown, county and state as well as the federal government.

There are several key types of taxation. You can divide some taxes by what is being taxed: (1) taxes on income, (2) taxes on wealth, and (3) taxes on transactions. You can also divide them by how they impact different income levels: (1) a proportional tax applies the same percentage to people of all levels of income or wealth, (2) a regressive tax applies a larger percentage to people of lower income or wealth, and (3) a progressive tax applies a higher percentage to people with higher incomes or wealth.

DOI 10.1515/9781547400751-021

In the framework outlined above how do you look at sales tax? It is a tax on transactions. If a sales tax is imposed on coffee and every adult drinks one cup of espresso per day (just espresso in this example, no mocha lattes) this is a regressive tax because it accounts for a bigger portion of the earnings of people with lower incomes. In the United States, gasoline taxes are often cited as regressive. However, if a sales tax is placed on boats that cost over $500,000 that would seem to be a progressive tax, assuming lower income families do not buy these.

Taxes can have a major impact on spending but sometimes not as much as planned. There is debate over the benefits of big nationwide tax changes. A study by the New York Federal Reserve Bank[ii] showed that the impact on spending from tax cuts does not usually effect spending until it actually hits people's take home pay and it is a bigger impact on spending habits when it is considered a permanent change rather than a temporary one.

Agencies of the government and other organizations try to anticipate the impact on the government's revenue and the overall economy of any new policies and legislation through the use of dynamic scoring. This tries to show the overall impact a tax change will have on government revenues. The Tax Foundation gives the example that if a $1,000 per family tax cut is shown to lower revenue by $70 million but not increase spending, then the government will have $70 million less than it had. However, if a tax cut on corporations would lower revenue by $70 million but stimulates more capital spending, that capital spending may increase tax revenue by a total of $100 million, thus a net increase of revenue for the government.[iii] Kevin Hassett, when he was chief economist for the American Enterprise Institute testified that while dynamic scoring can be effective in certain cases, it misses the benefits that accrue to the economy from overall economic activity that is generated when taxes are lowered.[iv]

Some recent research by Christine and David Romer[v] on past tax cuts added some logic to the debate as they pointed out that the impact of a tax change can be heavily influenced by the reasons for the tax cut and the economic environment in which it is being done. Additionally, it is rarely one or two items that are changed in a tax bill; the legislation in this arena is usually far reaching, this occurs in an effort to get broad political support and win votes by supporting tax breaks for every politician's pet project.

Taxes are not just used as a punishment but a reward as well. Tax incentives are frequently given in an effort to attract business to a region or change behavior, such as programs in some Scandinavian cities to reduce cars in inner cities. This has the potential to distort the competitive playing field; if the government decides to tax one product, service-type, or region differently from others (e.g., should the tax on whiskey be different than vodka or on chewing tobacco than cigars).

Big tax changes do not occur that often but minor changes happen frequently and can change the economics in some industries. It is not always easy to follow what might be happening on the tax code and trying to monitor all the rhetoric from politicians can drive anyone to the brink of reality. Monitoring some of the think tanks websites and lobbyist groups can be helpful for industry specific tax proposals. Sometimes trends start to develop and you can tell one industry or another are becoming out of favor and politicians are starting to see it as a source of revenue. For example, in the United States the courts ruled that internet retailers had to charge state sales tax, a possible blow to some of these companies and almost the same day a senator called for hearings on how to raise more federal revenue from internet companies. This is not saying that internet companies will become the next tobacco industry, but it is clearly a sign politicians may look to it for more revenue.

Taxation has lost its way; theoretically it is a source of government revenue, period. However, it has become a tool of policy, influence, and interference with free markets, often shifting the playing field for one company or another. This use as a policy tool is not questioned as often as it should be, when it gets used for policy it adds to the incredible complexity of modern tax codes. The tax sector has become an industry unto itself to deal with this maze. Just as people in the past have worried about the military industrial complex unduly influencing the United States' military policy, one could easily theorize that the IRS-accounting-tax lawyer triad is impacting the complexity of what should be a relatively simple source of government revenue.

Tax code discussions often cause anger, debates on debt funding by the government often cause fear. Some view government borrowing as a perfectly acceptable tool to have in place at all times, others believe it should only be a temporary tool for funding. In the large developed countries and most developing countries national sovereign debt is a fact of life. Sovereign government bonds have come to serve as the benchmark "risk-free" interest rate within countries (though that is not its purpose) and therefore the yield on these bonds are used as a tool to measure risk, rates, and inflation expectations between countries and relative to corporate debt instruments.

Typically when doing comparative country analysis ratios on debt levels are one of the most important metrics. A common ratio is the debt/gross domestic product (GDP). When data is available, monitoring debt service payments to tax revenues can be a powerful analytical tool as well. It is worth noting, that when national debt ratios are analyzed it often focuses on the national debt, not all of the public government debt in the system. It is important to look at both national debt as well as all government debt when doing country analysis. Currencies need to be considered as well in lesser developed countries. The ability to issue debt in their own currency reduces risk; the level of debt issued in nonlocal currency can be a big risk factor for these countries. Debt issued in foreign currencies has been the root of some major crisis in the past.

Debt may be used to fund the government, but debt is just a loan and needs to be paid back, so big debtor countries are perpetual issuers, as tax revenue is often not able to actually repay the principle. Additionally, as it is debt it ultimately needs to be serviced by cash flow and for the government this cash flow is usually from taxes. When a government looks to increase the amount of debt they are issuing the government needs to attract capital, and that means the capital has to come from somewhere else and typically this means less capital available to the private sector. This is referred to as a crowding-out effect. Technology has not yet disintermediated the government funding process at this point. However, we would expect to see some new methods of taping capital at the national level, most likely from developing countries.

Governments such as the United States, United Kingdom, and the European Union have been giving more information generally about their funding plans and future expectations since the great recession. The amount of advanced information about their plans that government treasuries and central banks choose to give can change the level of volatility in the securities markets. In the age of social media there is pressure on these agencies to be transparent about funding plans, timing, and rates. This may not always be the best idea, as markets and business planning may become too wed to this government guidance. This may then put more pressure on the treasury or central bank to stay on their preannounced path as they fear bad economic reactions from a change in plans, even if the data is starting to signal to them that they should diverge from their prior plans. These entities may be better served to give less guidance and be allowed to be more flexible and responsive to what they see in the market rather than being wed to what they have previously said.

Governments continue to use a combination of taxes and debt funding to pay for the services it provides. How they choose to use these financing tools can change capital flows and growth rates and at times can specifically advantage or disadvantage selected regions, industries, products or services. Disruption to the traditional political process may cause an increase in the speed at which policy changes and that can increase uncertainty in your career and investment decisions.

i Hodge, S. (2016 June 15), The Compliance Cost of IRS Regulations. *Tax Foundation*. taxfoundation.org

ii Steindel, C. (2011 December), The Effect of Tax Changes on Consumer Spending. Current Issues in Economics and Finance. Federal Reserve Bank of New York.

iii Hodge, S. (2015 February 11), Dynamic Scoring Made Simple. *Tax Foundation*. Taxfoundation.org

iv Hassett, K. (2015 July 25), On the Dynamic Scoring of Fiscal Policy. American Enterprise Institute for Public Policy. Retrieved from Aei.org

v Romer, C. and Romer, D. (2010 June), The Macroeconomic Effects of Tax Changes: Estimates Based on a New Measure of Fiscal Shocks. *American Economic Review*. American Economics Association.

Chapter 22
Expense Management and the Government— A Misnomer?

Government should be able to utilize a long time frame when choosing where to spend its citizens' money. However, this does not usually occur as election cycles ruin long-term planning. More often when a group is in power there is a sense of urgency to get things done and spend ahead of the next election cycle. Sometimes the spending favors groups that support the winning side rather than what is best long term for the country.

Government budgets are enormous compared to most corporate budgets. Therefore, where and how governments decide to spend money has far reaching consequences on the economy and specific sectors.

Governments spend money related to running the every-day business of a nation, and then there are also large projects and contracts associated with the operation of the government as well. There are periods of profligate spending as the bureaucracy adds people in scores. There are also periods where a political party may look to drive some fiscal austerity, at least on projects that are not important to them. The policies of high spending and austerity go through swings of popularity. However, the bias is toward spending, because giving people things generally wins more votes than taking things away.

The cost and number of government employees can create strong political biases. Government employees are critical to the smooth operating of a country's infrastructure and enforcement of rules. However, government employees tend to increase in numbers, but not always add to economic efficiency. Political leaders interact with bureaucratic government employees every day. The politicians want their votes and, human nature dictates that they are not likely to publicly take responsibility for making these people lose their jobs. Therefore, headcount cuts are not common in the government. As more employees work for the government they become an important political block. However, they are not necessarily generating revenue and if they increase in number they must be supported by taxes and those taxes effectively are coming from a smaller proportion of people in the private sector if more people are working for the government, problems can clearly evolve in this scenario. Redundancies in government add to costs. There are often multiple agencies with similar responsibilities and many layers of government. For example, if you commute to work into New York City from New Jersey, which is quite common, your taxes are going to support at least seven different governments.[i] Common sense says that there must be an inordi-

DOI 10.1515/9781547400751-022

nate amount of redundancy in such a system. The bureaucracy of the European Union is redundant almost by definition.

In times of economic stress in a country, what actions the government should take has typically created much controversy. Stimulus projects can be particularly valuable if unemployment has reached epidemic proportions and if the government has the wealth to pay for the stimulus. Not only is the increase in employment good sociologically it can also be better if it replaces pure transfer payments. One of the risks of stimulus spending is if it is just "make-work" on unnecessary and ineffective projects. This leads to tax revenue being taken from the public that if left on their own could redeploy money more effectively in the economy with a more positive long-term impact. If an economy has evolved into a heavily service oriented economy traditional stimulus programs, that involved physical infrastructure, may prove to be less effective economically and socially.

Government projects can be a major undertaking and typically require cost benefit analysis. This is a valuable type of analysis for all kinds of projects that has been utilized for more than a century. This field evolved rapidly shortly after World War II as work done by entities affiliated with the U.S. Department of Defense developed tools to analyze theoretical nuclear war scenarios during the Cold War. This scenario analysis has also proven to be useful in cost benefit analysis for non-military projects. This type of analysis can get very complex given the multitude of layers in the economy that a government project can impact.

Government cost-benefit analysis should factor in social aspects, generational impact, and financial returns (and, while not officially part of the process, the political risks). This analysis can get mind boggling and often leads to illogical exercises such as having to put a numeric value on a human life or calculating the economic benefits of a tree. Cost benefit analysis is a great approach to all investment decisions as you factor in the opportunity cost of committing to one investment over another and try to calculate multiple ramifications of each investment or project. However, trying to reach a conclusion can be a never-ending discussion as you add factor after factor. To be successful this analysis needs to be approached pragmatically.

Imagine a simple decision about whether a government will build a road from a large highway to a nearby town. Below is a sample of just a few things that would be analyzed in such a project:
- The cost of the road
- The increased revenue and taxes from businesses in the town
- The loss of any sales and related tax revenue to any retailers that are currently located along the highway and may have paid a franchise fee for the right to be there

- The impacts on revenue and taxes of other towns near-by that may already be getting revenue from highway traffic
- The lower cost of transportation for any people and businesses in the town getting the new road
- The long-term environmental impact on the area from higher automotive traffic
- The cost of other services that might be needed to service the increased traffic to the town (e.g., an extra traffic officer)

Of course, the list can go on and on like winding your way through a labyrinth. This analysis might also have to be factored against where else such a project might be undertaken. One of the problems with this type of analysis is that it can be very time consuming and add to the cost of a project. This type of work can also have a large subjective factor and can clearly be manipulated by people if they have certain biases. Increased computational speed and a matrix of best practices should allow for more efficient analysis, more probability scenarios, and less human bias.

Once a project is decided upon, governments needs to decide how they are going to get it done. They typically have a choice of using government employees or awarding a contract to a private sector company. In the United States and many other regions, there are guidelines on how to award contracts, in the hopes that it will avoid corruption. The specifications are often onerous and do not allow for innovation. While there are specifications on how the job must be done, contracts are typically required to be awarded to the lowest cost bidder. This does not always result in the best execution, simply going by price does not always result in a happy outcome, if you just bought music based on the lowest cost, you might end up having to listen to *Two Sides of Leonard Nimoy*, rather than The Who's *Quadrophenia*. Unfortunately, too often the approach to awarding government contracts is designed to avoid a problem rather than to make something better.

The arguments against hiring the private sector for projects include that the private side is purely profit motivated and does not look out for the public good. However, the counter argument is that if they are incentivized properly to do a cost-effective job, they will be looking out for the public good. The argument for public resources to undertake a job is that they must answer more directly to the citizens and have the public's best interest in mind. However, the counter argument is that they do not have an incentive to do a better or more cost-effective job, and are driven by their own job preservation.

Homemade digital media is increasing the scrutiny on both public and private workers, and misdeeds can go viral quickly and unwind profitable relationships. A video of a public or private sector employee on a government construction project sleeping or doing drugs can quickly force a change in which company or agency oversees the project.

Government spending on profligate projects might be good fodder for digital media. However, despite the proliferation of social media, it seems to always go on. Dr. Tom Coburn is a former U.S. congressman and senator from Oklahoma. By almost any standard he is considered a political conservative on social and fiscal issues. When he was in office he was so appalled by the waste in the government that he decided to publish an annual "Waste Book." Each year it identified some of the most egregious waste and inefficiencies in the government. His "book" added up to billions of wasted dollars each year. Some of these include $1.5 billion to keep lights on in unused or underutilized government buildings, $3 million to educate NASA employees on how congress works, and about $280,000 to send twelve music executives and a government employee to Rio de Janeiro Brazil to promote the independent music business.[ii,iii] These are the types of expenditures that lead to less trust in the government's judgment. The more viral and wide spread publicity is about these abuses and foolish uses of the tax payers' money, the more efficient government will hopefully become.

---

i In New Jersey you pay taxes to support the town, county, and state you live in. In New York you pay taxes to support the borough of the city, the New York City government, and the state. Finally, you pay taxes to the federal government.

ii CBS News (2013 December 17), Wastebook Report singles out $30 billion in spending. CBSnew. com

iii Maccalmont, L. (2013 December 17), Coburn 'Wastebook': $125K 3-D pizza. Politico.com

Chapter 23
More Gray and Purple, Less Gridlock

When a government can not get anything done it crushes confidence, and a lack of confidence is bad for investments. This was apparent when political gridlock caused the credit rating of the United States to be downgraded in 2011. Politic extremism has almost made the word compromise a curse which is bad because compromise can lead to progress.

Politics has always been intertwined with the media and the two reflect each other. In the United States some of the early newspapers started as a sideline revenue source for commercial printers. They evolved into very partisan mixes of politics, news, and gossip. In many countries certain news outlets are very clearly identified with certain political parties. Despite the guise of an unbiased news media (especially over the public broadcast airwaves), the media is increasingly showing its biases as they each struggle to carve out an audience in a more crowded field of cable news stations, blogs, and tweets. This can fan the fires of extreme political views with an unwillingness to even take the best ideas from the opposite side of the political aisle.

The media can reflect what people want and those who want extremely biased views of their news typically want the same features in their politicians. This can lead to gridlock. It can also lead to a cycle of alienation and then retaliation, especially when the electorate is fairly close to being evenly split in its political affiliations. For example, if one political party with more extreme views has clear control it may result in much more biased policies that alienate a large portion of the public. If there is a change in power this often results in an inordinate amount of time being spent by the newly elected government trying to unwind the previously placed partisan policies of their predecessors.

Children are often taught that the majority rules. However, does a simple majority say much on what the government should enact as a policy? If a politician favors some extreme policy and wins an election with 50.5% of the votes, how tenuous will the life of any controversial bill be that is passed and how much of a mandate of support for an extreme policy view is that slim margin of victory? Can people really plan for the policy to be in place over a long period of time if 49% of a population disagrees vehemently with the policy? More compromises can accomplish great things and be more efficient. In the 1960s in the United States Hubert Humphrey reached out to Everett Dirksen in the U.S. Senate; they were in different parties and on opposite sides of the debate, but they hammered out a compromise and the Civil Rights Bill passed. Likewise, Tip O'Neill, the former Speaker of the House and a Boston liberal democrat was able to reach

DOI 10.1515/9781547400751-023

agreements with President Ronald Reagan, a conservative republican, and get several bills done including the social service reform.

Extreme beliefs and radical views can sometimes be vital to accomplish big things. Winston Churchill was unwavering in his view of Adolf Hitler; if there had been much more accommodation by the United Kingdom, history might have been very different. However, most modern politics and most situations can benefit from compromise. Unfortunately, the chronic need to get noticed in the digital age seems to require more extreme messages and often the message is that compromise is bad.

Willingness to compromise can help avoid shocks. Should the Brexit vote have been so black and white? A decision to leave one of the world's largest free trade zones is a radical decision, even if the European Union has a growing tendency to wander into regulatory overreach. Perhaps a stronger attempt to negotiate what the United Kingdom needed in the relationship with the European Union should have been undertaken. Perhaps the vote should have signaled that they demanded that they needed to negotiate diferent terms not exit. A little more gray may have been better than a choice of just black or white.

In the United States there are huge swaths of the country that on political maps are colored either red (republicans) or blue (democrats). It looks like a military map with armies staking their territories. Too many politicians only want to listen to their own view and refuse to take any ideas from people on the other side of the aisle. This is easier when there is a lack of diverse political views in a politician's home district and they can be assured of reelection. It would help if there was an increased understanding that compromise is necessary and can be positive, there are many areas of common ground, and it would be good to have a bit more purple on the political map.

Economies and asset valuations tend to do best when governments can show that they can get things done as well as exhibiting a level of stability and predictability. Warring factions glaring at each other across a demilitarized zone of gridlock is not helpful for asset valuations and is not a recipe for rapidly responding to economic ills when they appear.

Periods of government inactivity can lead to investor complacency about political risk. The status quo never stays in place and radical change in political policies can come ripping into market valuations. From Roosevelt's New Deal to the recent Brexit vote, policies can crush old valuation models and create new trends, if you adapt quickly and do not get trapped into anchoring bias based on old policies you can often recover from an investment standpoint when there is a radical shift. Mapping out the potential impact from various political scenarios before they happen can be valuable and should be done alongside any financial analysis.

Selected Ideas from Part 6

Topic	Concepts	Investment Impact
Approach to Government	Ideologies on the approach to political economy slide along a scale often based on the level of government intervention and control.	Currently many leaders talk about being at more extreme ideologies, but act more like a combination of several ideologies.
Political Change	Digital media rapidly brings new topics to the top of government agendas and shifts electorate's views.	Outside of elections, investors often assume political status quo will be maintained. This is less likely due to digital media, anticipating political change and using scenario analysis can be helpful.
Government Actions	In most cases legislation is taking a backseat to regulation as the biggest impact on the economy.	Overreach of regulation may be the biggest risk to the economic flexibility and innovation that is evolving and supporting positive economic trends.
Complex Taxes	It is not just the tax rates, but the complexity of tax codes that add to their cost.	Complex taxes take up intellectual time of management and can cause a poor allocation of resources and inefficient structures.
Taxes as Influence	Taxation originated to pay for the cost of government, but it has become a tool of policy.	Policy implementation through taxation can sometimes be a roadmap for which industries government is favoring or attacking.
Taxes and Debt	Taxation and debt issuance usually increase with more activist government policies.	Taxes and government debt pull capital away from corporations and individuals and limit the ability to invest in growth.
Government Expenditures	Government expenditures are often an easy way to get votes and are hard to roll back.	Government expenditures can temporarily improve society and an economy, but can also be inefficient. Profligate spending, government debt burdens and poor tax structures can easily upend the benefits from technology.
More Gray and Purple	Gridlock in government is not helpful, nor is disenfranchising 49.5% of a population base.	Ideological purity is not a pragmatic way to govern. Economies often do better when there is some compromise in government and the best ideas from all sides are incorporated into policy.

Part 7: **Business is Different Now, But It Always Is**

Chapter 24
Business Structures—Think Again

The creation of the limited liability corporation in England changed corporate history. It allowed for massive innovation in capital raising, greater risk taking, and innovation while allowing the founders to protect other portions of their wealth. It is not likely that technology will change the legal concept of the limited liability structure. However, technology and related social changes are influencing critical features within every corporation.

Due to a combination of generational differences in the approach to work as well as a spike in technology driven company start-ups that can evolve very quickly, many corporations are moving from traditional hierarchical structures to flatter more evenly weighted ones. Technology allows more work to get done by fewer people; small teams can get significant amounts of work accomplished using technology rather than having to throw teams of subordinate personnel at a problem to solve it. Use of technology still needs to be well thought out and organized, simply throwing every whimsical idea into a spreadsheet or a data search is not a valuable or efficient approach. Teams can solve problems if they are organized well and truly run as teams. This often works well with flatter structures, which have begun to permeate corporate organization charts.

A lack of hierarchy in a corporate culture is not always a utopian situation for every organization and can cause problems internally and externally. There can be free-rider issues where certain employees, or partners, are not carrying their own weight in the workload. People may not do their own work and feel they can still opine or criticize others, creating incredible time wasting, inefficiencies, and ill-will. There is the potential that it can evolve into an inability to make decisions, too many opinions are given, too much weight is applied to everyone's opinion, and no conclusion is reached. Certain times call for decisive action and sometimes that means someone must have the final word and dictate. If a nonhierarchical structure is going to be successful it usually needs some clarity of people's roles in the organization and accountability.

In previous corporate generations as a business grew they added people to add scale. Often a manager judged his importance by how many people worked for him, unfortunately, this often took precedence over their output. The leadership in the "C suite" had generally climbed the ladder through success in managing people and as they climbed they managed continually larger groups. Critical factors were getting the right people in the right job and the tools to do their jobs. This is still critical, but corporate organizations now depend much more on information than just people. Management of data and information are of more value, making sure it is in

DOI 10.1515/9781547400751-024

the right format and structure, gets to the right people and places all is increasingly vital. In many organizations this has led to the rise of the chief information officer and chief technology officer as key members of the "C" suite.

With more centrally accessible data and electronic communication people can work from distances and communicate through video chats. Business demonstrations can be done on your computer as someone else takes over your screen. Even e-mails are an easy way to give detailed information about work that you need to leave for somebody allowing someone in India to hand off a project overnight to New York. The ability to manage work flow and track projects electronically has made it easier to manage oversight and easily create paper-less paper trails. This has allowed for the growth in telecommuting, which allows a company the ability to leverage off their employees' capital (their home) in exchange for savings on commuting. Data and the internet have also changed corporate communication. Broad communication can be accomplished quickly through e-mail and other chat systems; though it has its drawbacks as everyone has a horror story of a "reply all" e-mail that was not intended for that broad an audience. Combine e-mail with video chats and telecommuting and satellite offices are more connected to work, but it can create various "classes" of employees. People in the home office are likely to develop tighter relationships. There has not yet been the invention that can change the value, focus, and insights you get from an in-person meeting. The ease of new methods of communication have increased the amount of interaction but reduced the amount of in- person encounters. This has increased the value of the times you do meet in person.

The ability to monitor workers remotely as well as reach them with information and regular communication has allowed once rigid corporate structures to be much more flexible. Companies do not have to commit to long-term leases and infrastructure to start new businesses or divisions; they can rent space for short-term periods from companies that offer shared flexible term work space, like WeWork or The Office Group. The development of logistics, outsourcing and supply chains, and even 3-D manufacturing can allow a company to manufacture and distribute goods without building massive factories or distribution networks. A corporation can manage the design, distribution, marketing, branding, and manufacturing of products but have each of these duties outsourced to other businesses. The organizational structure extends out from the center like spokes on a wheel, but all the spokes can be changed at any time. This growing number of expert outsourcers allows companies to be formed more quickly. It also allows these companies to be formed with less capital, fewer people, and therefore, perhaps, less commitment. A lack of imbedded structures can allow new companies to change their focus, alter strategies or fix structural issues more often and more quickly. This can all be good for a start-up company competitively. For existing incumbents it means more competition shows up more rapidly and from more directions.

Several generations in the United States had owning a home as a key component of their financial dream; it appears that many in the millennial age bracket have owning a company as the key component of their dream. The giant shift in employment from the industrial revolution was the move from independent agrarian farmers becoming employees of huge conglomerates to whom they sell their labor (as predicted by Karl Marx, even if he got the conclusions wrong). Now with the efficiency of technology we may see some of this unwind. Employees of major traditional corporations may increasingly move away from these companies and choose to form their own business and labor for themselves and a few partners in their own company.

It is not all rosy. This corporate flexibility and ability to start with less capital, can allow companies to close more easily. There are fewer costs associated with shutting down, fewer long-term obligations, and fewer employees that the law may require a company to deal with. This in turn can create a lack of stability in employment as well as a lack of a sense of loyalty in employees. This can hurt the ability to plan long term and cause more volatility in the business and employment world.

From an investment basis this all means:
- more opportunities in which to invest
- more opportunities in which to fail
- more competition from start-ups for incumbent operators
- less consistency in financial results of corporations
- less predictive value in historical financial results for a corporation
- increased value in understanding potential changes in the competitive landscape
- increased value of careful technology investment for incumbents
- the need for incumbents to develop structures that can evolve new revenues and sub-businesses even if they compete with their existing revenue sources

There are various measures of new business formation. It is unclear if the data are catching all the start-ups, in particular peer-to-peer businesses and some individually run online businesses are likely missed. However, Figure 24.1 uses the data from the U.S. Census Bureau for business applications, which are requests for employer identification numbers. This should be at least a reasonable proxy for new business formation, and the data shows a meaningful increase in recent years, implying significant more competition evolving.

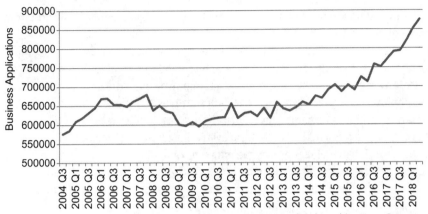

Source: U.S. Census Bureau, www.census.gov/programs-surveys/bfs/data/datasets, September 2018

Figure 24.1: Seasonally Adjusted Business Applications

Fast growing decentralized companies can develop other problems, some of which can be caused simply by a founder that is a creative mind but not a leader or can come from poor cultural evolution in an organization. This can be a problem of not having any hierarchy in the business structure and not instituting adequate checks and balances within the organization. Lack of internal controls and corporate culture has been an issue at some young, high profile and exceptionally fast-growing companies. These have included Uber and the alternative finance company SoFi, Social Finance. Both companies suffered very damning reports in the press of sexual misconduct and harassment and both of their high-profile CEOs were forced out.[ii]

Some new business models can have unique business risks. This is particularly evident in the internet media space. In many cases much of the asset value of the company comes from the community of users attracted to a site. Every business runs the risk of disenfranchising existing customers as a company tries to grow, but it can happen more quickly on the internet. Facebook has suffered by using data that they had gathered on their customers that left many users uncomfortable, it also hurt its image by allowing postings and advertising from extreme political groups, further alienating some customers.[iii] The most valuable capital for many of these firms is their customers, switching costs are very low so a few miss-steps could wipe out significant value. New industries and new companies are still learning how to manage these unique types of risks.

It appears that Amazon has been masterful at avoiding missteps. Reading one of CEO Jeff Bezos's quarterly shareholder letters reinforces an unbridled focus on the customer and he tries to imbue this ethos throughout his company.

The Amazon experience has made their customer base comfortable with buying an item by simply relying on a description and reviews by fellow customers rather than seeing an item in person. Amazon must contend with unscrupulous sellers manipulating these ratings or it could lose some of the trust of their customers. However, Amazon could take steps on its own and alienate customers, too. For example, Amazon appears to list "sponsored" products at the top of their searches more frequently, and there have been articles discussing more overt advertising and a push of its own brands. As it allows vendors to run "stores" on the Amazon site they also lose more control of the customer and the process. All of this could change the shopping experience and alienate some customers. Controls and management structures must be in place to protect their most important asset, which is their community of shoppers that they created. Fast growing companies do not always have these risk management tools within their corporate structures as they scramble for market share and subscribers.

Amazon is a good reminder that scale can still make a huge difference in business. However, many of the newer companies do not need the same level of scale to succeed. Lower costs and more flexible companies can go after "tail" customers. Focusing on these niche market customers and creating specific products for specialized groups, like banjo players or unicyclists, can create a unique business that can scare away competitors because of how small the markets for the tail products are. Exploiting a specific personal passion can often be the motivation for these types of start-ups and scale may not be as important for that entrepreneur.

The emotional force behind the technology driven start-up boom varies from founder to founder; Bill Gates probably had a different goal in founding Microsoft than Andy Grove had with Intel or Jack Dorsey with Twitter. However, it does seem that this era has seen an inordinate number of start-ups that are designed with the goal of selling the company. This means creating a company, not because it can thrive and prosper over time, but it can be sold to a buyer. This mentality can create risks for investors as it is not driven by a business success but convincing someone else that a business can be successful. Broadcast.com was founded as AudioNet by Christopher Jab, Todd Wagner and Mark Cuban. It was a pioneering company in audio streaming. While it is unclear what the goal of the founders was as they created it, the company was sold for billions of dollars to Yahoo. Ultimately it failed for Yahoo. This was probably due to the timing of the product given the lack of available content and quality of internet service at the time. However, it unintentionally showed a road map for some people as a way to make a fortune on a business with a great idea, regardless of its ability to be successful.

Corporate structures and the concepts of how to run companies are changing, this is also changing the roles and jobs of people in a business. How new companies are structured, potentially outsourcing much of their needs, is different than in the past. Businesses can come and go and change direction more easily. This means that even in extended periods of good economic growth the competitive pressures on existing businesses and industries can develop more rapidly and be more prevalent and investment returns can be more extreme.

---

i Isaac, M. (2017 June 21), Uber Founder Travis Kalanick Resigns as C.E.O. New York Times. Retrieved from NYTime.com

ii Yu, R. (2017 September 12), SoFi CEO to step down after claims of managers' sexual harassment. USA Today. Retrieved from usatoday.com

iii Frenkel, S. (2018 July 25), Facebook Starts Paying a Price for Scandals. *New York Times*. Retrieved from NYTimes.com

Chapter 25
Business Investment—What People Watch and Should Watch

Increases in business investment are generally viewed as a positive sign for the economy. Investments in human capital, out-sourcing partnerships, peer-to-peer businesses, and intellectual property are all less tangible and harder to track than many traditional business capital expenditures such as a physical plant or media content. These dynamics limit the usefulness of using traditional business investment figures as a measure of economic activity or potential future growth. In the United States, gross domestic product (GDP) report there is a break-out of "private nonresidential fixed investment," which includes structures, equipment and intellectual property. This data can give some color on business spending trends. There are at least two dangers in using this historical data. One is the dramatic changes in the last few years in the composition of non-residential fixed investment. Intellectual property investments increased to the second biggest category, moving from 27% of the total to 33%. When the composition of data is changing meaningfully you must be cautious how you use historical data. The second danger is that with the significant changes in how some of the most dynamic companies in the economy invest in their business, you must question if the data is truly capturing the actual level of business investment activity.

A factor that could also be distorting the impact of business investment is that technology is often allowing corporations to get more out or each dollar spent than once was achieved. For example, a copy machine can still copy but can also scan a document and simultaneously send it to thousands of people, while also sending a personal fax to a different person. The cost increase to buy such a machine is less than what it would be to purchase the three separate machines. This also results in derivative savings, such as the employee hours involved to accomplish the tasks. Simply counting the dollars spent on business investment is not capturing all of these factors. It is also worth considering that theoretically increased business investment in the latest technologies is also making all the existing assets that companies own worth less as they are less efficient and less attractive on a relative basis to the newest assets.

New media companies are investing in their businesses very differently than traditional media corporations have. Social media and gaming communities invest capital in the design of their service, but much of their value really comes from having more users that create a community. The users are often creating a large part of the "content" and enhancing the experience. Growing and main-

DOI 10.1515/9781547400751-025

taining this type of unique business requires a different type of investment. In a traditional movie or television studio the investment in the product is much more defined. The value of the product (e.g. a movie or a television show) increases if it is popular but the value is not enhanced by who is sitting next to you in the theater (it is often actually a negative experience). In the case of a video game community the experience might well be enhanced by who you are playing with. Social media sites are more popular if people post more content on them. Therefore new media companies often have to invest in making the experience of using their website easier and more attractive than having to invest in content.

Business investment figures also may miss some of the expenditures involved in developing an "asset-lite" business model utilizing outsourced vendors for much of the work. A new company at the center of a circle of third-party vendors may have engineering and design teams that will craft specifications for a product and then outsource the manufacturing and assembly as well as distribution and then have a separate team that coordinates marketing with an advertising agency. At the center of this circle is a company that will be investing in human capital for customer service and quality control but not that much in a physical plant. There will also be significant investment in legal and logistics planning and documentation involved in pulling this all together but this is a different type of investment. Perhaps 10 or 15 years ago all of this would have been done in-house for a company and it would have required significantly more capital to start up and build out these capabilities rather than just utilizing unused capacity of other companies. Much of this is possible because of technological improvements in logistics and communications. These changes are distorting capital investment figures relative to historical data. Investment in intellectual property, including design, brands, contracts, logistics, and so on, are not all easily captured in the traditional macro data.

Trying to capture true business investment is valuable for many reasons. From a macro thematic view increased investment by businesses should lead to growth and this activity can give a good sense of an economy's direction. From a micro investment point of view understanding how well a company can monetize its invested capital is an incredibly valuable tool for investors to measure relative value. If you are analyzing companies in the same industry you can combine various line items in their financial statements and cobble together a reasonable view of true investment. If you are looking across industries, it gets more difficult.

Some newer economy companies have an advantage over their incumbent competitors, in that they do not have to answer to the same metrics, such as earnings per share or return on capital. If you read research reports and articles Amazon gets to benefit from a different valuation framework than many other traditional retailers. Theoretically, this gives Amazon an advantage over its peers, as they can attract capital without having to show profits, while most incumbent retailers do not get this benefit and their stock valuations are typically measured relative to earnings. By this measure start-ups can get rewarded for expensive launches into new arenas that add to revenue but not profit and can be aggressive on pricing, traditional companies would likely have to discuss the impact on earnings to any new venture. This can get carried to the extreme and allowing companies to avoid having to rationalize an investment by showing positive cash flow generation can eventually result in meaningful capital losses. The combination of easy money and bad business investments is clearly a risk to economic growth and can destroy capital. However, right now, capital seems to flow to companies that are innovative and can grow the revenue and market share line, with the promise of strong profits in the future.

Mergers and acquisitions are an important way in which corporations invest capital. Corporate combinations have increasingly resembled pieces of a puzzle being put together than vertical or horizontal expansion. Technology companies are often about products. These products will have a life cycle and often as top-line growth slows for a product line it will become a significant cash generator, though not as much of a growth vehicle. This cash can be used in the pursuit of acquisitions of new products that can fit its existing customer base. A company that provides customer relationship management tools, like Salesforce.com might add an e-commerce software company. This is not traditional horizontal integration but adds to a suite of services that can be marketed to an existing customer base. Part of Dell's acquisition of EMC was rationalized by "revenue" synergies as Dell believed it could sell EMC's storage and cloud computing services to its existing customers.

A high level of capital availability and a large amount of business investment have appeared to be prevalent during much of the technological revolution. How business investment needs to be allocated for a company's success can be very different in start-ups than it has been for more traditional companies as asset-lite models utilize third-party vendors. This has made measuring the quality and the quantity of business investment more difficult and has changed the make-up of corporate asset value.

Chapter 26
Business Cycle Theory: It's Wrong and Slow

Business cycles are dead. Well, if not dead inexorably changed. If new companies can grow more quickly than they could a decade ago, if technology continues to get adopted more quickly, if information can be found and shared at speeds not even thought of a few years ago, and if trade in goods and securities happens much faster, then why would business cycles still follow the same pace as they did decades ago? It is logical that if the pace of everything else has increased so has the business cycle, and it needs to get measured differently. Business cycles still can happen but, like everything else in business, they just start and finish much faster.

The traditional framework of the business cycle has five phases. The economy goes from a peak, into a recessionary decline, hits a trough, then starts to recovery, and shifts into an expansion and then a new peak. In the United States the National Bureau of Economic Research (NBER) defines expansions, contractions, and recessions. It traces business cycles back to 1854.[i] The traditional definition of a recession is usually two consecutive quarters of gross domestic product (GDP) decline, but the NBER states that it uses several indicators including jobs, income and, even, industrial production to determine a recession.

Since World War II through 2018 the NBER measured eleven recessions, with the typical length of about eleven months. The great recession was measured at eighteen months. Keep in mind that typically final GDP numbers are not available until about six months after a quarter ends, on average recessions could be more than half way done before they are declared. Expansionary periods typically lasted fifty-nine months. Clearly there is more expansion than contraction in the trend lines.

Note that recessions and expansions are usually measured in time. This measurement has validity as extended economic downturns can cause more damage to businesses and the social fabric of economies. However, the extent of the impact on the overall economy should also be considered, measuring the compounded growth during the recessions can put downturns in perspective, too. The compounded growth impact on GDP during the 2001 recession was not much worse than the weakness in the economy in 2011, when no recession was declared.

The expansion after the great recession has been very shallow. Perhaps this should not be looked at all as one part of a cycle. Figure 26.1 shows that there have been at least three quarterly periods of negative GDP since the great recession in the United States. There were two periods in 2011 and one in early 2014. Perhaps these were full economic cycles that were simply more shallow and recovered more quickly than traditional measures, maybe this is the new economic cycle in

DOI 10.1515/9781547400751-026

the technology era. In the third quarter of 2011 stock levels dropped and the S&P 500 was within 4% of the Great Recession average, this was during a time of economic uncertainty as the United States government looked like it was in gridlock and might shut down and the country's debt quality was downgraded by a credit rating agency. The Chicago Fed National Activity Index (CFNAI), that measures business activity, is very broad in scope and more volatile and responsive than GDP and during this period it had contractionary indications. Similarly, when oil prices collapsed in mid-2014, large parts of the economy acted and smelled like they were in a recession through 2015 and very early 2016. This was not an official recession by current definitions using measures such as GDP, but "soft" economic data like the CFNAI and the Purchasing Managers Indexes (PMI) trended weaker and the S&P 500 Index posted some very poor results. This bump-in-the-road business cycle may prove to be more common as greater efficiencies keep the overall economic trends positive for a longer time period than in the past.

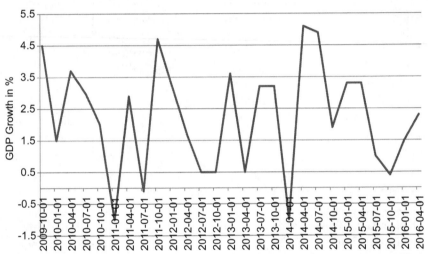

Source: Chapter U.S. Bureau of Economic Analysis, Real Gross Domestic Product, retrieved from FRED, Federal Reserve Bank of St. Louis; https://fred.stlouisfed.org/series/A191RL1Q225SBEA, September 2018.

Figure 26.1: Post-Recession U.S. Quarterly GDP Growth Quarter-to-Quarter Seasonally Adjusted

So-called soft indexes, such as the CFNAI and PMIs, respond much quicker to changes in the economy than larger government driven macro measures. This is due in large part because they were designed with different purposes in mind, the soft indexes are supposed to be more responsive. While these survey-based indexes may give more false signals, the overall trends of these indexes, such as the CFNAI, is probably more telling of how modern rapid business trends are moving than slow moving data sources like GDP. This can be especially true when some of the most followed data may be undercounting the most dynamic and rapidly changing parts of the economy.

There are many theories about the causes of business cycles. None of them are right all the time, because while many periods have similarities the context of the economy, the excesses, and the mistakes are very different each time. There-fore, it is most likely that the various theories have their time and place and none of them are right for every country, industry, or event. One of the larger historical economic debates has been the view on the business cycle of the Austrian School of Economics, generally associated with Ludwig von Mises and Friedrich Hayek, and the Keynesian school. A brief, over simplified and probably flawed synopsis of the two theories follows:

The basic theory laid out by Mr. Keynes is focused on recessions caused by shocks to the aggregate demand in an economy. Generally, the argument is focused on investors and suppliers responding to aggregate demand. Once a change in that demand happens, due to a shock of some kind, the anticipated returns on investment realign changing the climate for business reinvestment and this further exacerbates the downward cycle. The Austrian theory focuses more on supply and points to artificially low-cost credit being made available to businesses and entrepreneurs. This leads to a boom in investment. However, too much cheap capital drives more supply into the market and bad investment decisions are made because of the abundance of capital. This then creates a credit crunch as these "malinvestments" fail, capital is lost, and a recession occurs.

Both theories have been picked apart for flaws and both have been altered, improved, and rearranged by subsequent generations of economists. However, these two views have been the seeds from which most strains of business cycle research have grown. Not surprisingly, the solutions offered by the two schools of thought differ, too. The Keynesian model follows on that government stimulus spending can trigger demand and smooth out business cycles. Meanwhile, the Aus-trian school calls for more market-based solutions with less interest rate interven-tion to create a natural supply and demand for goods and products rather than allowing the recovery to be dictated by artificial government-induced demand.

A recent research paper about the Great Recession and the investment hang-over (Rognlie, Shleifer, and Simsek, 2018) discusses the real estate boom and bust that contaminated the financial sectors and household values. However, in a sur-prising move, in an era that seems to have forgotten compromise, the paper built a model that utilized both the Austrian theories of overbuilding and investment and the Keynesian ideas of demand shortages.[ii] Business cycles will always be caused by different things because business and the economy evolve. The cycle in 2011 was triggered by a frozen government in the United States, but at that same time there was a crisis in Europe due to profligate spending by a member of the currency union. The next cycle may be caused by overly aggressive interest rate hikes, over-regulation, government deficits or trade wars, it is hard to tell.

The obsession with pundits that are always calling for the next economic collapse damages the market. Looking at triggers from the past is valuable, but the data is not always useful for the current situation, it is like a goalie thinking of the last penalty shoot-out while a striker bears down on him at full speed. The situations are loosely related but not really relevant. False calls for the next crisis happen all the time and even the best signals are hard to time. An opportunity for capital appreciation can be lost by leaving a trend too early. False negatives have hurt more than false positives as the average expansion to recession ratios show.

Do not think that there is a timer running that rings loudly and reminds you when an economic expansion is fully baked and about to end. Recessionary bumps will still happen but should not last as long or be as extreme. They may even occur more often, but have less impact. More economic and financial flexibility in the economy will mean that cycles should look more like trend lines with a few bumps. The time and depth of those bumps should be smaller than in the past given increased technology-driven flexibility of capital flows, supply chains, and company formation. One of the major risks to such a scenario is that government interference could disrupt these self-correcting measures in the broad economy. However, even though economic flexibility creates an environment of longer positive trends and quicker recoveries it does not mean that volatility disappears.

There will also be "pocket" recessions that hit an industry or a region. Pocket recessions will occur more often because of the rampant changes in competition and capital flows. Pocket recessions will get noticed, some investors will lose meaningful money when they happen. Sometimes they may be large enough to impact asset valuations in other areas for a period of time. However, pocket recessions will be relatively contained and problems inside of the pocket will not be such a large burden that it will cause the economy's pants to fall down.

---

i http://www.nber.org/cycles.html
ii Rognlie, M. Shleifer, A. and Simsek, A. (2018 April), Investment Hangover and the Great Recession. *American Economic Journal*. American Economic Association

Chapter 27
Tearing Down and Running Around the Barriers to Entry

Barriers to entry form a wall that is built around an existing company protecting it from competitors. A start-up does not care how they breach the wall, they just want to get to the other side and take some of the revenue and customers that are inside. They want to find the weakness in the barrier and exploit it. There have been many lists of critical barriers to entry. Michael Porter, a Harvard professor, has done a significant amount of work on business strategy and his work on five forces of competition highlights barriers to entry. Below is a list of some of the key barriers to entry inspired by Mr. Porter's work and work by others:

- Economies of scale: this typically gives larger operators cost advantages
- Brand loyalty: this requires unique positioning or marketing spend
- Product differentiation: sometimes linked to b., but this offers something unique in product mix, price, accessibility, or service
- Capital: running a business costs money, an incumbent will likely have cash flow and access to capital with which to compete, a start-up must spend a significant amount of management time on finding capital
- Switching costs: there is a cost for a customer to switch away from a product, the bigger the cost or disruption the better the barrier to entry
- Distribution access: whether physical or digital, setting up access for customers is costly and tricky
- Management time constraints: highly complex businesses require huge amounts of time, start-ups usually have limited manpower and only so much time available, time is a very limited resource
- Government policy: in many industries a significant set of rules are set around an existing business, there may be considerable licensing or registering costs and new services may be competing with the government.

Outlined below are details on how relevant, or not, some of these barriers are in the current era of innovative technology. The internet has changed economies of scale. It has given people the potential for almost immediate scale by being able to reach many potential clients at once without needing to build out physical locations. It seems as if every time someone says a specific item can not be sold on the internet, it becomes available and people adapt to buying it, clothes, cars and dog food all come to mind. Scale is often considered an effective way of lowering your price and leveraging your fixed costs. Using multiple global value-added supply chains can help lead to cost advantages as well and counteract the advan-

DOI 10.1515/9781547400751-027

tage of a larger competitor to some extent. More often though success is achieved by figuring out a new way to do something cheaper, for example, using peer-to-peer car services rather than buying an entire taxi fleet. Additionally, cost savings through scale matters less if a company is willing to compete without having to make a meaningful profit and it can still attract capital.

The advantages of brand loyalty and product differentiation can disappear quite quickly. At one time many people would go to the supermarket, but remain loyal to their butcher. Then eventually the ease, cost, time and, perhaps, even the quality of the supermarket meat drove customers to leave the local butcher. People may have had their favorite grocery store. Now the supermarkets are being challenged by internet grocery delivery companies like FreshDirect in the northeast United States or Ocado in the U.K. and as for the butcher a whole bunch of people do not even eat meat anymore. People still care about brands, but it is more fleeting, and ease of access seems to have outweighed brand value. An outgrowth of this is that since unique products are rare, this has also caused pricing power to be rare.

There are more ways to access capital and more different types of capital available. Thanks to the ability to gather and share financial and credit information, funds can be raised more quickly than in the past. Like other eras of great positive economic change, capital is increasingly available for growth opportunities, even if the risks are high. This is causing capital flows to favor newer start-ups. The ready availability of capital is also taking away the advantage of capital as a barrier to entry. Technology, the internet, peer-to-peer networks, and other developments are also lowering the amount of capital needed for new businesses. A consequence of these business "lite" models where much of the process is outsourced is what happens if the company fails. The assets of the company may be worth significantly less than older style companies that owned significant cash flow producing assets. Detailed and specialized computer codes from a failed business may not be as easy to sell off as the real estate of a shopping mall to help repay investors.

Switching costs, in some cases, can still be a solid barrier to entry. If a company has an outside vendor manage an elaborate suite of software that allows a company's various operating systems to communicate between sales, logistics, and production—it might be quite time consuming, risky, and expensive to switch vendors. There are many areas where switching costs are minimal. For example, in the past there was some disruption in switching your video service from cable television to satellite, however, switching costs are very low to switch to watch a show on Netflix or Amazon Prime. While technology has generally helped to lower prices, increase competition, and weaken barriers to entry, the complexity of technology has made switching costs in some areas much higher, but in other areas it has made it virtually painless.

Nowadays distribution can be bought. Federal Express, DHL, even Amazon, along with a multitude of other operators can come in and provide a huge portion of distribution for a company. This does not mean that there are still not some unique protected logistical advantages, think of a gas pipeline or a port. However, many companies can save a huge amount on infrastructure spending by farming out much of the distribution to vendors. Getting a product noticed may be the more difficult part of the process, but the internet can lower the costs and paying for placement may be more effective and time saving while also reaching a broader audience than paying to get actual shelf space at thousands of locations.

If an industry is highly regulated it remains a significant barrier to entry. Licensing, registration, and supervision are all major costs and cause delays in developing a new business, the more burdensome the steeper the barrier. There have been significant peer-to-peer projects that have moved ahead with their offering in regulated businesses and just chose to fight the legal battle after they had scale.

While not often listed in classic barrier to entry, time can be a massive barrier to entry. An existing or entrenched incumbent business company has more of a first mover advantage, this is a time advantage. Starting, capitalizing, and organizing all aspects of a new company or a new business line take time away from competing in the market place. If the incumbents are efficient and flexible it may be difficult for a start-up to catch-up, especially if the incumbent sees the competition coming.

In many cases a start-up has an advantage because an incumbent is not willing to adapt. An incumbent is often not as willing to change the way they are doing something because they have invested so much capital into that process, moving forward to newer methods may destroy the value of capital they have already invested. If a company has built out and staffed 1,000 restaurants, they may be reluctant to switch to a prepared food delivery service that could lessen the value of those dining establishments that they own. It takes bold leadership to undertake these types of big changes in an established business and it takes management time. However, as new generations of management come in to leadership roles it may be a more common place to see incumbents switch business models more quickly. As big incumbents try to be more nimble and adapt technologies more quickly it may get harder for start-ups. New companies will need more creativity in developing ways of doing something.

Overall, many traditional barriers to entry are weaker than in past eras. This can cause the value of invested capital to shift more quickly. Theoretically it can lead to more volatility and impact the value of traditional business assets.

Traditional balance sheet measurements of asset value in a company like book equity value and property, plant and equipment can be of little meaning in the real world when innovative technologies are causing the real market value of old assets to decline very quickly.

Many of the traditional moats that have protected companies from competition are getting narrow enough to jump across. This will increase market share battles and likely cause more frequent industry centric pocket crashes, recessions, and booms. When market leaders show a leak in any of their barriers to entry, such as their brand getting lambasted in the press or service failings, competition will pour in through that breach in the barrier. However, the same is true for new economy start-ups. Companies with a good idea on the internet or in peer-to-peer businesses will quickly see imitators, many of which will correct some of the problems they see the pioneers struggling with. There will have to be more and more differentiation between a company with a good idea, and a good company with a good idea. It can not just be a good idea, it must be able to be executed with a better product, process or cost and have long-term demand.

Chapter 28
Incumbents Can Fight Back

Do not expect incumbents to lose every time they face competition from an innovative start-up. Incumbent businesses are not all fat, drunk, and stupid. They can be powerful and viscous when they fight back and often have unique resources at their disposal.

As time marches forward incumbents can see where mistakes have been made by other companies that have come under attack from technology-driven competition. There is more of a playbook now and they can use their position of strength. They are also unlikely to be as surprised to see competition as they might have been ten years ago.

Some companies may choose to retrench. That may mean changing what they do. Consider IBM, which was an exceptionally early tech company. At one point it was a typewriter company, then a major mainframe computer leader, and then a leader in laptops. It clearly seemed to lose its way for a while but retrenched and focused on artificial intelligence and cloud storage services.

Some incumbents have the strength of brand to be able to act like a spoiled child on the playground who stomps their feet, takes their ball and goes home. A company like Disney may believe their franchises and brand value is strong enough that they will choose to compete with exclusiveness. They may intend to pull movies or television shows from video streaming companies like Netflix and only make them available on their own service. Several incumbent television networks in the United States originally formed Hulu, which was their own streaming service.

A counterpunch is an effective move by an incumbent if they can pull it off. As network television in the United States has lost viewers to anytime video services, they have changed their offerings. They have moved to more event style programs. These might be live events that people do not want to miss because they will be excluded from the conversation the next day. This is part of the attraction to programmers of reality television (at the low-cost end) and live sporting events (at the high-cost end).

Cherry-picking is often an effective way for an incumbent to defend its position. An incumbent may not want or need to do everything a start-up does. However, they can observe and pick out some of the best practices of these companies and what works for them. Large financial institutions currently appear unlikely to adopt crypto-currencies as a mainstream store of capital or means of exchange. However, it is quite likely that they will adopt the use of block chain technology (i.e., distributed ledger technologies) for record keeping and confir-

DOI 10.1515/9781547400751-028

mation systems. Supermarket companies may not close up their local stores, but will offer internet ordering and delivery services that they may see being done by start-ups.

In some cases incumbents may form partnerships. For example, many companies have partnered with Amazon and eBay to have their own "store" on the site. However, on the other hand, Wal-Mart has struck back with their own website and online presence, a move into foods, and their own style of retail focus and brand positioning.

If you can't beat them, buying them is always a strategy for an incumbent to take. This strategy has had mixed success. Time Warner had been a media giant and to some extent had foresight and saw the potential early on for the internet and bought AOL (America Online), which unfortunately turned out to be an epic failure. In a more specialized niche, retailer of pet supplies, PetSmart, chose to buy online competitor Chewy, but is still facing off with Amazon.

Incumbents have played the legal card, too. This has occurred in some peer-to-peer businesses like Uber. In addition to Uber's avoidance of long-standing regulation of the taxi industry that is central to its initial success, there are safety and social issues that cities legitimately will want to manage over internet accessible taxi service, but some of the legal challenges are just about money. Legal challenges are generally temporary as ignoring regulation has often led to success for start-ups that have been able to avoid or fight their way through the regulatory pressure. Companies such as Uber and Airbnb (providing lodging in noncommercial residences), Google, Facebook, and Amazon have taken advantage of the lack of regulatory will, or understanding, to push their agenda. This is not a new phenomenon; going back a bit further, DHL's overnight services were illegal at first in most every country, and the music industries' streaming saga is another very public example. These companies have pushed until they met resistance and kept pushing. It has not prevented them from being able to raise capital and they have found it to be quite a successful model. This is also occurring today in the fintech areas where companies are popping up, challenging regulation at an extraordinary pace, including the cybercurrency markets, which have had some spectacular breaches, but continue to fight their way through attempts at regulation. In the United States, the fledgling marijuana industry may face this issue as state and national laws are not aligned. However, if there is an elimination of the national ban it may bring on more competition from major corporations than the start-ups want. Great marketing and broad public acceptance can sometimes overcome the pressure to uphold regulations. In such cases, the existing regulations often leave the incumbents defenseless (or at least disadvantaged) to compete. If a new service or product is in high demand and is better than what is offered, it will keep coming back to the market. It may come from a different company and the legal challenge may crush the pioneers, but it will be back.

Incumbents have access to technology and can innovate, too. They will not all go quietly into the night. Challenges from start-ups can sometimes make the incumbent better. In many cities, hotels and taxi companies have become more adaptive and flexible because of Airbnb and Uber, supermarkets now have delivery services, and years ago, we saw postal services improving their package delivery services. These are all reasons why competition and choice are good for the people and the economy.

Chapter 29
Food and Energy

It is always important to track large industry categories and how they might be impacting the wider economy, whether you plan on investing in them or not. These are sectors that are the big components of the gross domestic product (GDP) and can have a major impact on labor markets and inflation as well as overall supply and demand. In many countries housing and health care are the largest household expenditures and are huge components of the economy. The cost associated with housing and healthcare in people's budgets is large in the United States but it is a fairly stable and predictable expenditure from year to year. Therefore, it is unusual for pricing changes in these categories to cause a shock to spending and demand.

The next two biggest categories of household expenditures are usually energy and food. While a smaller portion of expenditure, these items typically have very volatile prices. The movements in these prices can disrupt and influence peoples' inflation, spending, and savings expectations more than housing and health care because of how significant and unexpected the price movements can be. Prices are so volatile in these two industries that they are excluded from "core" inflation results, which are widely used by central bankers to gauge near term inflation trends. There are numerous widely distributed and well followed macroeconomic reports on housing and health care. There is somewhat less on energy and much less food. Because of the ubiquity and price volatility in food and energy they are vital to follow to get a sense of how consumers are being impacted. Both industries are also going through considerable change due to shifts in technology and sociology.

Fossil fuels, like oil and natural gas, have been the key source of energy for much of the world for some time. The economies of the nations that produce most of the oil and gas tend to be dominated by that industry, such as Saudi Arabia and Russia. High energy prices help these economies and, in some cases, are vital to their well-being. However, for most companies and consumers higher energy costs are a burden. Energy costs that cause increase in gasoline, heating, cooling, and electricity draw income away from other sectors. When companies get hit by higher energy costs, their customers are too, and this makes it harder to pass along price increases, so margins can get squeezed.

Traditional analysis of the energy industry focus on supply and demand dynamics and the supply factors have been controlled in part by the major oil cartel, Organization of the Petroleum Exporting Countries (OPEC), which accounts for about 40% of the world's oil production, based on many estimates, but much

DOI 10.1515/9781547400751-029

more of its proven reserves. Geopolitics and technology have changed things for OPEC as the United States has become a much bigger producer of energy. There has been increasing tensions among OPEC members and major political problems in countries such as Iran, Libya, Venezuela, and Nigeria. The development in technologies that have allowed shale production in the United States to boom and this has appeared to be a huge factor in energy prices and the result is that OPEC has less control of pricing than it once did. The fracking production is much more flexible and can come on and off stream at lower costs and more quickly than other sources of fossil fuels, such as deep-sea offshore production or a sovereign nation's development program.

The demand side for fossil fuels is being changed due to technological and social aspects. Oil's transportability has always had an advantage over natural gas. However, now there are facilities to produce liquefied natural gas (LNG) that can easily be transported and that could be changing the value of gas heavy fields. Then there is the push toward ecological and sustainable alternative energy sources ranging from nuclear, wind, solar, biofuels, water turbines, and other sources. Many of these are being subsidized by government programs. From 2000 to 2016 renewable energy production grew by approximately 40% in the developed countries.[i] There are several reasons that alternative and sustainable energy sources are being increasingly developed, countries want (a) less dependence on a supply from a few concentrated nations, (b) a greater understanding of the finite nature of fossil fuels, (c) they are an alternative to turn to as a way to combat cost spikes, and (d) ecological concerns have increased as countries and individuals focus on decarbonizing the energy stream. In the more economically developed countries there is significant focus on energy efficiency and overall reductions in usage, too. Automobiles, a major user of oil products, have been lowering fuel usage using everything from energy efficient windows to lighter car parts and getting more power from batteries. The same is true in housing. Of course, other energy sources may develop their own problems, for example, the demand for lithium used in batteries is very strong and mining activity has accelerated in South America and Australia for this mineral.

While developed countries are making major efforts to reduce carbon producing energy sources and new production methods are causing changes to the energy industry, demand is also changing in emerging markets. Faster growing less developed countries are still often seeing increased use of traditional energy sources, while energy and efficiency are important to many of these countries, expediency often calls for them to deploy capital in areas to enhance growth other than on ecological enhancements. Overall, this is gradually causing a shift geographically where energy demand and specifically demand for oil is coming from, causing more erratic and complex factors to impact prices of energy, power projects, and logistics.

Electricity usage has been increasing and electrical utilities are becoming more varied in their generation methodologies and more efficient. Many large utilities have developed sustainable energy projects and have diversified their energy sources to become less wed to one type of feedstock. They are looking to improve efficiency through smart grids and load shifting as well as developing better energy storage with newer technologies like super-capacitors. Better monitoring technology and data on usage has had a major impact on utilities' operational improvements and their ability to inform customers on better energy usage patterns.[ii] More developments in storage and transportation of electricity may reduce generation needs over time as well.

Energy demand is shifting, and the cost equations have seen important new variables added to the equation. Economic growth will likely continue to lead to increased demand, but the demand may be for different types of energy sources and in different locations than in the past. It will continue to be a huge expense factor at the micro through the macro levels of the economy.

Food supplies energy to humans and animals. The food industry has become vastly more efficient over time as fewer people have been needed to be able to produce more food. This is especially true in the United States where major technology changes in the food industry have driven efficiencies and allowed for more and varied food to be widely distributed. These technologies have included bio-engineering that have made many food stocks more hardy, selective breeding, logistic improvements and more efficient and flexible refrigeration. However, given the dependence on weather for the clear majority of food, there are uncontrollable vagaries that impact the food supply chain and the cost of food. There are also periodic diseases that can wipe-out crops or require culling of animals.

Energy is a huge expense in the overall cost of food as well. Some studies have estimated in the United States food chain from production to storage to preparation energy usage accounts for somewhere in the low to mid-teens of all energy costs in the United States and energy accounts for about 6% of each dollar spent on food by consumers.[iii] The industry is always looking for energy efficiencies within the food chain.

Food demands are changing. In the more advanced economies there is an increased focus on health and ecologically sustainable food, this is changing eating habits and causing differences in demand. While knowledge and education are driving more people toward healthier choices, it can be somewhat cost prohibitive for some. It is often difficult to eat on a budget and to eat healthy. In countries where there is a significant millennial population, there has tended to be a bias toward organic foods and there are some increased incidence of food allergies which have reduced demand for gluten and starches versus other generations. Millennials also tend to eat out of the home more. In the countries with advancing economies the demand for proteins tends to rise as affluence increases. The United Nations, the OECD and other agencies, track and predict changes in food demands and publications predict things like increased sugar demand in Africa and lower pork consumption in China in coming years. These reports highlight how food demand changes.[iv]

The food chain requires consumers to have a high level of confidence in the safety of foods. Therefore, companies must take responsibility for all aspects of the supply chain because a tainted product can destroy a brand or a company and change long-term demand. There is significant ability for customers to switch who they buy from and what they buy. This substitution effect can be driven by health, price or scandal. These factors lead to more volatility in demand for specific products as well as more extreme successes and failures of individual brands than in many other industries.

Food is critical from a humanitarian aspect. Hunger and famine are devastating to societies, countries and regions. Nations with excess food supply really must feel an obligation to help where possible. When there is a humanitarian need to redirect food supplies, it is the right thing to do, but does disrupt normal supply and demand. Normal supply and demand in the food industry can be massively skewed by government policies as well. The interference with market forces can be significant. Sometimes it might be done to protect agricultural production, from a security stand point, even if economics is not supporting it. Other policies that can skew the food market place can be a program that includes transfer payment style food programs, export policies, or changed agricultural regulation used to impact certain regions or products.

Agriculture is intertwined with real estate. Like many other energy sources, most food is developed from the ground. As the agriculture industry changes so does land use. In some cases, greater efficiencies can free up more land, but sometimes crop switches to certain more profitable products can demand more space. Similarly, the food service industry and the out of home dining industry are increasingly taking up real estate at places where retail stores used to be. Shopping malls across the United States are effectively becoming higher end dining malls, food courts that offer upscale steaks and seafood, Chinese, Italian, or barbecue cuisine. Science may lead to land use changes too. There are rapid developments in using plant fibers in new ways. These include using plant fibers to strengthen products like paint and lumber. These developments could lower the carbon footprint of these products and make them last longer.[v] While on one scale using these sustainable more natural products instead of those developed from fossil fuel may prove to be a great business and better for society, there are always ramifications, and it could crowd out food production, given the limited real estate dedicated to agriculture.

Energy and food are huge volatile portions of company and make up a large portion of personal expenditures. It is hard to follow or understand any economy without paying attention to these two industries. Monitoring these industries can give good insight into demand, inflation, capital flows, prices, logistics, and infrastructure as well as sociological changes that are driving demand more broadly in the economy. Almost any meaningful change in these two industries eventually ripples through an economy. Every major nation has government agencies that oversee these aspects of the economy and usually have significant data available, choosing a few industry leaders in these industries and monitoring their financial reporting and stock prices can be helpful, too. Keep in mind when looking at data the significant changes to both the supply and demand side that have been taking place in both the energy and food industries.

---

i https://data.oecd.org/energy/renewable-energy.htm#indicator-chart

ii Deloitte (2015 September), Electricity Storage Technologies, impacts, and prospects. Deloitte Center for Energy Solutions. Deloitte.

iii Canning, P., Rehkamp, R., Waters, A. and Etemadnia, H. (January 2017), The Role of Fossil Fuels in the U.S. Food System and the American. U.S. Department of Agriculture. Economic Research Service. www.ers.usda.gov

iv Food and Agriculture Organization of the United Nations (2017), The future of food and agriculture: Trends and challenge. United Nations.

v *The Economist* (2018 June 14), Making buildings, cars and planes from materials based on plant fibres. *The Economist*.

Chapter 30
Supply Chains, Outsourcing, and Innovation

Supply chains are as simple and as complex as chicken and egg problems. To have your breakfast you have to get the egg from the chicken and then get the egg into your skillet. That is a simple supply chain. Of course, you must have gotten your skillet from somewhere, which had to get the raw materials that were combined to make your skillet. Then your heating source, probably a stove had to come from somewhere and that fuel used to heat the skillet likely got mined and transported. As you take apart the components involved in your breakfast, the supply chain has become more complex. Supply chains have been critical to business forever. During the nineteenth century, pioneering industrialist Andrew Carnegie saw the benefits of combining and controlling an integrated supply chain of coal, railroads, and steel production. Supply chains have evolved dramatically and are now global. They add value, flexibility, and risk to the modern corporation.

In the making of a product, a supply chain is the process that takes raw materials, organizes them and assembles them into a final product that is then packaged and marketed and moved out to the end customer. While it is usually associated with manufacturing, it could be applied to intellectual properties too. For example, you could have people that develop a concept for a customer order system, then software coders that prepare the code to make the system operate, a separate team that prepares the end user interfaces and legal and accounting teams that make sure the information on the system is processed right. Supply chains can get quite complex and the construction and management of efficient supply chains has become its own field of study.

In many cases when an organization is vertically integrated a large portion of a suply chain may be managed within the company. When part or all of a product or service comes from another organization it could be considered outsourcing. Sometimes that outsourcing can be from local third party vendors or it can come from another region or country. When it involves a company using products and services from outside its home country it is often called off-shoring. Off-shoring can be more controversial politically.

Use of outside supply chains, outsourcing and offshoring can allow companies to tap into the most cost effective and efficient methods of production, but require detailed logistics, vigilance, careful design and quality controls. Increasingly there are start-ups, younger companies and innovative incumbents that run a large portion of their company operations using outsourcing. This can allow a business start-up to require less capital, be formed quickly and, if necessary, change strategy rapidly. Even the physical logistics of the supply chain can be

DOI 10.1515/9781547400751-030

outsourced all the way to having the mail delivered in your office. There are consequences to consider for the investor, for example a heavy use of outsourcing can result in a company's primary value being in the form of intellectual property, rather than more tangible assets.

The evolution and exploitation of the supply chain does not necessarily mean that the supply chain has to go global; but it often does and global value chains have helped to drive global trade. Apple's innovatively designed products that have impacted music, communications, social inter-action, business, education and language have utilized the global value added supply chain for many years. In a much cited research paper in 2008, Jason Dedrick, and others, analyzed the supply chain for Apple's iPod and some other computer products. The study tracked a staggering number of countries from which Apple sourced low cost components that included items to run the screens, video, memory, processing and other functions of the iPod[i] that were eventually assembled in China.

There have been numerous innovations in logistics that have increased confidence in using complex supply chains. Additionally, the development of the concepts inspired by just in time manufacturing (JIT) have further increased the willingness of companies to utilize outsourcing. Improvements in logistics have tapped into developments in everything from fuel efficiency to better satellite technology. Logistics have benefitted due to better, package tracking, routing, transportation, energy efficiency, computerization of manufacturing specifications, and customer-vendor communication that have allowed supply chains to be more flexible and precise. JIT has shown companies the benefits of running with little to no inventory and the financial benefits of lower working capital needs. This allows companies to be more flexible in their offerings and can allow for more customer specific requests. There are now specialized third party vendors that allow an innovative corporation to outsource almost all of its logistical and production needs and have just the right amount of inventory in place to fill current orders.

Federal Express (FedEx) was a major innovator in the field of logistics. FedEx was founded by Fredrick Smith. As a teenager Mr. Smith became a pilot. While studying economics at Yale he wrote a paper about delivery logistics. However, before he got to see if his theories worked he served two combat tours as a United States marine in the Vietnam War. After he was discharged he raised money and started a delivery company, effectively competing with the United States Postal Service (USPS). According to Mr. Smith, one of the key changes that allowed his company to revolutionize the logistics industry was the government's deregulation of the air cargo industry. This allowed more flexibility in air routes and for overnight competition with the USPS. Mr. Smith realized that there was greater efficiency in delivering everything to one central hub and routing the packages to their destinations from there. However, it did not stop at the hub and spoke innovations, as he wrote in 2015, "Innovation is the holy grail of both businesses and consumers around the world."[ii] His company had the first global tracking network for shipments, the first system for customers to electronically request pickups, the first to use barcodes in ground transportation, and the first to have internet package tracking available for customers. FedEx is now one of the most successful logistics companies in the world. Third party logistics firms like DHL, FedEx, Li & Fung, and United Parcel Service (UPS) can all effectively run all the logistics at a company. These companies operate around the globe. This allows a company to focus management and capital on other parts of the business.

Improved logistics have allowed supply chains to be less dependent on prox-imity and this has led strategies like JIT to expand and be able to use the best priced and best quality components from around the world. Just in time, man-ufacturing has also helped to innovate outsourcing supply chain management. The Japanese car company Toyota has been credited with truly exploiting the benefits of JIT. Taiichi Ohno has received much of the credit for championing this strategy. He was born in Manchuria to Japanese parents and moved back to Japan and spent his career at Toyota. He started off working in their textile machinery company and moved to the automotive operation in 1943. He was tasked with making his division more efficient. He constantly studied inventory levels and questioned the existing manufacturing methods. In his efforts to eliminate waste, inventory costs, and space he developed the JIT system. This involved careful tagging of each part used in manufacturing and studying the manufacture and delivery time for each piece of the final product. The system allowed Toyota to wait for a customer order before manufacturing and then once the specs for the order were in it would have all the parts for that order arrive just ahead of when they were needed for manufacturing.[iii] As the advantages of JIT became appar-ent, and because of Toyota's success, the focus on more efficient supply chains increased throughout the business world. Computer driven technologies have allowed for more precise specifications of parts. Better communication, precise computerized manufacturing specifications, package tracking, and labeling of products has made JIT more accessible to a variety of industries. Manufacturing with the use of 3-D cameras should also enhance the ability for JIT to be more widly used.

These developments in logistics and JIT have increased the benefits of out-sourcing many of the components in the manufacturing process. Outsourcing has become a modern day version of the classical economist David Ricardo's theory of comparative advantage. Mr. Ricardo's famous example was where he suggested that even though both Portugal and England could produce port and good linen cloth, the world would be more efficient, and enjoy port more, if the Portuguese stuck to the port and the English focused on the textiles. A modern analogy is a company that just focused on axles for cars should do a better job making an axle than a car company that made seventy-five different car parts, although the axle company may be more at risk given its high level of specialization. This system allows the central final product company in a supply chain to be more flexible, use less working capital and be able to respond better to demand changes. It should also free management to be more forward looking. A car company's management might be more willing to look at cutting edge opportunities in something like designing a flying car if they do not have to rationalize how much they had spent on an axle factory or tire inventory. They will not care as much that the axle company spent the money. A move to a flying car will likely hurt the specialized axle company, but may allow the car manufacturer to adjust more quickly to fend off a rival upstart. The supply chain is often thought of in terms of physical products. This is not always the case; there is an increasing use of outsourcing in less physically tangible products and services. This can include everything from research and development to product testing, design, legal work, and coding.

Increased use of supply chains and outsourcing is not without risk. Problems can erupt, such as the delays and electrical problems that occurred in the production of Boeing's Dreamliner airplane due to the use of subcontractors in the supply chain that were used for many of the components and that did not meet Boeing's specs. There are also scandals such as with Menu Foods, a pet food company that appeared to have included contaminated wheat in its food from a manufacturing partner in China. Companies like Nike and Apple have also faced scandals over some of their parts suppliers following inhumane employment practices. Interruptions from natural disasters like an earthquake or flood can create significant moral dilemmas for the end customers about switching suppliers when the affected country or region may be in need of revenue. A high use of supply chains also can make a company much more sensitive to transportation costs, rising fuel costs or transportation shortages can suddenly become nightmares to the smooth operation of a business. All these issues present problems involving loss of control for companies that have tapped into outsourcing and need to be factored in to an investment assessment.

The supply chain and outsourcing evolution changes the value and need for inventory and working capital. Also, if specialized suppliers are building cutting edge manufacturing plants with the latest technology it decreases the value of the invested capital that other operators may have in their older plants. Supply chains increase the amount and value of intellectual property, such as manufacturing specifications, supply chain design, and contracts. The value of the intellectual property and the barriers to entry they may present are difficult to truly value in financial statements. The specialized nature of these types of assets may make them more difficult to monetize if the company becomes distressed. This can all change the value of comparing capital expenditures and other business investment over various time periods and may make it more difficult to compare two businesses that compete but have chosen very different business models if one has chosen to vertically integrate and one to outsource.

The use of diverse supply chains and JIT can be a great help to a company's profitability and flexibility, but it also allows new entrants to come in to a market with less capital. Companies can be more flexible and may have the ability to rapidly change parts, adjust business design, and be more responsive to customer needs. However, the outsourcing company may have less control over its business. On the opposite side of the ledger the companies within the supply chain typically will develop specialization and perhaps a more narrow focus, which may make them more susceptible to revenue disruption.

---

i Dedrick, J. Kraemer, K., and Linden, G. (2008 May), Who Profits from Innovation in Global Value Chains? A Study of the iPod and notebook. http://web.mit.edu/is08/pdf/Dedrick_Kraemer_Linden.pdf

ii Smith, Fred (2015 September 8), Continuous Innovation Fuels FedEx Success. Fedex.com. Retrieved from about.van.fedex.com/blog/continuous-innovation-fuels-fedex-success/

iii *The Economist* (2009 July 3), Guru Taiichi Ohno.

Chapter 31
Measure of Trade

International trade should allow the world to be efficient and provide more and better things to people. However, it does not always work that way because trade causes domestic disruptions and that pulls politics and policy into the equation. If Canadians can buy Spanish wine that is cheaper and better than their wine, people with capital invested in the Canadian wine industry will not be happy. This may lead to the Canadian wine industry complaining to politicians that then get involved and trade then becomes quite complicated, even though it should not be. Tariffs and quotas might get imposed and you could imagine that in this hypothetical example an entire sub-industry evolves that uses capital to keep trade barriers in place to protect the Canadian wine makers, rather than getting the industry to focus on how to make Canadian wine more competitive (which might be a tough task). Even when free trade zones are formed, bureaucratic cultures grow up making them operate less freely and imposing more rules.

Despite government caused distortions in trade, the data on trade can be a good indicator of the economic direction of various countries. Usually these figures get released more frequently and are sometimes considered more accurate than gross domestic product (GDP) data. Trade data is a good tool to use to compare and contrast the different key economic forces when comparing countries' economies. Some countries and regions are much more dependent on international trade than others. In the Post-World War II era, for example, Europe has generally been more dependent on trade than many other regions, while the United States has been much less dependent.

Cross-border trade has almost always been a part of economic history and was written about as far back as the ancient Greek philosophers.[i] A major explosion in trade has happened since the 1970s. The onslaught of technology, improvements in tracking and transportation, as well as high speed communication have all played a huge role in increasing trade. However, the change in the currency regime that took place in the 1970s played a significant role as well. In 1971, the major currency markets moved from fixed exchange rates that had been in place roughly since the end of World War II to a regime of floating rates. The ability of currencies to fluctuate in value based on demand allowed for better adjustments in exchange rates relative to trade. This appears to have resulted in a greater and more agile transfer of capital across borders. The free floating exchange rate regime certainly brings some other positives and negatives, but it has allowed for much greater flexibility in the relative value of products. Some writers also point to improved geopolitical relationships as having helped trade

DOI 10.1515/9781547400751-031

increase. However, one could turn it around just as easily and say the increased intertwining of trade between countries has improved geopolitical relationships. Transportation and communication improvements have been crucial to increased trade in goods and services. In the trade of goods, the basics of transportation costs always make proximity matter. In the trade of services, proximity can matter less, but commonalities like language and time zones can play more of a factor. Despite much conversation about China and the United States as two of the world's largest trading partners, neighbors still tend to be some of the biggest trading partners for most countries. Geographically designed trade agreements like NAFTA that link Canada, Mexico, and the United States together or the European Union (EU) can further strengthen this geographically driven flow of trade in goods. There are other variations of regional trade agreements as well, like the *Alianza del Pacífico* (Pacific Alliance) that link four Pacific Ocean facing Latin American countries together to try to forge more trade with Asian Pacific countries. Many of these organizations have grown their focus beyond just trade. The EU has expanded past their initial focus on trade and economic enhancement and now appears to try to change all aspects of people's lives within their region. This can cause the organizations to become politically unpopular and political pressure can mount to unravel what initially was a positive economic relationship. The EU has moved to the point of undertaking actions that are sometimes seen as anti-sovereign, such as passing proclamations and regulations on topics from how countries should restructure their banks or run their judiciary all the way to making it illegal to sell eggs by the dozen rather than by weight or not allowing labels on water bottles to claim they can prevent dehydration.[ii,iii]

Trading agreements, for many years, were increasingly unilateral in nature. These agreements involved a number of countries and usually took years of negotiating before an alliance would be finalized. This is often advantageous for countries with small economies as they tend to have the most to gain from being part of a larger body. Increasingly there has been a push to do more bilateral, one-to-one, international trade agreements; in theory these agreements could be more customized and work well as they address the specific relationships between the two countries.

International trade in services requires many different facets than trade in goods. Service trade requires significant communication and legal scrutiny as it involves things like intellectual property and copyrights. Common language, economic rules and infrastructure between countries can help improve trade in services. In many developed countries, there has been significant growth in services as percentage of total trade and this has caused greater differences in the mix of trade by country. Cross-border trade in services appears as if it may not be as accurately measured as trade data involving goods. This could be distorting some of the value of trade data when used to analyze economic activity.

In many countries, including the United States, there is a monthly report on international trade in goods and services. The report typically breaks-out exports and imports and further cuts up each of those categories by goods and services. The relatively rapid report time, compared to other economic reports, means these trade reports can give significant insight into economic trends. In the United States the report gets its goods data from actual transactions; therefore, the timing of transactions from month to month can skew numbers. Export figures typically include cost of transportation, while import figures use what is referred to as custom value, or the value that would be declared at customs. Services are measured by a survey of companies and associations. Therefore it would appear that the more services data that show up in trade reports increases, the likelihood that the figures are inaccurate. Given the changes to the global flow of information, international trade in services, almost by definition, will be more digitized may not be as easy to track, and may be done on more of a peer-to-peer basis. It would seem reasonable that a good percentage of this will likely not be captured in reporting figures. On a quarterly basis trade figures are rolled up into a report on the current account balance. This report is much less timely than the monthly trade reports. However, one of the major values in the quarterly reports is that it includes data on the flow of capital. It has an income account for things such as gains in the holdings of foreign stocks as well as loans from country to country and direct government aid flows.

There has been a push by many organizations focused on trade policy to change how trade is measured, at least as a tool for analyzing trade agreements and flows of goods and services. The methodology that is often being championed is known as value-added trade and it can be a valuable tool to understand economic drivers and international interdependency. Understanding these connections has become more critical as global supply chains have become larger and more vital to corporations and economies. However, it is hard for any of the studies to keep up with the dynamism that exists in the modern supply chains.

Value-added trade does demonstrate how complex trade has changed. As an example, in the past a car may have been made in Japan and then shipped and sold to a car dealer in Australia. For illustrative purposes the example will be kept in Australian dollars. If we imagine an Australian auto dealer paid A$10,000 for the car from Japan, that amount showed up in the trade figures between Japan and Australia. However, now that car might get its parts from a thousand different locations due to the global value supply chain. The axles might come from Mexico, a brake system from Singapore, and it all gets assembled in Japan. If all the parts that were imported into Japan cost A$9,000, then after the assembly was completed in Japan it was sold to the Australian car dealer for A$10,000. The Japanese sale of the car to the Australian dealer would be counted as A$1,000 in value-added trade between Japan and Australia. Australia still spends A$10,000 on imports but it only shows A$1,000 of this trade with Japan. This methodology can clearly start to change how countries think about policy, especially on a bilateral basis. It also changes how analysts should think about the revenue truly flowing into Japan. This methodology also illustrates why "net" balance of trade numbers between exports and imports are typically what make headlines and draw comments from politicians. Jason Dedrick of Syracuse University has studied supply chains and in a 2012 presentation he wrote that in the supply chain for a $299 iPod, he estimates that there is $144 of the value that shows up as part of the United States trade deficit with China, but China only adds $5 in to the product.[iv]

The globalization of trade has changed the roadmap for how many lesser developed countries look to gain wealth. At one point the model to advance a country's economy was to build a deep and diversified industrial base like Germany, Japan, and the United States. This takes enormous time, requires capital flow, and a certain amount of sheer human capital or natural resources to make this practicable. Globalization of business has allowed an economy to try to specialize to capture part of the global supply chain and this can become a realistic route to success in improving the wealth of a country. A nation could focus on manufacturing semi-conductors, circuit boards or car parts. Specialization and dependence on other countries corporations to make end products can cause a country to lose some control over its economy, but this is a decision each nation can make. Over-dependence on a narrow sleeve of business can become a risk, but a reasonable plan should allow for some diversification even in a relatively small economy. Open economies that can be part of global trade generally do better than closed economies, even if they are dependent on a fairly narrow set of businesses. If you think of examples, closed economies such as North Korea or Venezuela, under the policies of Hugo Chavez, have not had a great economic track record.

Globalization changes risk analysis. It can expose even large domestic economies to disruptions that occur in other regions of the world that they may have little control over. If planned and utilized properly, however, global trade can allow for multiple sources and quick reaction time to changes and disruption, which can minimize the impact of natural or geopolitical problems. When bad events do happen globalization can give an economy more optionality in its paths to recovery after a disaster. Concern about trade and control can lead to policy mistakes or a desire of policy makers to limit trade which can cause economic distortions. Utilization of globalized trade impacts the valuations of corporate assets. In many cases design, logistical skills, marketing, and product placement drives more of the value at a corporation than the actual manufacturing process does now. Companies in the middle of the supply chain have less control over demand for their products as they are not interacting or managing the final customers.

---

i Rothbard, M. (2006 February 1)

ii Leake, C. (2010 June 10), EU Ban selling eggs by the dozen: Shopkeeper's fury as they are told to sell all food by kilo. Dailymail.co.uk

iii Ward, V. and Collins E. (2011 November 18), EU Bans Claim that Water Can Prevent Dehydration. Telegraph.co.uk

iv Dedrick, Jason (2012 March 21), Who Profits from Innovation in Global Value Chains? iPhones and Windmills. Syracuse University, retrieved from www.usitc.gov/research_and_analysis/documents/Dedrick_USITC_3-21-12_0.pdf.

Chapter 32
The Invisible Consumer: Customer Retention, Big Data, and Customer Service

The customer is always right, because they supply the money. Customers used to be relatively predictable, consistent, and loyal. Now given the number of options available to the consumer, the ease which they can be accessed and the low cost of switching, consumers can change directions like squirrels on amphetamines. The age of digital information has made consumers much better informed, more mobile and more demanding of shopping when and how they want to than in the past. The dispersion of media audiences, in some ways, have made customers harder to reach, but the move to diversified and mobile communication sources has created more ways for businesses to reach them. All of these factors, in many cases, have made consumers' attachment to a product or a service more fleeting and this has impacted how you have to value a customer when analyzing a corporate investment.

As an example, consider consumers of news media. Centuries ago they started reading news sheets that eventually grew into newspapers, this was the dominant medium of news for a few centuries. During the time newspapers dominated the media, people tended to have "their" newspaper and were loyal to it. This transitioned to listening to radio as a news source and newsreels in theaters. This lasted for a few decades until consumers began watching television news. Now they can take television with them wherever they go and can choose when and where to watch it. Ironically, now many consumers have gone back to getting much of their news by reading. However, they are not reading one newspaper, they are getting their news from a multitude of sources that can be downloaded. A customer that you know would be there every day to read your paper is more valuable than one that is jumping between twelve different media outlets to get the same information. This proliferation of options for consumers is happening in almost every business. It is obviously not just in media. With more easy access to more choices, all consumer brands seem to have less loyalty because of how easy switching has become. A company can compete for customers through pulling a few levers: price, quality, and service. Brand loyalty is created by trying to capture some combination of these characteristics. Price is an extremely tough way to compete in the modern world. People can walk into a store, scan a bar code on an item with their phone and see immediately if it is cheaper elsewhere or on the internet. They can go shopping in a store but make the purchase when they are home. Some start-up companies can put significant pressure on pricing and

DOI 10.1515/9781547400751-032

undercut the competition. If a start-up can attract capital and get healthy equity valuations without being profitable, they can feel free to cut prices almost to cost as long as they are gaining market share, or hitting whatever other metrics their investors care about, they do not need to worry about profit margins. New companies may also have cost advantages against incumbents because they are using the latest technology. Quality is a way to compete, however, in many cases technology has decreased the differences in quality between products. With better global logistics, so many components of products being outsourced and technology being able to replicate higher levels of craftsmanship there seems to be less differentiation of product. A high end Ford automobile now appears to resemble a high end Mercedes sedan much more so than any time in the past. Unique design can still make a difference and increased complexity or service interconnections can create switching costs that can help retain customers, all of which have been meaningful factors in the longevity of the success of Apple. Service can make a difference, but what service means is changing. Sometimes it is the ease by which you can return products or sometimes it can be the ease by which you can find products. The biggest factor in service is that if it is bad, a customer can be lost for life and with social media that impact can multiply.

Increasingly many companies are trying to create communities of like-minded people to retain customers, to do this requires a high quality and consistent level of service. Some of the gaming companies, like Activision and Take-Two Interactive, may be the most successful at this right now. For the gamers it is creating a shared common experience among people with the same interest (this is not dissimilar to what sports teams do). This type of business is typically dependent on subscriptions but benefits from its subscribers making connections with other subscribers. Newspapers, cable companies, and software services have all used the subscriber concept to retain customers, however, none of them have the same unique bond among their subscribers that is seen within the gaming communities. For businesses like cable television, mobile phone services, music streaming, and on-demand video, subscribers have been a huge factor in the valuation that the stock markets put on these businesses. However, these types of businesses do not appear to have the same subscriber stickiness that communities in gaming have created. All of these subscriber style businesses tend to face the risk of customer loss when greater flexibility and choice are offered by competitors

Businesses have also been undertaking a huge effort to gather data on customers and try to use it to retain them either through targeted advertisements or product offerings. Customer retention techniques have moved from couponing to affinity groups and now to scanning data trying to capture and monitor how people buy things. Some systems try to predict what individuals want to buy before they know it themselves. How well these techniques truly work over time is still yet to be seen. Forcing customers to give up too much information could backfire on any company trying to capture data. The information is often gathered under the guise of making the "customers experience better" but it is a tool for retention and upselling. These tactics face the risk of creating a "big brother" backlash, especially if security breaches occur.

To win and retain customers, proximity and timeliness can still be an advantage that is hard to beat. There are some products where proximity is critical; few people will order a cake or a spicy tuna roll through the mail and when needed they want a plumber or an electrician to be accessible. Logistical strengths are critical too. A bad experience in getting an item delivered can cause a company to lose a customer forever. Niche services may be able to maintain greater customer retention through the use of hyper-specialization; companies with focuses on services for special needs may become more valuable, like a concierge service for wealthy shoppers or specialized services for elders or a website for left-handed mandolin players. If there are more specialized niche services that are successful, this may make it more difficult for giant conglomerates to retain regular large segments of their customer base and another round of customer fragmentation may occur.

Perhaps there is no customer retention anymore. All customers fly to the best deal and the best "rated" product. There certainly seem to be fewer businesses that have customer loyalty. As customers have more choice and are more mobile it seems ill advised to think companies can easily retain them without constant investment. As an example, Netflix has been adding customers in a very competitive market, but it is doing so at an enormous cost as it invests heavily in new content and burns through cash each quarter. The investment to retain customers can squeeze profit margins and cause issues for individual companies, even in a strong economy. The less loyal consumers become the harder it is for investors to give a company a high valuation for their customer base, especially if the cost of customer retention is regularly rising.

Selected Ideas from Part 7

Topic	Concepts	Investment Impact
Business Structure	New organizations are flatter. Managing information is now more valuable than managing people.	Flat structures may make decisions slower more difficult. Lack of hierarchy can be accompanied by a lack of controls and increased risks.
Business Formation	Flexible organizations and lower capital requirements can lead to increased business formation.	Rapid business formation and disintegration can be good for economic flexibility, but increases competition at micro levels.
Business Investment	Increases in service companies and corporations heavily invested in intellectual property, distorts traditional business investment data.	Technology investments can rapidly decrease the value of older assets relative to their balance sheet figures. Intangible assets may be harder to monetize in distressed times.
Business Cycles	Traditional view of business cycles has not adapted to how much faster, everything in the economy moves.	Recessions may appear like bumps in trend lines as they recover quicker. Pocket recessions in industries or regions may be more prevalent but they should not be large enough to cause broad based economic wardrobe malfunctions unless bad government policy is enacted.
Barriers to Entry	There are several types of barriers to entry. Barriers to entry are all weaker in today's economic world.	To be successful it is unlikely that one barrier to entry is enough for any company. Switching costs have been an increasingly prevalent barrier in areas of complex technology.
Barriers to Entry II	Capital is flowing to companies that can breach barriers to entry and some new companies can attract capital without any profits.	When companies can attract capital without profits, it gives them an advantage to compete for market share with costly services and low prices. Meanwhile incumbents may need to focus on traditional profit metrics to maintain their valuations.
Incumbents	Incumbents will fight back and have resources.	There are various tacks incumbents can take when challenged, they are not as complacent about start-ups as they were a decade ago.
Food and Energy	These are two vital segments of the economy; they are especially important to watch as their price volatility can lead them to have an inordinate impact on how consumers act.	Society and innovation are changing these industries on a global basis. When these prices rise, they are such a large part of household budgets that they can pressure the consumer and shift expectations.

Topic	Concepts	Investment Impact
Supply chains	These have become more wide-spread and more complex, but allow for increased efficiency at corporations.	Understanding a company supply chain is increasingly important in valuing a company and understanding its risks.
Outsourcing	This allows more flexibility for a company making the end product, but potentially more risk in the mid-stream suppliers.	Outsourcing may allow for better decisions, it may allow a traditional company to innovate with less worry about debasing invested capital.
Outsourcing II	Increased outsourcing may mean that lead companies have less hard but more intellectual assets.	If a company that significantly utilizes outsourcing gets into trouble, creditors may have fewer saleable assets to get value from.
International Trade	Trade figures are a great way to understand trends and differences in economies.	The trade in services may be more difficult to track than the trade in goods.
Customers	The value of a customer to a company is declining, because in most cases it is increasingly easier for customers to switch.	Investments that are heavily dependent on customer count may require greater valuation discounts. Unique product or service factors that retain customers are rare.

Part 8: **Value, Volatility, Uncertainty—Different Arrangement but the Song Remains the Same**

Chapter 33
Value

The value of any asset is subjective. It is worth what someone is willing to pay for it. People may use similar methodologies to value an asset and arrive at the same conclusion, but at times of greater uncertainty they may not. With the recent plethora of high tech and innovative early stage companies in the economy, people may value these companies on their longer term potential more so than on their near-term expectations, this is different than they would value more mature companies. People may consider what an asset cost to make or cost previously to buy, this may add to a buyer's knowledge, but this sunk cost does not determine the value, it just may give the potential buyer some insight as to what price the seller may be willing to transact. The buyer may also consider what else they could do with their money rather than buy the asset and this opportunity cost is a major factor for both the buyer and the seller. Lastly, a buyer will want to consider how other potential buyers might value a specific asset, because that will set the price where they can sell the asset should they decide to do so.

With typical investment assets like stocks, bonds, loans, convertibles and real estate there are common methods that are often, but not always, used by investors to access value. Ultimately the methodologies are not that different from the past. The value of a project or a company is based on the cash flow that it can generate over time. However, there is lots of subjectivity in how these methods are used. Some investors will value current cash flow significantly more than future cash flow; while others may be more willing to defer current cash flow because they believe the future pay off has so much greater potential. When a company has little or no current cash flow compared to future expectations investors will sometimes use other metrics to monitor potential cash flows. These metrics might include revenue, customer website clicks or market share gains. Companies that are being valued on the potential for future cash flows will often have market valuations that have more volatility because the valuation can be so sensitive to even minor changes in expectations. It is not that cash flow does not matter for these companies, investors are still looking for it; they are just willing to wait for it. They are willing to defer their gratification in part because they believe that these companies can dominate or innovate enough that when the cash flow eventually comes, it will be enormous and will be more than enough to rationalize the current valuations. New economy companies like Microsoft, Google, and Apple have shown a path to enormous cash flow generation.

When evaluating how a company is doing, the media and analysts often discuss earnings. Earnings can have different definitions; net income is often

DOI 10.1515/9781547400751-033

referred to as "earnings" and in fact is the bottom line. It is the figure after all the accounting adjustments, special charges, and taxes are deducted. Because of all that accounting noise that occurs before you get to earnings it may not be the best way to measure the cash generation potential of a business or an asset. Often when assessing the value of a project or a company, an analyst will utilize some measure of cash flow to get more of a "normal" sense of the cash generation. Popular cash flow measures are EBIT and EBITDA (earnings before interest and taxes, and adding in depreciation and amortization for the latter calculation). These figures often also exclude items that are considered a one-time event, such as gains on a large asset sale. It is always worthwhile to look at a company's financial statements of cash flow and compare any calculated measure of cash flow to the financial statement line item typically labeled "cash flow from operations" as a gut check. Any cash flow figures can be adjusted further by subtracting on going expenditures for capital investment. Because of the variety of definitions of "earnings" and "cash flow," which one is used can add high levels of subjectivity into a valuation.

The traditional methodology for valuation is to take the stream of expected cash flows over a period and apply a discount to the future values of each cash flow (i.e. discounted cash flow analysis). The discounted value simply means that the cash flow you are expected to get ten years from now is worth less than the one you get next week. This is because you must wait for that future cash flow, but also because there is more uncertainty as to what that cash flow will be the further out you go. So your cash flow projections and the discount value you choose will have a major impact on your view of valuation. Too often people view these projections as absolutes, they are not yes or no questions. It is often better to think of them as scenarios, and to build a few of them with different macro and micro expectations and apply some probabilities than to just build one and think it is a perfect predictor of the future. Scenarios should include potential actions that management might be motivated to take that could change the business model and how the company will capitalize itself. These choices can dramatically impact risk and value. The discount rate is another area of subjectivity; theoretically, the discount you apply to these projected cash flows should factor in the time, uncertainty, and what you can get paid in a risk-free government bond.

There are other factors that increase the subjectivity of value. Each investor will have a different time horizon and what that time horizon is will influence their valuation methodologies and determine the type of investments they will favor. Investors' time horizons also change during an investment period. Time is the ultimate depleting resource and, despite all the various ways to measure time, no one can be certain how much of it they have.

It is important to understand how others value assets because someone else's subjective value will determine where you can ultimately sell the asset that you own. The decision to buy something and determine a value is always influenced by the relative value of other opportunities. This opportunity cost is based on how much utility you could have received by buying something else, or doing nothing. Factor in that each investor is assessing their own personal valuation to all these other opportunities in order to determine what they are willing to pay for an asset and you see that value is quite subjective.

Momentum can also drive asset valuations. The value of an industry sector, a company's stock, or any asset that begins to attract capital and rise in value will often attract more capital; and that in turn will likely push values even higher. Part of this is driven by the fact that investor's may feel there is less uncertainty in an asset if other people are buying it. Momentum buying gets support, in part, because of studies that have shown the success of various momentum trading strategies. Index funds, technical traders, and some program trading can all add to this momentum. This valuation may be caused by the change in some risk or uncertainty around the investment or it might be driven by an over-reaction to a price move or a news item that triggers a piling on effect as investors buy based on a fear of missing out (FOMO in millennial parlance) rather than any fundamental change in the ultimate value. Momentum can, however, also change directions and assets can fall out of favor. Sometimes this can happen when data doesn't back up the rationale for the momentum.

Some of the best insights about the perception of value can be gleaned by watching how market valuations for an asset moves and react in different periods and to different types of news. Markets tell you other people's perceptions of value. Through watching the markets you can gain knowledge that can help reduce your uncertainty about how the asset will act. Ultimately this can help you determine value and give you an idea how the asset will be valued by others when you decided to sell the asset.

When you can get market valuations they are good to use. Markets may not always be right about the valuation of an asset, but they are definitely giving you a signal on values and what other people believe they are worth. Even if a company does not have a public stock you can often look at comparable companies or acquisition transactions to get a sense of valuation of a company, just as you would compare prices of similar cars in the car market to get some sense of what you should pay.

Mr. Milken and his team at Drexel Burnham Lambert were early champions of using the market value of equity as a measure of asset value rather than the book value of equity that gets recorded on company balance sheets. They also developed a solvency measure using market values. Instead of measuring a debt/equity ratio using the balance sheet, they used a market adjusted debt (MAD) ratio using market values instead of book values. Some of the complaints about this methodology have been that since the market value can fade or boom so quickly it may be less reliable and markets are fallible. These concerns are valid, but, book equity also has flaws as it is adjusted by many accounting issues and may not reflect what anyone is willing to pay for the assets. As asset valuations change much more quickly than in the past, due to factors like barriers to entry and working capital shifting so rapidly, the measurement of market value of equity becomes a more valuable tool as it is much more responsive to change.

When public companies report their earnings, valuations of that company, and sometimes similar companies, will move in response. Similarly, broad market valuations of stocks, bonds and loans might move when economic data is released. However, often this is not due to the actual earnings figure or the economic data. Valuations often move because of other information the company gives or text that is attached to an economic press release. Valuations move on this news because it changes people's perceptions of the outlook. Management may hold a conference call and make confident statements that could increase or decrease uncertainty. Some typical items that can trigger valuation changes include:

- Did the company change its guidance?
- Did it announce plans to raise capital or pay dividends?
- Were there changes to key performance indicators (KPIs)?

Of course, sometimes management can act erratic and if management throws a fit or starts singing a song during an earnings conference call, it is likely that it would increase uncertainty, too. You may disagree with how the market reacts to something in a corporate or economic report and may believe that over time the market will come around to your point of view or that future news will change their minds. If this is the case, then this is an opportunity to react–whether it is on a macro, medi or micro basis.

Much of what drives value can be uncertainty. However, you must make decisions with a certain level of uncertainty. Otherwise, there would be little to no reward. Differing views in the level of that uncertainty can lead to different views on valuation and as uncertainty increases or decreases, valuations will change. Sometimes a news release changes the perceptions of uncertainty. Markets and how they react can add to your knowledge of how other people are viewing uncertainty, and this is powerful because part of how you value an asset may be based on how you believe you can get the market to value it in the future.

Even Real Estate Changes

Real estate is often viewed as the ultimate tangible asset. People always want to own it because they are not making any more of it. Of course for centuries land and wealth were linked. However, it is not just corporate and intangible asset valuations that can change due to societal and innovative developments. Real estate valuation can be impacted by sociology and technology as well. In the United States and parts of Europe, a major revaluation of real estate occurred in the Great Recession. Some argue that this was the root cause of the economic set-back. An investor can monetize real estate through the cash flow of a rental stream or through making it attractive to someone as a home. The drop in real estate values during the Great Recession was a bit of a shock to the net worth and the overall mentality of home ownership. This could have a long-term sociological impact on real estate value as people who experienced the shock, or saw their parents struggle, may be more reluctant to own real estate, and these changes could impact valuations. Some countries, like the United States, have had active policies to promote home ownership in the belief that it will help family formation and a community, which are probably true. However, promoting such policies can result in distorting valuations as it drives more buyers toward an asset that they might not seek otherwise. When there is an economic downturn in a region, home ownership can severely restrict the ability of people that are out of work to move to find employment elsewhere because they cannot sell their home. A new generation of workers may increasingly value mobility and not want it limited by ownership. There has recently been an increase in urbanization with younger people moving into urban areas. However, this could unwind. If younger people get married and have children and the schools are not good in urban areas, then they will leave. Technology could shift values of property as well. Real estate is valued higher in desirable locations. A location's value is often due to an attractive setting or proximity to areas of high employment. Additionally, the improvements in telecommunication and increased acceptance of telecommuting could lead to significant decentralization and unwind the benefits of employment proximity in real estate values. While real estate is a classic investment that may seem above the fray, even these types of investments are not immune to technological and social changes impacting their valuations.

Being able to show the ability to generate actual cash flow helps decrease uncertainty. When a company fails it is usually because they cannot generate enough cash flow or attract capital. When this happens, the question arises as to what the assets of the company are worth. If it owns a building and a production plant that makes boxes, another investor may look at it and figure if they can transform the building or repurpose the machines, they can generate cash flow from these hard assets and use this anticipated cash flow to decide what they will pay for the assets. However, new companies may have fewer tangible core assets. Sometimes their assets are very specialized and it is difficult for someone else to monetize them. For example, a company has built a complex supply chain, but does not own it. The new economy company may have intangible intellectual property that someone else wants, but the audience of purchasers may be small. The more specialized that intangibles are, the harder they will be to monetize in a time of crisis. When intangible intellectual property accounts for the bulk of a company's value, the recoveries for investors may be more challenging and this all should be factored into valuations as well.

New technology can change the value of existing assets. Music streaming has changed the value of recorded music and music rights. The incredible dispersion of large television audiences into a multitude of smaller diverse venues has oddly increased the value of an event, which can draw a large national audience. More efficient and green technology companies over time could dramatically impact the value of older power generation equipment or fossil fuels. Broad based, rapid, technological innovation impacts value because it unleashes potential growth but it also increases uncertainty.

Chapter 34
Volatility and Risk Measures—A Point of View

From an investment point of view, risk is about the potential to lose money. Other risk measures are just ways of trying to analyze the probability of losing money. Changes in the business world should cause people to be careful how they analyze risk because so many risk models are based on using data from the past. The linkages between this older data and the current markets are likely to be different and you need to take some time analyzing the current period to see what risk measures really apply.

While loss is the real risk in an investment, it is quite common to use volatility as a measure of risk. Changes in the value of an asset and the comparison of the value between two assets are often linked with volatility, but volatility is not a measure of loss. Volatility of returns is usually measured utilizing standard deviation of returns over a specific time period typically using daily, weekly or monthly returns. Much of the work on using volatility as a measure of risk was developed as part of modern portfolio and efficient market theory. This work focused on the returns of stocks. The research utilized data on liquid assets in which investors had symmetrical information flow and good record keeping and disclosures of transactions and volumes traded. Part of the key when using volatility as a measure of risk is that you have good data and that means the asset you are examining should be actively traded. Volatility in the valuation of an asset does tell you whether there are big or small changes in the market perception of the value of that asset and how often that happens. Higher levels of volatility does add risk because it increases uncertainty of how the market is valuing the asset. If the volatility is related to a corporate investment, it may signal things about the company's operational stability, too. When you have shorter investment time frames, the volatility of valuations matters more as you will have fewer entry and exit point options, and if an asset has more volatile pricing, your time horizon probably has a bigger probability of aligning with a valuation that is a bad valuation for you. Volatility in the price of an asset indicates that the market place is less certain of an asset's prospects, and volatility in a company's operation metrics can indicate less predictability. However, volatility is not loss. One of the problems of just measuring volatility is that you could easily devise a scenario where you look at two investment assets over a twenty month time period. The first asset we will call asset Alpha. It might be down about 40% from the price you bought it and asset Bravo could be up 400% and not had a single month of negative returns, but asset Alpha could have a lower standard deviation of monthly returns. In this case, the lower volatility does not help to measure the greater level of risk. In theory, this

DOI 10.1515/9781547400751-034

occurs in part because the use of standard deviation assumes that the returns will be normally distributed, and nothing is always normal. It appears that asset Bravo's returns are not normally distributed. There are many adjustments you could apply to the data by choosing selected time periods, looking at volatility only in periods of price declines or using statistical smoothing techniques, but blindly using volatility to measure risk can be misleading.

Analyzing periods of loss can be a valuable tool for understanding risk. However, measures of loss can be tricky because you need to analyze what caused the loss and how applicable it may be to current risks. If you take an average of periods when investment losses occurred over an extended time period, it might include months that had losses that were triggered by rising interest rates, a global collapse in commodity prices, a war, or trade tensions. One of these periods of "drawdowns" might have been wide-ranging and impacted every asset's valuation or it might have been a period when drawdowns only impacted a specific commodity, region or industry. Just as you can measure volatility in various ways you can measure drawdowns in various ways. The time frame you choose is important, both the decision over how many years you want to analyze the data and then whether you care about the drawdowns during a day, week, month or year. You must make sure the data is applicable to the current time frame you are analyzing. You also can analyze different types of drawdowns such as the average drawdown during these periods or the maximum or minimum drawdown. It may not be only for periods of drawdowns. You may want to look at any time period where the returns were under a selected threshold. Comparing the frequency and the amplitude of the drawdowns between specific assets or asset classes can be a valuable risk assessment tool, though it is not as widely used as volatility.

Value at Risk

Instead of measuring risk through volatility, measuring the risk of loss is sometimes viewed as a better measure. Values at risk (VaR) methodologies have tried to do this. It has been heavily used by banks and securities trading firms as a risk management tool. These firms may at any time in a given day have hundreds of thousands of positions in commodities, options, stocks, bonds, and currencies. VaR can help tell them what their potential risk of loss is based on past data. VaR can also be used in portfolio management. VaR uses historical pricing data and probabilities to calculate potential losses during a set period, such as a day. There are flaws in this methodology. If shocks happen to move prices out of the historical range, losses may be greater than the VaR models predicted. Also, if there are fundamental shifts in correlations, VaR can get thrown off. VaR is still based on historical prices and does not factor in changes in the fundamental drivers of risk. VaR is not perfect, but it shifts the focus of risk to examine potential loss rather than just volatility.

Volatility has other uses than just measuring the risk of an investment return. You can look at the volatility of other factors and metrics. For example, when examining the operations of a company, you can look at the volatility of cash flows or the volatility in capital expenditures. A more consistent metric can give you a higher level of confidence in you projection scenarios for that company. Greater volatility could indicate greater business risk. You could also compare the volatility in a cash flow metric of a company to the volatility in the asset valuation of that company and see if they are reasonably correlated and if the business risks are reflected in valuation. There are numerous other possibilities. Similar functions could be constructed using macroeconomic data; you could do a comparison of the moves in volatility in food prices to the demand for out-of-home dining. These types of comparisons can give you some insights, but you must be sure to understand the context of the time periods you are examining relative to the time period that you are investing in and carefully analyze the logic of comparing the data.

It is often important to compare different asset classes and to decide how you wish to allocate your investments across them. For example, consider how you want to be invested in stocks, bonds and real estate. There is an endless body of writing on asset allocation, and the right allocation can shift over time and can vary greatly depending on the investor's goals. Volatility is often part of the toolset used to compare asset classes. Much of the research that utilizes volatility is concentrated on very liquidly traded assets. This means the market is giving investors regular data that can be used to calculate gains and losses at least every day and frequently every second. These highly liquid assets are typically stocks and currencies in developed country markets and sovereign government bonds in the strongest credit quality countries. There are many assets that do not have nearly the same amount of trading volume or liquidity as equities, government bonds and currencies. These might include corporate bonds, real estate and tranches of securitized debt. Sometimes these markets are very inefficient and illiquid. An asset that is illiquid may have very low volatility, but that may be because there are no transactions for several days so that prices have not moved. A lack of transactions does not mean that there is less risk in the investment. As a matter of fact, you could make quite a case that if something rarely trades, then there are fewer valuation data points and possibly fewer buyers so it has greater risk even though it may have mathematically lower volatility. There are also structural issues that have to be considered when comparing various asset classes that can distort relative volatility. For example, much of the return in stocks price has historically come from appreciation or depreciation of the value of the stock and much less from the stream of income from dividends, whereas in corporate bonds the bulk of the return comes from the interest income stream. The structural issues are real and given these structural differences it is probably of limited value to compare volatilities of these types of asset classes. Differences in liquidity and trading volumes make comparing volatility across asset classes difficult to do consistently. It does not mean that this type of comparison does not add some value, but it should not be the sole tool used in comparing the risk and the risk reward ratios of various asset classes.

Measures of Fixed Income Risk

Bonds and other fixed income investments have many unique features that have led to the development of some unique risk tools. The most notable characteristics are the payment of regular stream of interest and that they have a finite date when the investment gets paid back. In fixed income, investors often look at measures of duration as a measure of risk. Duration highlights the sensitivity in the price of a bond relative to a move in interest rates or relative to a change in the expected credit spread of the bond issuer (we will use 'bond' as a proxy for fixed income investments in this section). The spread is often viewed as the market's valuation of the risk that you will not get paid back for your investment in the bond (as explained earlier the spread is the yield on the investment minus the risk-free rate on a government bond with the same maturity). Duration therefore measures the potential volatility of the price of a bond. The simple explanation of duration is that if a bond has a duration of 3 years, interest rates move up 1% and the bond moves in lock step, then the bond price will lose 3%. The return would be this loss net of any interest income that the bond pays. There are many types of duration including option adjusted duration and spread duration, which are both widely used. To analyze risk in fixed income duration can be compared to data on historical drawdowns, volatility and volatility of interest rates, to name a few examples. It can also be compared to credit quality measures using rating agency data, your own credit rankings or it can utilize spread as a proxy for the market's view of risk. Adding in these credit factors can help to measure how a bond will perform if the perception of credit risk changes, duration does not measure this credit risk, but it can be coupled with measures of credit risk to better analyze an investment in a fixed income asset.

Risk and returns are intertwined; comparing the apparent risk you are taking to the potential reward is a common and valuable process. However, not all tools that are available to analyze return and risk fit all situations. These tools can be used to analyze an individual investment, but are more commonly used to analyze an entire portfolio or to compare asset classes in order to make decisions on allocations. The most popular measure to compare return versus risk for investments is, refreshingly one of the simplest, the Sharpe ratio. This ratio takes the return of a portfolio and subtracts the theoretical "risk-free" rate of return (which is usually assumed to be a government bond), and then divides it by the volatility of returns of the portfolio. The result is a simple return per unit of risk measure, assuming you accept volatility as a measure of risk. There are at least two important variations on this formula. The Treynor ratio changes the measure of risk, in the denominator. It uses beta as a measure of risk rather than overall volatility of returns. Beta measures how much of an investment return is due to changes in the market and how much is specific to that investment. A beta of 1 means the investment moves in line with the market; if it is 1.5, then it means it moves more. Making sure you utilize the right market from which to measure beta is important. The Sortino ratio adds loss into the equation and that is very valuable. In the Sortino ratio, the denominator utilizes the standard deviation of periods when the asset had negative returns, which is sometimes referred to as downside deviation. This tries to separate out good volatility from bad. It could be adjusted. Rather than just including periods of negative returns, it could utilize the volatility during any period in which a certain threshold return is not met. As an example, for a bond portfolio, this could be counting any period in which returns fell below the average coupon rate. The Sortino ratio may help when the data on the volatility of returns does not follow a normally distributed pattern. Which ratio you use will also depend on what exactly you are trying to measure. They can all be helpful, but all have flaws.

For any investor or decision maker, risk versus reward is a constant exercise. For security, investing the simplicity of the Sharpe ratio makes it very attractive to use, its simplicity has led to over use. Analysis should include an understanding of any idiosyncratic events that might have occurred during the period you are examining and how the constituents in the universe might have changed relative to the current time period. The distribution of returns should also be analyzed.

Risk and return are intertwined. Valuation changes are generally what drive returns, and valuation is driven by the perception of potential upside versus potential downside. Both of these perceptions can move significantly due to change in uncertainty.

Chapter 35
Uncertainty—The Opportunity

A good joke and a good horror movie both depend heavily on the unexpected. Markets are not as entertained by the unexpected and can react violently when the unexpected resets the level of uncertainty. Volatility occurs when asset values move up or down. Increased uncertainty tends to only impact asset values in one direction and that is down. Uncertainty reduces asset values and can immobilize the decision process. Eventually, however, new levels of uncertainty are like a bad smell in a room. It takes time, but people adjust to it, and it becomes the norm. If there is not a certain level of uncertainty associated with an investment there would not be opportunity.

With the global economy going through a rapid innovation driven transformation coupled with demographic changes, uncertainty is declining in some areas and increasing in others. The efficiencies and flexibility being driven by technology are lowering uncertainty in broad macroeconomic trends. Counterbalancing this is greater uncertainty over how politics and policy will be changed by cultural transformations. In addition, uncertainty is increasing at the more medi- and micro-economic levels as regions, industries, businesses, and jobs experience more disruption with uncertain outcomes.

There is a classic book in financial economics entitled, *Risk, Uncertainty and Profit*, published in 1921 by Frank Knight, who was a pioneering University of Chicago professor. In the book he defined different types of uncertainty.[i] In the first type of uncertainty you can predict the risk, quantify it, and maybe even mitigate it. For example, if you are playing backgammon and you need a specific roll of the dice to win, there is uncertainty what you will roll, but the possibilities can be calculated. You know what the outcomes are. Sometimes in finance uncertain risks can be partially mitigated with different strategies such as short-selling, the use of options or careful diversification. When you do not know what the potential outcomes are or the outcomes can not be calculated, that is true uncertainty (sometimes referred to as Knightian uncertainty). For example, all the possible ramifications from a war can not be calculated.

When people have been living within a certain range of risk, and have made assumptions about this risk, economies and markets can function well. It does not mean that volatility will not exist; it means there is a framework of risk within which investors will be relatively comfortable even if the movements within that framework have a high level of volatility. If these parameters are shattered and true uncertainty replaces the previous assumptions of the ranges of risk, it can lead to panic. You might think of risk as bound within a set of lines. As uncer-

DOI 10.1515/9781547400751-035

tainty increases or decreases, those lines are moved. If they are moved so far apart that investors cannot even see them, they lose their way. As an example, prior to the financial crisis in 2008, many financial firms used derivatives to limit their risks. They knew these instruments did not eliminate risk but it gave them a range of potential losses. When major financial firms, like Lehman Brothers and Bear Stearns, failed, they did not know if those derivatives, many of which were obligations of the failed firms, would be honored and suddenly these financial firms had a different level of risk on their balance sheets, and the lines of uncertainty blew out so wide they could not be seen.

Investors do not like uncertainty. However, to make money you must invest with a certain level of uncertainty, which is where the return comes from. As an investor you must go to uncertainty, determine if that uncertainty impacts your thesis, or just increases the range in which your investment will be valued. You may also have a view if uncertainty is going to increase or decrease. This could be a view about the outcome of a close election or a lawsuit that impacts a company or it could be a view on the expected consistency of economic results over the next year. When uncertainty increases, the value of risk aversion goes up. For example, the demand for safe haven investments like U.S government treasury bonds and the Japanese yen have historically risen when uncertainty increases. When the markets move toward safer havens, prices of these assets rise and it is often a signal of risk aversion.

Various investment vehicles react differently to uncertainty. Owning the shares of a company typically has little intrinsic value (assuming you do not have controlling shares) unless someone else wants to buy them from you. Therefore, they tend to have more uncertainty than many other assets. Commodities have some intrinsic value, but they are still dependent on who ultimately wants or needs the commodity. Bond valuations can be impacted by almost every feature of the economy but offer less uncertainty because of their structure—if the borrower fulfills its obligations that are part of the bond's contract, you know what you will get paid in interest and principal and when. This removes a large uncertainty from the investment.

There are events that commonly increase uncertainty; ironically the uncertainty is often scheduled. Elections and central bank meetings often increase uncertainty. The uncertainty around elections has increased recently as political factions have become more extreme from each other. Assume one candidate is like an angry mongrel dog, denigrating his opponents and advocating for government takeover of some private companies and that any private companies pay for increased regulation. Then assume the other candidate is like a feral cat screaming to rally its supporters and guaranteeing to shut down all regulatory agencies and have corporations not pay taxes. It is not hard to see how such an election will increase uncertainty no matter who wins.

When the uncertainty rises or declines you need to question the cause and the impact of the change in uncertainty and try to determine how much it might affect your investments directly or indirectly, such as through changes in the opportunity cost of choosing other investments. Innovation increases uncertainty, especially for those that are not the innovators. At the corporate and industry level there are many items that can increase or decrease uncertainty; management with a successful track record, an understandable business plan, assets that are easily valued and healthy levels of cash flow all impact uncertainty. Companies with less tangible assets may have higher levels of uncertainty, but perhaps this can be mitigated by other factors like the ability to attract a significant amount of customers or capital.

Mitigation of uncertainty is difficult. One way of reducing uncertainty within a portfolio is through diversity. Uncertainty is unlikely to strike all regions, businesses and assets at the same time or in the same ways. While diversity does not eliminate uncertainty, it can mitigate some of its impact. Communications can reduce uncertainty. When government officials or corporate leaders lay out plans and explain their actions and rationale, uncertainty can decrease. Some research has shown that the stock valuations of companies that communicate more actually perform better,[ii] or of course it could be that because they are doing well they are willing to communicate more. There is a flip side for an organization that communicates heavily. If it publicly lays out its plans, goals, and targets, it opens public scrutiny of all its actions. It may limit the organization's flexibility as it partially boxed itself into its guidance and increased the cost of adapting to change.

It is understandable that people want to develop ways to quantify true uncertainty, but it is not easily done. You can try to calculate some possible outcomes and apply probabilities, but the danger comes if you start to assume those are the only possible outcomes and that your analysis is more complete and quantifiable than it is. As you move farther away from calculating the numbers yourself and computer simulations do more of the work, it is even easier to assume a higher level of confidence in the results than may exist. For example, it is certain that a computer could calculate a series of potential actions that a person would take in each situation, but people are unique, and it may not be able to factor crazy into its model.

Doing nothing because you have not decided is bad, but making an active decision to do nothing is fine. Uncertainty can often trigger a freeze reaction, and this is not good. Decisions must be made even in the face of uncertainty. Sometimes this immobility in the face of uncertainty is insidious. Assume that within a company a team meets to address a high-risk problem, but there is significant uncertainty. The group decision is to get more information to address the level of uncertainty. This can be valuable. However, they must make sure this is not just a subconscious postponement of deciding. Someone in the room has to question if the additional work is really going to lower your uncertainty and help reach a meaningfully better answer or if you are doing additional work to postpone a decision and using unsolvable uncertainty as an excuse. If it is just an "uncertainty stall," you are not achieving a better answer, and you are wasting one of the most precious assets of the firm, and that is people's time, an asset lost forever.

An economy that is defined by innovation will logically increase the levels of uncertainty in certain arenas. While it allows for more rapid macroeconomic solutions, there is more disruption to people's lives, and this can increase political uncertainty. Disruption at the business level has materially increased uncertainty. The best models can not factor in what they do not know. The expanding economy should lead to more choice, more growth, and more things available for more people, but it comes with some creative destruction that Joseph Schumpeter wrote about so famously.[iii] This creates greater risks but a greater number of opportunities for investments and adds to the excitement of uncertainty.

---

i Knight, F. (2014), *Uncertainty Risk and Profit*. Martino Publishing.

ii Jiao, Y. (2011 September 21), Corporate Disclosure, Market Valuation and Firm Performance. *Financial Management*. Financial Management Association

iii Schumpeter, J. (2008), *Capitalism, Socialism and Democracy*. Harper Perennial Modern Thought.

Part 9: **Random Ramble and Concluding Topics**

Chapter 36
New Industries and What to Do about Them

Joseph Schumpeter was an economist who did most of his work during the first half of the twentieth century. He wrote extensively about innovation in the economy and is generally credited with coining the phrase creative destruction. In his construct of creative destruction, innovation and entrepreneurs disrupt, displace, and sometimes destroy existing industries, companies, and jobs, which causes upheaval. Like Mr. Keynes, Mr. Schumpeter's ideas evolved over time and changed with more research and took into account events that were occurring in the world. He was a man of many ideas, and you may not want to accept all of them but just because you disagree with some of the concepts does not invalidate all of them. Much of his work culminated in his book *Capitalism, Socialism and Democracy* published in 1942. His work often features the entrepreneur as a hero in society. Some of his other views may seem a bit more radical today. He did not view creative destruction as the end of the process; in his thesis creative destruction would eventually cause the collapse of capitalism. He also, controversially, questioned the value of democracy. He was unsure whether most of the people understood what was best for the public good.[i]

There is no question that the twenty-first century has been ripe with the evolution of new industries and new businesses. The development of new industries raises questions about the economic, sociological, and political impact on existing companies and industries. All these developing industries present new and challenging potential investments. When analyzing the opportunities in new innovative investments categorizing the business by their approach and their reason for existing can be helpful:

a) Is the industry bringing a new innovative product?
b) Is it developing a new production methodology? Does this include use of new raw material or new methodologies?
c) Is it opening a new market, such as giving access to more people for an existing product?
d) Is it a new industry structure, such as some of the new peer-to-peer offerings?
e) Is it truly a new product or replicating an existing one?
f) Is it solving a problem with a process or an invention?
g) Is it competing on quality (i.e., product, service, access) or price?
h) Is it gaining an advantage by specialization or broadening the customers' choice?

DOI 10.1515/9781547400751-036

If you invest in early stage companies some of these themes may appeal to you more than others and you may favor innovators with certain traits. At the same time incumbents may be in a stronger position to fend off certain types of approaches from new entrants than others. With all this change, strategies can be developed that focus on rotating industries based on where you believe they are in the cycle of transformation and similar rotational strategies can be undertaken by geography as different economies are in different phases.

Innovation and new industries can take market share from existing companies and even push them out of existence. Operators in the existing businesses will not just roll over, but will fight back. Existing companies must be willing to invest and stay on the right side of technology to survive. The cynic has to question if the innovative business idea is just a great idea or an idea for a great business. If it is the former, the incumbents can often just usurp it. As an investor you can look for validations on a new industry. Two common validations for a new business come from customers and capital. If a new business or industry can attract and retain one or the other, it is often a strong validation of the business.

You will also want to analyze the ability of a new industry to keep its advantage. Today barriers to entry are weak and capital can flow quickly to competitors. One barrier that seems to lend itself to technology companies is switching costs. Switching costs can be actual cash expenses, annoyance, or risk of business interruption. As a retention tool, companies try to raise the switching costs for customers in different ways and one is to cross-sell them multiple services. In technology, embedded multiple offerings of complex services, the risk of downtime and malfunctions as well as loss of customer data and the effort of having to learn new systems can create a meaningful barrier from losing customers.

Israel Kirzner, a professor at New York University, for many years has written extensively on entrepreneurship, its importance, and impact. One of his themes is that entrepreneurship is often ignored in economic theories that focus on equilibrium. Economies do not stay in equilibrium as they are dynamic. He pointed out that new businesses and new industries are vital to competition and successful capitalism.[ii] The destruction, disruption, and draw on capital that new industries create have impacts throughout the economy. On a macro basis these factors can initially hurt the economic environment through job disruption and changes in the status quo, but generally lead to long-term growth and improved employment and quality of life.

Analyzing new industry developments is difficult because of how subjective the process is. There is often no data on the new industry. You can examine the opportunity set and the strengths and weaknesses of existing operators. You can conduct surveys and game theory to analyze possible outcomes, but there is no certainty. Investors in start-ups are often very industry focused as understanding the entire economic sphere around a new industry can be very valuable in making investment decisions but it still does not guarantee success. The level of subjectivity, uncertainty, and unknowns in the analysis is what can make an investment in new industries so exciting.

---

i Ibid.
ii Kirzner, I. (1973), *Competition & Entrepreneurship*. Chicago: University of Chicago Press.

Chapter 37
Emerging Economies—New Paths

Emerging market investment involves several regions and types of investing. Even the concept has a variety of names including emerging markets, developing countries, or advancing economies and probably a few others. It is misleading to lump all the different emerging markets into a "category." There are at least four major geographical regions that include Asia, Africa, Latin America, and Eastern Europe. You could then divide the countries by size of their economy. You might include Brazil, China, India, and Russia in one category and form others for the smaller economies. Some people increasingly have a separate category for "frontier" markets. You could also divide investments by government structures, such as dictatorships/authoritarian rule and democracies. As a final example, you could divide them by economic drivers such as: commodity, manufacturing, supply chain specialization, or services. All of this can help you define thematic investments.

Emerging economies may get a jump start on economic growth from a strong commodity base or cheap labor, but they usually need to expand from that base to experience broad-based sustainable growth. Generally, just ripping things out of the ground and selling them to more developed countries is not a good long-term economic plan for development. Success in these countries can come when capital gained from commodity or low-cost labor driven businesses can be redeployed into infrastructure that can help diversify economies. This can include government, legal, or physical infrastructure. Investments also need to be made in structures that help cultivate human capital, such as health care, communication, education, and housing.

Historically, physical transportation-focused infrastructure was always at the top of checklists when analyzing emerging market countries. However, economic drivers are more varied now. It is not that infrastructure does not matter, but in some cases communication infrastructure may be more critical. Infrastructure in general is important to attract capital and help growth, but it also must be scaled as the economy grows.

Technology can make infrastructure investment more efficient, which can help transform countries and regions more rapidly. For example, countries that did not have full coverage of wireline phone service for many years have been able to rapidly reach more people with service through the build out of wireless phone networks which can be more efficient in many regions. Once a mobile telecommunications service is set up, access to many other services can grow rapidly. In many regions in Africa the primary access to banking and financial transac-

DOI 10.1515/9781547400751-037

tions is through mobile phones. Additionally, in remote places access to services like medical consultations are available through mobile phones or other wireless devices.

There are many ways to invest in emerging markets, just as there is in all cross-border investing. One aspect of the investment that can play a bigger role in emerging markets is the currency in which you choose to make the investment. Typically, you can invest in instruments in the local currency or investments issued in one of the major currencies, usually U.S. dollars or Euros. One of the differences in emerging markets versus other cross-border investments is that it is usually more difficult, or costly, to hedge the local currency. Emerging market currencies also tend to be more volatile than the larger developed country currencies.

There is typically a full variety of investment vehicles available in emerging market countries; this includes government debt, quasi-government debt, equities, or the debt of companies that are in the emerging market. There are also forms of direct investing. The level of development of the local capital markets vary greatly and should be a consideration in how you choose to invest. There is also the potential to invest in major international companies that are based in developed countries that do a significant amount of business in emerging markets, which is a more indirect way of investing.

When you are making investments away from your home market there are always at least two layers of risk and opportunity. The first is the potential improvement or deterioration in the overall economic conditions of the country in which you are investing relative to your home country and opportunities in other markets. This can cause any form of emerging market investment to increase or decline in value. The overall perception of the quality of a country will typically shift much more in emerging markets than in developed countries. The other major opportunity, and risk, is through the vehicle in which you choose to invest, meaning the specific bond or stock or real estate that you purchase. There have been times when corporate bonds in a country trade better than the national government bonds. The entity in which you invest will impact your returns, but it will also be impacted by how the country is doing.

To undertake analysis at the country level there are many financial factors to consider and many areas of analysis that do not always lend themselves to quantitative measures, such as how good is the rule of law, government stability, and financial infrastructure. On the more quantitative side you can analyze trends in trade and capital flows. Government finances can be important, as can some measure of trends on general economic activity, strength of the government budget and debt levels at the national and local levels. You will also want to get an understanding of the country's more critical industries. Analysis of a country's financial system is also important. This should include an analysis of the major banks. Bank analysis should include capital ratios, mix of liabilities, and asset formation trends. Additionally, analysis of the financial system should include examining overall access to capital, as well as the flexibility and variety in financing sources. All these factors impact the ability to attract capital flows and make the capital stickier, which can be critical for emerging market nations.

Developing a framework for investing in emerging markets and all cross-border investing does require examination of some less quantitative factors and the use of checklists and matrices on these topics can often help categorize strengths and weaknesses and aid with the decision process. Some of the factors you would want to include on a matrix checklist at the country level might include:
- Rule-based economy
- Political stability
- National financial stability and resources
- Physical infrastructure
- Economic drivers and industries
- Access and consistency in reporting of economic and financial data
- Health and education
- Key trading and financial partners

The factors to consider in emerging markets investing are not that different from doing any other cross-border global investing. However, there is typically more volatility and greater variations by country than in the developed world. The impact of technology can be different on emerging market economies as the introduction of technology-driven competition may not face as many incumbent competitors, so changes can happen more rapidly and can have a larger impact on the overall economy. However, in some cases the existing industry leaders are even more powerful and entrenched than in the developed markets. Technological adoption may prove to be another key differentiator between emerging market nations.

Chapter 38
Socially Responsible Investing and Environmental, Social, and Governance Factors

Environmental, social, and governance (ESG) issues, socially responsible investing (SRI), and activist investing are driving major changes in the process of asset valuation, and are already influencing investing patterns, access to capital, and in some cases corporate operating performance. Whether the issues are of importance to you on a personal basis or not, they must be considered on an investment basis. Definitions are evolving in this arena and what can be considered socially responsible investing to one organization may be viewed very differently in another. ESG can be viewed as a risk mitigation tool that can be utilized for active investment decisions and should be part of all prudent investment decisions. SRI and impact investing are more of a stylistic decision that can utilize ESG data as well as other factors and SRI can materially impact the opportunity set for an investor. Stylistically impact investing is somewhat different, as it attempts to drive change in behavior around SRI or ESG issues.

ESG has become important due to scientific, sociological, and technological transformations. Concern over the environment has been steadily growing over the last several decades. This has been accompanied by more scientific evidence about environmental issues on a myriad of topics. Social issues have also been increasingly relevant as evidence has shown the economic (and moral) advantages of treating customers, employees, and counterparties fairly. Proper governance of corporations and organizations has always been important to investing but a period like the great recession highlighted these issues. Any bad behavior on these topics is increasingly captured through activist digital media outlets that are so prevalent and can quickly transmit and reach a large enough audience to hurt a company's business. The ramifications of corporations failing on critical ESG factors can result in limited access to capital, loss of customers, government fines and higher legal and operational costs. It is vital to manage and monitor these risks when investing.

Companies must be aware of all facets of its operations to avoid ESG risks. These concerns can be harder to manage if a company grows rapidly and as the use of supply chains and outsourcing increase. Apple faced issues when its contract manufacturing partner Foxconn had problems reported about the treatment of its employees. Apple had to quickly respond to this indirect social problem as if it was its own and it rapidly and successfully changed things at its partner. Governance should always be a major part of any analysis, how a company is

DOI 10.1515/9781547400751-038

managed and how it is organized, this has to include understanding what checks and balances it has in place. This must include all aspects of its operations even if it means checks on its vendors and suppliers.

ESG analysis helps an investor to understand all the risks of an investment and these can be balanced against the potential rewards. SRI may limit certain investment outright or actively seek to overweight certain types of assets. SRI can be designed enumerable ways to reach specific goals that are important to an investor. For example, an SRI strategy may focus on a broad diversified portfolio but with no fossil fuels and a minimum of 10% allocation to renewable carbon free energy sources. You could argue that SRI decisions are driven by factors beyond pure financial issues, though an investor with an SRI strategy may disagree if they believe that a type of company is doomed to become extinct because of SRI issues in its business. Just like different investors may disagree about how much to weigh certain investment metrics in the decision process, investors may have different views on what are important SRI issues and what tolerances to accept.

There are an increasing number of styles of activist, or impact, investing. In these cases, investors use their capital to influence how a company acts on ESG and SRI issues. This is typically through pressures on the board and perhaps even through threats of proxy fights to wrest control from existing management if changes are not made. It can also come in the form of more cooperative engagement with management. In other arenas groups have pressured government to change certain issues, such as quotas for female representation on the board of directors; rules have been put on these issues in some places such as in France.[i] Green bonds, that reward a company with better lending terms if certain ecological targets are met, can also be considered a form of impact investing. Whether any of these issues are important to you or not, they will impact the returns on investments and may impact the ability of a company to survive. When these factors are big enough risks there will be fewer investors to supply capital and there may be a backlash from customers. Some fund managers have become very active in impact investing and ban investments in some areas under SRI policies; it is unclear yet how this is impacting long-term performance so far. Initially it is likely that studies in this area will be run by people that have invested into using ESG and/or SRI systems so there may be some confirmation bias in the research. However, whatever the studies show, ignoring ESG and SRI factors is not a prudent approach because it is influencing capital flows.

In some cases, SRI positions are being taken by pension funds, which have certain fiduciary responsibilities to protect and grow the money it manages for current and future retirees. It may become an interesting debate as to what legal obligations a pension manager has should it choose to follow a set of moral standards with its investments that its membership may not agree with. The plan's beneficiaries could challenge the management on whether this SRI policy is actually in the best interests for preservation of capital and growth of the capital base that employees have contributed for their retirements.

Everyone can undertake economic activism, and it is likely to become more common as people become more financially literate and realize the power of economics. Nations have realized this for some time, from historical blockades to modern day sanctions and tariffs. These techniques can work at the consumer level as well. Economic activism can be more quickly mobilized now than in the past and when a company has a misstep it will need to undertake more swift corrective actions. If you, as a consumer, do not like the way the American National Football League is handling brain injuries or are upset about safety at Formula 1 races, you could write nasty letters to the television networks and tell them they must stop showing them. They will likely not listen. However, if you organize enough people and get them to stop watching, it may have more impact, and then if you get all these people to stop buying the products of the sponsors of the sports, it may get an even larger response.

You do not fully understand the risks of investing if you ignore ESG, SRI, and activist investing. It is a reality that is influencing asset valuations and cash flows and will become increasingly important. It will evolve as a field, and digital media is likely to accelerate the impact of these factors.

---

i Zillman, C. (2017 November 20), The EU Is Taking a Drastic Step to Put More Women on Corporate Boards. Fortune.com

Chapter 39
Trends, Data, Correlations, and a Few Other Things—Again

A trader may be able to exploit an intra-day trend in a stock and have it play out, but economic trends tend to last longer. They can be driven by bureaucratic or politically controlled "regimes" or from unplanned forces that dominate the economy. An example of a controlled regime would be the "easy money" low interest rate policies put in place after the great recession by many central banks around the globe. An example of a more unbridled trend was the digitization of media, which started in the early 1980s with music CDs[i] and has since included all forms of media and data. While the intra-day trade is valuable, shifting capital to invest in a major trend is very powerful for long term investors. Medium- and long-term economic trends tend to transition rather than collapse and often include a long unwinding tail that can give ample opportunity for an exit without too much degradation of asset value from the peaks. These trends do not follow straight lines; there will always be some divergence along the way. If you have a long-term time frame, these undulating waves that occur during a long-term trend can cause entry and exit points around a core position. Tsunamis are much less common than waves.

Economic trends can be very narrow or broad in their impact. For example, a shortage of cubist paintings and a growing demand among collectors may prove to be a long-term trend, but is unlikely to impact the broad economy. Whereas, a massive new oil discovery will have broader impact on the region in which it was found but also possibly across the globe. Major broad reaching trends typically are signaled by multiple data points and impact values across several types of assets. For example, the structural long-term decline in interest rates that started in the early 1980s in the United States was signaled by actions by the Federal Reserves, moves in the dollar and measures of inflation. The decline in rates impacted home values, bonds, currencies, equities, and the investment decisions of businesses. The global economic impact of an increase in the prices for cubist paintings would probably not transmit as broadly through the economy.

You want to monitor data and look for trends, but the data you are using is always old. The components of the economy may be very different now in critical ways than in past cycles, which can limit the value of using historical data blindly. Analyzing which historical data is relevant and putting it into context for the current economic situation will lead to better decisions. No single piece of data is "always" the best to use. Various environments will require the use of

DOI 10.1515/9781547400751-039

different data, especially as change happens more rapidly. Analysis that is aware of the forces of change and how they are impacting the value of the data being used is what is valuable.

Markets often lead the economy; they can react quicker than the economic data does. However, markets are reactionary and often give false signals. A market price on an asset, despite some false signals, is still valuable data. It is fleeting but it gives you the best real-time data point on value. It adds to your knowledge on how others view the value of the asset. Long-term patterns of prices can be more critical data than one data point in time and you can always overweight the latest price point relative to the one from a year ago. Focusing less on individual prices or variances and more on the broad changes in the direction of asset prices can help spot trends.

It seems like almost every investor is drawn to try to find correlations between data and asset prices, hoping to find the magic formula. Investors often grow dependent on correlations between some specific data set and a specific asset valuation. Sometimes the strength of these correlations breakdown and create an opportunity because they quickly revert. However, sometimes things have changed and the correlations no longer work. This is happening more rapidly in the economies of today. Correlations do not usually last forever, and analytical logic can be critical in recognizing when a change in correlation makes sense.

Simplicity has been popular through the ages. William of Occam, a medieval logician, is still remembered for teaching to avoid complexity when simplicity will do.[ii] Albert Einstein, the legendary physicist is best known for a simple formula $E=MC^2$ that changed the world. Simplicity can often be the best path for good decision making. With constant changes in the economy the value of using any data point is going to vary considerably over time. The more different data sets you are utilizing in a model the more likely some of them have become irrelevant. Keep it simple, fewer moving parts, fewer things break. Despite timeless advice about simplicity, there are some people that take delight in building complex models or doing things the hard way.

Models work well when the data inputs are easy to track and monitor. Trying to find investment themes through highly complex models with a multitude of variables can confound an investor with many false signals. Simple models allow more careful tracking of how the data interacts and affects the economy. This does not mean advanced concepts and ideas are not valuable. However, investment themes work well when they are based on inputs that can easily be analyzed to see how they are changing over time. Models also should not be binary; several scenarios with probabilities can drive better decisions than a single view of the future.

No investment trend will move in a straight line. At some point prices will move against a thesis and if the data and the thesis have not changed, the investor needs fortitude. Alternative viewpoints should be examined and ancillary data looked at, but investors should not be afraid to stick with their convictions. For example, just because something has been going up for some time is not enough of a reason for it to go down.

Asset values often move when results vary from expectations. Missing or beating expectations is very different than a change in a long-term trend. However, for very short-term trades, results relative to expectations are more important than the actual result. An over-reaction in the market to miscalculated expectations can create an opportunity for investors with long-term convictions. Understanding what is driving the expectations of others is important because that will be part of how they set the price at which they will be willing to sell you an asset and where they will be willing to buy something when you are ready to sell.

Changes in the level of uncertainty cause valuations to reset. If uncertainty increases enough, shocks can happen. Like a championship fighter takes some punches but does not get knocked down, shocks can happen but don't always lead to a crash. Valuations can adjust to the uncertainty over time and just as uncertainty can increase it can also decline. A few shocks, or sometimes even a single good one, can change people's tolerance for risk. When this happens people will pay more for risk aversion. Monitoring a market's tolerance for risk can be quite useful, and following relative movements in data points such as credit spreads and prices of safe haven investments can help.

The time horizon that you have for your investments needs to be matched with the types of investment themes that you choose to pursue. The decisions you would make managing a pool of money that is not going to be touched for fifteen years will likely be different than a pool of money that might get taken out after twelve months. The time periods you choose to measure investment performance can also greatly impact how you invest. It is human nature that you will think and act slightly differently if your performance is questioned twice a day, quarterly or annually. It is odd that everyone seems to measure performance off the same calendar year; a study of how performance varies if someone is measured off-cycle, such as every five, or every fifteen months, would be a good project for a behavioral economist.

It is not worth changing investments every time the wind blows. However, any investment thesis should be questioned constantly and examined using various sources of data because everything is always changing rapidly.

i Generally, ABBA's album "The Visitors" is considered the first music CD produced. However, Billy Joel's "52nd Street" was considered the first one commercially released.

ii Occam's philosophy is often called Occam's Razor as it recommends shaving away unnecessary hypotheses.

Chapter 40
Never Close Your Eyes or You Will Miss Something

It is hard to think of a time in history when technology has become more rapidly accepted or economic change has been more widespread. This is impacting economic activity and how society functions. Together innovation and sociological impacts are making this era very different than in the past. It has been typical to use historical data to make decisions, but you must understand that this era has changed the value and relevance of much of the historical data that is typically used to develop opinions on the value of an investment. Data must be looked at differently now. Similarly, revisiting and reexamining theories about economic interactions are critical because so many relationships in the economy are being transformed.

Technology is allowing information and transaction flows to be much more flexible than in the past. More varied sources of capital are available, and it can be more rapidly deployed to more areas of the economy. This is helping to increase company formation and destruction. On a macroeconomic basis economic problems should be caught sooner and resolved quicker. This means that broad-based positive economic trend lines should last longer and when trouble hits, the shock should be shorter and shallower. This could create long, positive economic trend lines with relatively small readjustments. Figure 40.1 gives a visual representation of what this type of trend line might look like.

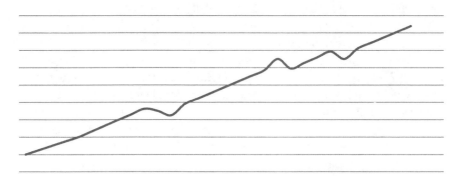

Figure 40.1: A Hypothetical Trend Line for an Innovation Driven Economy's Growth

Crashes are hard to predict and are not very common. People often obsess about finding a data point that was the sign of the last crash, but a piece of data that in, hindsight, looked like a trigger for the last event is not always relevant for the next

DOI 10.1515/9781547400751-040

one. This is even more true in an economy that is shape shifting. Timing matters as well. If someone calls for a crash and it takes three years to come about, then the returns on your investment for those three years may have more than made up for any future losses. But those returns were obtained only if you did not panic and pull your money out of the investments and bury it in your yard.

The current economic trends appear to be heavily influenced by a series of revolutions in technology, and it does not appear to be abating. While history is not always a guide to the future, it is worth putting the current environment into some context. The first industrial revolution is generally considered to have started in 1760 and to have lasted sixty to eighty years. This was followed by a second industrial revolution that began in 1870 and lasted about forty-four years, up to the start of World War I. For context the first e-mail services were launched in 1995 and the iPhone was introduced in 2007. Based on this backdrop, the current era has time to run. Currently, innovative developments are still occurring at a rapid pace and in multiple areas such as artificial intelligence, virtual reality, the internet of things and quantum computing and impacting the economy and all parts of society. At some point, people will look back at this current period as an exceptional epoch of economic evolution.

Just like all good parties, the macroeconomic party is unlikely to go on too long without something getting broken. While the overall macro figures and economic conditions should continue to advance, there will be much more volatility and uncertainty at the medi and micro level. New competitors are changing the competitive landscape constantly and in some arenas barriers to entry seem to barely exist anymore. This will cause pocket style recessions in selected industries with more severe investment losses and gains. This means more successes and failures at the regional, industry, and corporate levels.

More thoughtful work needs to be done for investing success because manipulation of historical data will not be enough to tell you who the winners and losers will be. Start-ups are nimble and unencumbered by legacy assets and can attract capital like never before, but incumbent operators are increasingly innovative and are clearly fighting back more successfully than earlier in the century. Risks are heightened as changes in corporate structures will likely make failures more painful than in the past. For all these reasons, despite expectations of long range positive macroeconomic trends, careful investment selection will likely matter more than it has during previous macroeconomic runs.

The biggest risk to this scenario of macro growth coupled with more medi and micro uncertainty is the amount and type of government interference. Sociological changes driven by new media outlets and methods of communication and the millennial population bubble could lead to more radical and rapid swings in politics and policy. There is clearly a need for structure and rules from the government, but over-regulation, or poor regulation, may crush innovation and damage the economy in any country. The further the government apparatus is separated from understanding people's well-being and how the private sector works, the more likely poor regulation will be enacted. The economy could also be disrupted by heavy handed miscalculations on interest rates by central banks and, especially, by governments having to face deficit challenges due to overspending and a lack of expense management.

Keep your eyes open. Constantly looking for new sources of information on the economy is healthy. Too much of the traditional economic data is too late and changes too slowly to be useful in an economy of innovation. In many cases the more frequent releases of "soft" data can be more valuable than "hard" data. Public releases from industry leading businesses at times can give greater insight into the economic trends than gross domestic product (GDP) reports often can. The amount of publicly available research from governments and agencies around the globe can be staggering. The work can sometimes be obscure and valuable at the same time. It is good to always look at events and data from outside your home market or your industry of choice. The modern economy is very intertwined and myopics never see the trends until it is too late. Just because something worked well for a long time does not mean that it works in the new economy any more. Throwing something out when you find something better is not bad to do. For good or bad, nothing stays the same.

Selected Ideas from Parts 8 and 9

Topic	Concepts	Investment Impact
Value	Assets are usually valued based on their current or potential cash flow generation.	There is a multitude of subjective factors that are used in discounted cash flow analysis that can lead to differing results. Opinions of growth, risk and uncertainty will impact discount rates used.
Value Differentiation	Tech driven innovators are being valued more on potential than incumbent companies are.	Analyzing the value of new growth companies still focuses on cash flow, but it often is based on future cash flow, different metrics are used to measure the progress and the value of the company.
Volatility	Volatility is often used as a measure of risk, but volatility is not loss. Volatility can be a measure of perceived uncertainty or consistency	Volatility is a useful tool in liquid markets when you are unsure of your investment horizon. It is difficult to compare volatility across asset classes with varied liquidity. Measure potential loss as well as volatility.
Risk and Return	Comparing adjusted returns to volatility ratios (Sharpe ratio) are popular for measuring risk/return.	Real risk is investment loss, not potential loss due to volatility. There are tools that explore loss more than volatility, like VaR and the Sortino ratio.
Knightian Uncertainty	With risk uncertainty you know potential outcomes but not the results. In true uncertainty, you do not even know the potential outcomes.	Markets do not like true uncertainty; it puts risk assumptions into question. Innovation can increase periods of uncertainty. With time, markets learn to live with uncertainty, but it may re-price assets.
Investment Uncertainty	Complete knowledge is not possible; if outcomes were known there would be no return. Changes in levels of uncertainty reset the parameters of expected risk	Uncertainty can become an excuse for inaction; time spent trying to answer the unnecessary and unanswerable is waste of an asset. You always have to be willing to invest with some level of uncertainty.
Uncertainty	Changing demographics, politics, and technology may raise uncertainty in some areas and decrease it in others.	Benefits of technology and innovation should reduce macro uncertainty but may increase medi and micro uncertainty.

Topic	Concepts	Investment Impact
New Industries	There are certain themes that new companies and industries tend to fall into.	New businesses and industries need to be analyzed for their competitive advantages and disadvantages, their potential, and derivative impacts on the existing economy.
New Industry Validation	Sometimes new industries can be validated.	Growths in customers and/or capital are common ways a new business can be validated. New businesses can weaken the value of incumbent assets.
Emerging Markets	Emerging economies are using different methods to expand and develop their economies.	Capital flows are now more flexible for emerging markets; global interaction has brought benefits and risks.
SRI & ESG Factors	ESG factors should be part of risk assessment for investments.	ESG and SRI factors are changing how people invest and will impact valuations and the ability to raise capital. They must be part of the investment process.
Data, Trends, Correlations	Technology is making everything move faster, including economic factors and sociological changes.	Historical data is less valuable. Capital flexibility makes macro trends last longer. Rapid change disrupts micro factors and can rapidly make correlations from the past meaningless.

Index

A

Activist government policies 145
ADP (Automatic Data Processing), 65
Age groups 25, 77, 123
Agencies 57, 91, 93, 109, 134, 136, 142, 160, 174
Agreements 129, 144, 184
Agriculture 91, 174–75
Amazon 21, 25, 41, 66, 152–53, 156, 165, 168
American Economics Association 137, 162
Analysts 91, 118, 186, 197–98
Apple 25, 78, 178, 180, 190, 197, 223
Aristotle 115–19
Asset Bravo 203–4
Asset classes 40, 50, 204–6, 234
Asset prices 12, 228
Asset valuations 3, 5, 7–8, 92, 96, 144, 223, 225, 228
Asset values 3, 13, 94, 105, 108, 199, 209, 227, 229
– corporate 157
Asset values move 209
Assets 13, 102–3, 105–7, 111, 197–201, 203–5, 210–12, 227–29, 234
– existing 155, 202
– hard 77, 201
Asymmetrical information 95, 108
AT&T 41
Australia 33, 172, 185–86
Authers, John 33–34
Autocorrelation 46, 50

B

Bank lenders 103, 116
Banks 31, 79–80, 82–84, 91, 96–97, 101, 103–4, 106, 115–16
Barriers 7, 22, 163–66, 180, 192, 200, 216
Benchmark inclusion 31–32
Benchmark indexes 30–31
Benchmarking 29–34
Benchmarks 6, 30–33, 135
Benefits 12, 67, 71, 116, 134, 144–45, 156–57, 177–79, 234–35
Beta 94, 206

Biases 8, 68, 95, 124, 127, 139, 141, 143–44, 173
Bonds 79, 81, 83–85, 104, 108, 115, 197, 200, 204–6
Book equity value 105, 166
Booms 5–6, 153, 161, 166, 172, 200
Borrower 83, 116, 210
Bottoms 11–15, 38
Brand loyalty 163–64, 189
Brand value 111, 167
Brands 153, 156, 164, 166–67, 174
Bulk 6, 83, 103, 115, 201, 205
Bureaucracy 124, 130, 139–40
Business applications 151–52
Business cycle theory 159–62
Business cycles 125, 159, 161, 192
Business formation, new 151
Business investment 55, 84, 94, 96, 155–57, 181, 192
Business models 14, 181, 198
Business risks 118, 205
Business structures 149–54, 192
Businesses 3–4, 19–21, 62–63, 102–6, 149–56, 177–81, 186, 189–90, 215–16
– existing 154, 163, 216
– new 56, 101, 150, 164–65, 215–16, 235
– peer-to-peer 151, 155, 166, 168
– traditional 3, 71
– unique 153, 156

C

Calculations 37–39, 198
Capital 84, 101–10, 114–19, 155–57, 161–65, 183, 192, 199–201, 223–25
– access 108, 164
– equity 102–3
– excess 68, 102
– financial 101, 119
– foreign 107, 109
– liquid 102–3
– new 33, 99
– return on 105, 156
– short-term 104
– venture 68, 103

DOI 10.1515/9781547400751-041

Capital availability 103, 157

Capital expenditures, traditional business 155

Capital flows 101–2, 106–8, 110, 116, 119, 162, 164, 185–86, 220–21

– data on international 109

– foreign 110

Capital formation 73, 101–6

Capital investment 119, 198

Capital markets 101

– diversified 115

– fluid 115

– local 220

Capital, raising 104, 116, 149

Capital sources 80, 108, 119

– new 116, 119

Capital spending 134

Capital spending trends 62

Capital structures 117

Capitalism 125, 132, 212, 215

Capitalization companies, large 30

Cases technology 67, 76, 190

Cash 80–81, 101, 106, 108, 157, 163, 191

Cash flow 103, 105–6, 136, 197–98, 201, 205, 211, 225, 234

– current 197

Cash generation 102, 198

Census Bureau 151–52

Central bankers 78, 82, 171

Central banks 69, 72, 77–78, 80–82, 84, 86, 88, 97, 136

CFNAI (Chicago Fed National Activity Index), 60, 160–61

CHF 87

Chicago Fed National Activity Index. See *CFNAI*

China 19, 25, 68, 124–25, 174, 178, 180, 184, 186

Commodities 88, 109, 204, 210, 219

Communities 152–53, 155, 190, 201

Companies 65–68, 101–8, 111–17, 150–53, 155–57, 164–69, 177–81, 189–93, 197–201

– existing 163, 215–16

– innovative 105, 117

– internet 135

– private 210

– supermarket 168

– traditional 157, 193

Comparisons 50, 105–6, 203, 205–6

Competition 117, 125–26, 151, 162, 164–69, 190, 192, 216, 221

Competitive advantage 117, 119

Competitors 31, 72, 117, 153, 163–64, 190, 216

Complex taxes 145

Consumer confidence 73, 92

Consumer price index. See *CPI*

Consumer sentiment 92

Consumer spending 69, 75, 96, 137

Consumption 19, 55, 77, 94, 101

Contagion 108–9

Contraction 6, 55, 159

Contracts 108, 129, 139, 141, 156, 180

Control 75, 80–81, 84, 97, 101, 116–17, 125, 180–81, 186–87

Control markets 12

Core numbers 76

Corporate bonds 81, 205, 220

Corporate levels 7, 111–12, 232

Corporations 56, 58, 66–69, 112, 114, 149–51, 155, 192–93, 223

Correlations 4, 43, 45, 48–50, 52, 70, 204, 227–30, 235

– negative 45, 49

Cost 31–32, 75–76, 84–85, 106, 130, 139–41, 163–66, 190–91, 197

– legal 130

– lower 104, 141, 153, 172

– switching 152, 163–65, 190, 192, 216

Cost benefit analysis 140

Cost-effective job 141

Countries 55–58, 65–68, 75–77, 86–88, 107–11, 113, 172–74, 183–86, 219–21

– developing 102, 114, 135–36, 219

– new 101

CPI (consumer price index), 75–76

Credit spreads 83–84, 229

Crisis 6, 58, 116, 123, 136, 162, 201

Cultural changes Make Economics Change 25–27

Currencies 40, 76–77, 85–89, 97, 109, 135–36, 204–5, 220, 227

– local 87, 220

Currency exchange rates 75, 87
Currency markets 49, 85, 88, 183
Customer retention 189, 191
Customers 104, 152–53, 163–64, 171,
    177–81, 189–91, 193, 215–16, 223–24
Cycles 3–8, 51, 70, 72, 86–87, 143, 159, 162,
    192

D

Debt 14, 62, 83, 87, 101, 103–7, 133–37, 220
– national 135
Debt capital 103
Debt issuance 81, 145
Debt levels 135, 220
Decision process 11, 209, 221, 224
Democracies 124, 129, 212, 215, 219
Demographics 4, 25, 126
Denominator 106, 206–7
Depreciation 106, 198, 205
Destruction, creative 212, 215
Developed countries 4, 25, 56–58, 67, 77,
    109, 114, 172, 219–20
– lesser 77, 109, 135, 186
Diffusion indexes 60–61
Discounted cash flow analysis 198, 234
Disruption 17, 19, 21, 51–52, 123, 126,
    163–64, 186, 212
Disruptors 19–23, 52
Distorting capital investment figures 156
Distorting valuations 13, 201
Diversity 26, 124, 211
Dividends 105–6, 200, 205
Dollars 49, 85, 87, 89, 123, 153, 155, 220, 227
Drawdowns 204
Drivers 29, 55, 78, 102, 108, 119
– economic 185, 219, 221
Dynamic scoring 134, 137

E

Early stage companies 103, 216
Earnings 61, 71, 91, 105–6, 134, 156–57,
    197–98, 200
ECB (European Central Bank), 87
Economic activism 225
Economic activity 6, 25, 55, 58, 60, 62–63,
    77, 97, 134
Economic analysis 7, 56, 71, 160

Economic change 4, 6, 65, 231
Economic conditions 60, 220, 232
Economic data 12–14, 19, 21, 26, 52, 67, 91,
    160, 200
– historical 3, 25, 51
Economic data points 69–70, 93
Economic factors 25, 75, 93, 235
Economic flexibility 51, 145, 162, 192
Economic growth 55, 61–62, 79, 91, 124, 157,
    173, 219
Economic policies 22, 69, 123–24
Economic reports 185, 200
Economic results 87, 210
Economic theories 3, 13, 58, 65, 216
Economic trends 62, 66, 69, 160, 185, 227,
    233
– current 232
– global 61
– long term 73
– long-term 5, 227
– new 73
– positive 51, 145
Economists 57–58, 63, 65, 80, 82, 87, 91,
    175, 181
– chief 91, 93, 134
Economy 3–8, 12–14, 55–56, 58–63, 83–86,
    123–27, 129–34, 159–62, 231–33
– bank-centric 115
– closed 186
– country's 55–56, 107, 186
– current 8, 69
– developed 7, 129
– expanding 77, 212
– global 20, 61, 67, 209
– market-based 115, 126
– market-oriented 115
– modern 5, 59, 233
– political 123–24
– real 63, 97
– strong 87, 191
Economy companies, newer 156
Efficiencies 3, 20, 78, 151, 160, 172–74, 178,
    209
– economic Egg 85–89, 177, 184
Elections 69, 129, 143, 145, 210–11
Electricity 19, 171, 173
EMA (exponential moving average), 39

E-mails 150
Emerging economies 219–21
Emerging market countries 219–20
Emerging market economies 221
Emerging market investment 219–20
Employee headcounts 70
Employers 66, 70–72
Employment 21, 60, 65–66, 68–73, 80, 97,
     112, 114, 151
Employment data 65, 69–70, 73
Employment figures 65, 69–71
Employment levels 65, 69, 78
Employment market 67, 70
Energy 20–21, 61, 75–76, 171–75, 192
Energy costs 171, 173
– higher 171
Energy efficiencies 172–73, 178
Energy prices 76, 172–73
Energy sources 21, 61, 172–74
Entities 106, 136, 140, 220
Entrepreneurship 25, 216
Entry 39, 163–65, 227, 232
– barriers to 7, 163–66, 180, 192, 200, 216
Environment 8, 68, 72, 86, 93, 108, 114, 223,
     227
– current 3–4, 41, 96, 129, 232
– economic 58, 69, 93, 134, 216
Equities 14, 71–73, 79, 83–84, 104–6, 199,
     205, 220, 227
– market value of 106, 199–200
Equity market capitalization 38
ESG 223–25
ETFs (exchange traded funds), 30
Euro 85–86, 88, 220
European Central Bank (ECB), 87
European Union 71, 136, 140, 144, 184
Exchange rates 86–88, 183
Exchange traded funds (ETFs), 30
Expansion 6, 19, 55, 58, 101, 110, 124, 159
Expectations 55–57, 60–61, 77, 86–87,
     91–97, 105, 136, 229, 232
– composite 91, 96
– economic 93, 95
Expectations theories 91–97
Expenditures 76, 142, 156, 171, 198
Expense management 139–42, 233
Experience 4, 33, 95, 155–56, 219

Exponential moving average (EMA), 39
Exporting countries 86, 110
Exports 21, 56, 185–86

F
Facebook 41, 152, 154, 168
Fairness 12, 102, 104
Falsehoods 79–84
FDI (foreign direct investment), 107–8
Federal Reserve 61, 66, 75, 80, 82, 227
Federal Reserve Bank 6, 23, 60, 81, 84, 87,
     92, 116, 118
Federal Reserve System 6, 49, 81
Financial Times 33, 88
Financing 104, 115
Fiscal policies 80–81, 125, 127, 137
Fitted line 47
Fixed income investments 83–84, 206
Flaws 12, 55, 68, 161, 200, 204, 207
Flows 102, 109, 157, 163, 184–85, 216
Food 75, 112, 163, 168, 171–75, 180, 187, 192
– cost of 76, 173
Food and energy 75, 171–75, 192
Food chain 173–74
Food industry 173–75
Forecasts 91
Foreign capital investments 109
Foreign direct investment (FDI), 107–8
Foreign portfolio investment (FPI), 107
Form, liquid 101–2
Formula 39, 43–44, 106, 111, 206, 225
Fossil fuels 171–72, 174–75, 202, 224
Founder 14–15, 25, 149, 152–53
FPI (foreign portfolio investment),   107
Fracking 20–21
Free market economy 67
Funding 62, 115, 133–37
Futures 86

G
Gas 20–21, 171–72
Gauge 31, 60, 88, 171
GDP (gross domestic product), 3, 43, 55–63,
     77, 91, 155, 159–61, 171, 183
GDP reports 55–56, 58–59
Generations 25–26, 113, 123, 151, 161,
     173–74

Global value chains 178, 181, 187
Global value supply chains 107, 185
Globalization 87, 97, 107, 110, 186
Gold 86, 107, 123
Goodhart 29–34
Goodhart's Law 29–30, 33, 52
Goods 20, 68, 75, 77, 87, 159, 161, 184–85, 193
– basket of 75, 86
Google 25, 41, 168, 197
Government 55–56, 67–69, 83–84, 123–26, 129, 131, 133–37, 139–45, 232–33
Government bond 79, 105, 205–6
Government debt 55, 82, 135, 220
Government debt pull capital 145
Government employees 139, 141–42
Government expenditures 145
Government interference 124–25, 162, 232
Government policies 51, 123, 163, 174
Government projects 140
Government revenues 134–35
Government spending 55, 58, 62, 142
Government's job 129–32
Government's role 123–27
Gray 143–45
Great recession 161–62, 201
Gross domestic product. See GDP
Growth 60, 62, 69–70, 80, 102, 108–10, 124–26, 155–56, 234–35
Growth rates 43, 47, 55, 136
– economic 70

H
HC. See human capital
Health care 72, 129, 171, 219
Higher interest rates 72, 87
Hiring 12–13, 70, 141
Historical data 3, 7, 40, 43, 50–51, 155–56, 227, 231–32, 235
History, economic 67, 183
Home ownership 201
Housing 60, 171–72, 219
Human capital (HC), 111–14, 119, 156, 186, 219
Human capital
– focus on 113–14
– investments in 111, 155

– quality of 111
– value of 66, 111
Human capital index 113

I
IMF (International Monetary Fund), 91, 109
Immigration 26, 111
Imports 56, 75, 77, 87, 185–86
Income 33, 60, 62, 66, 71, 94, 102, 133, 159
– fixed 77, 83–84, 206
– personal 69, 71
Incumbent businesses 19, 106, 167
Incumbent companies, uneven field benefitting 104
Incumbent operators 126, 151, 232
Incumbents 106, 117, 119, 151, 163, 165, 167–69, 190, 192
Index companies 32
– largest 31
Indexes 3–4, 13, 29–34, 38, 41, 48, 60–61, 85, 160–61
– soft 160
Indicators 57, 60–61, 63, 69–70, 75, 81, 159
Industrialized economy 13
– modern 13
Industries 7, 59–60, 116–17, 135–36, 161–63, 171, 173–75, 215–16, 232–33
Inflation 70, 72, 75–78, 80, 91–93, 96–97, 125, 127, 171
– demand pull 76–77
– measures of 75, 227
Inflation expectations 77, 80, 88, 93, 135
Infrastructure 110–11, 114–19, 124, 126, 150, 175, 184, 219
Innovation, rapid 8, 105, 119, 209
Institutions 12, 25, 32–33, 91, 93, 108, 113, 115–16, 124
Intellectual property 155–56, 177–78, 180, 184, 192
Interest 75, 79–80, 87, 106, 190, 198, 206, 210
Interest rates 13–14, 69, 79–80, 82–84, 86–88, 94, 125–26, 204, 206
Interest rates and falsehoods 79–84
Interest rates move 80, 206
International capital flows 102, 107–10, 119
International Monetary Fund (IMF), 91, 109

Internet 21, 72, 76, 102, 104, 150, 152, 163–66, 168
Inventories 56, 60, 69, 178, 180
Invested capital 105, 112, 117, 156, 165, 180, 193
Investment assets 197, 203
Investment decision process 4, 79
Investment decisions 3, 8, 13, 19, 22, 67–68, 103, 136, 140
Investment economics 7
Investment hangover 161–62
Investment Impact 51–52, 97, 119, 145, 192–93, 234–35
Investment losses 204, 232, 234
Investment performance 32
Investment portfolios 7, 32–33
Investment return 205–6
Investment themes 5, 228–29
Investment time frames 203
Investment trends 51, 229
Investments 29–30, 38–40, 49, 116–17, 119, 156–57, 205–7, 209–12, 219–20
Investors 32–33, 82–83, 93–96, 103–5, 107–10, 197–99, 201–3, 223–24, 228–29
Investors' time horizons 198
Invisible consumer 189–91, 193

J
Japan 61, 67–68, 83, 115, 179, 185–86
JIT 178–79, 181
Jobs, good 93, 95, 131–32

K
Key performance indicators (KPIs), 91, 200
Kodak 117–18
KPIs (key performance indicators), 91, 200
Kraemer 181

L
Labor 65, 70–71, 73, 76, 151
Labor markets 65–67, 171
Laws 5, 12, 29–30, 48, 108, 115, 119, 126, 129–30
– rules of 12, 108, 220
Lazarus 14, 25
Legislation 130–32, 134

Legislature 129–30
Liquid 107–8
Liquid assets 40, 102, 105, 203, 205
Little Bit 75–78
LNG (liquefied natural gas), 172
Loans 79, 83, 101, 103, 106, 108, 116, 197, 200
Local capital commitments 110
Local capital commitments to infrastructure in exporting countries 110
Logistics 20, 72, 104, 150, 156, 164, 173, 175, 177–79
Long-term trend 5–6, 26, 39, 63, 73, 227, 229
Loss 49, 85, 106, 109, 203–5, 207, 216, 232, 234
– potential 204, 210, 234

M
Macroeconomic data 12, 205
Macroeconomic trends 209
– long-term 7
– positive 232
MAD (market adjusted debt), 200
Management 32, 112, 114, 117, 145, 149, 198, 200, 224–25
Management time 163, 165
Manufacturing 3, 56, 58, 60, 123–24, 150, 156, 177, 179
Marginal utility 12, 15
Market adjusted debt (MAD), 200
Market capitalizations 30, 33
– company's 31
Market data 5, 8, 29
Market forces 67, 124–25, 174
Market place 62, 125, 165, 203
Market prices 21, 71, 228
Market reactions 69, 82, 88
Market share 114, 116, 153, 190, 192, 216
Market systems 102, 115, 126
Market theory, efficient 94, 203
Market valuations 144, 197, 199–200
Market values 105, 199–200
– real 166
– total 55
Market-based economic structures 126
Marketing 150, 156, 163, 168, 187

Markets 4–5, 12–14, 56–57, 81–85, 87–88, 91–93, 115, 199–200, 205–7
– emerging 172, 219–21, 235
– foreign 107–8
– home 88, 107–8, 220, 233
Maturity 79, 83, 206
Measure of Trade 183–87
Medi 7, 19, 23, 51, 200, 209, 232, 234
Media 56, 61–62, 73, 76, 82, 143, 189, 197, 227
– digital 123, 132, 141–42, 145, 225
Media companies, new 155–56
Median 37, 49
Metrics 156, 190, 197, 205, 234
Microeconomic Trends 7
Microeconomics 7
Microsoft 41, 43, 197
Milken,Michael 111–14, 117–18, 199
Models 78, 82, 123, 125, 161, 164, 168, 204, 228
– complex 51, 228
Momentum 13, 30–31, 199
Monetize 156, 181, 192, 201
Money 6, 11–12, 76, 79–80, 86–87, 101, 115–16, 139, 229
Monitor 60, 62, 84, 88, 109, 112, 117–18, 131, 135
Mortgages 75, 81, 116
Moving averages 37–40, 60
– 200-Day 38–40
Music industry 4, 59, 168

N

National Bureau of Economic Research (NBER), 159
National level 111–12, 129, 136
Nations 101–3, 108–9, 111–14, 127, 129, 139, 171, 174–75, 186
– emerging market 221
NBER (National Bureau of Economic Research), 159
Netflix 41, 164, 167, 191
New companies 150, 152–53, 156, 159, 165, 190, 192, 201, 235
New economy companies 197
– innovative 117
New industries 58, 106, 215–17, 235

New industries and new companies 152
New role of capital and capital formation 101–6
New York Times 15, 27, 154
News 31, 71, 88, 97, 108, 143, 189, 199–200
– economic 13, 67

O

Obligations 63, 83, 174, 210
OECD (Organization for Economic Cooperation and Development), 57, 63, 92, 109, 174
Officials, elected 129, 131, 133
Oil 20–21, 48, 76, 93, 105, 171–72
Oil prices, crude 49
OPEC (Organization of the Petroleum Exporting Countries), 91, 171–72
Organization for Economic Cooperation and Development. See *OECD*
Organization of the Petroleum Exporting Countries. See *OPEC*
Organizations 91, 93, 109, 111–14, 149–50, 152, 177, 184–85, 223
Outcomes 11, 43, 45, 95, 106, 141, 209–11, 216, 234
Outsourcing 150, 154, 177–81, 193, 223
Ownership 102, 107, 125, 201

P

Parties, political 123, 139, 143
Part-time jobs, multiple 73, 97
Passive investors 31
PCE (personal consumption expenditures), 56, 75
Perception 88, 103, 199–200, 206–7, 220
Performance 30, 33, 38, 45, 95, 105, 123, 229
Periods
– current 203, 232
– extended 3, 93, 96, 154
– long 5, 87, 119, 143
Personal consumption expenditures (PCE), 56, 75
Physical capital investments 105
Physical infrastructure 115, 129, 219, 221
Plans 58, 60, 67, 101, 136, 143, 151, 171, 211
Plant, physical 105, 111, 119, 155–56
PMIs (purchasing managers index), 60, 160
Pocket recessions 7, 51, 162

Policies 29, 123, 126–27, 129, 132–33, 135, 143–45, 183, 186
– extreme 143
– public 4, 22, 129, 137
– regulatory 131
Policy makers 68, 73, 75–76, 78, 186
Policy tool 125, 135, 145
Politicians 56, 61, 69, 135, 139, 143–44, 183, 186
Politics 82, 123–24, 143, 183, 209, 232, 234
Population 11, 19, 26–27, 66, 73, 93, 95–96, 113, 143
Port 165, 179–80
Portfolio 7, 30–31, 38, 83, 206, 211
PPI (producer price index), 75
Price effects of stock market indexing 34
Price stability 77, 80
Price volatility 171, 192
Prices 13–14, 38–40, 71–72, 75–79, 83, 171, 189–90, 203–6, 227–29
Pricing power 72, 97, 164
Private sector 22, 26, 58, 62, 129–30, 133, 136, 139, 141
Producer price index (PPI), 75
Producers 75–76, 94, 172
Product differentiation 163–64
Production 55, 60, 62, 76, 101, 164, 173, 177–78, 180
Products 59–60, 76–77, 156–57, 165–66, 174, 177, 179–80, 186–87, 189–91
– new 19, 45, 157, 215
Profits 68, 70, 72, 94–95, 157, 187, 192, 209, 212
Prosperity 65, 111, 115, 126
Purchasing managers index. See *PMIs*

Q
Quality 101, 108, 111–12, 153, 157, 164, 189–90, 215–16, 220

R
RA (real assets), 111
Rates 6, 69, 77, 79–81, 83–84, 87, 94, 97, 135–36
– short-term 81, 94
Ratios 55, 105–6, 112, 200, 206–7
Real assets (RA), 111

Real data 111–14
Real estate 13, 25, 164, 174, 197, 201, 205, 220
Real estate values 201
Recessions 4–7, 25–26, 58, 76, 78–79, 159–61, 166, 223, 227
Regions 7, 109, 134, 174, 183–84, 186, 209, 211, 219
Regression 4, 43–50, 52
Regression analysis 43, 45–46
Regression and correlation analysis 43, 50
Regulations 29, 71, 116, 119, 126, 130–32, 145, 168, 233
Regulations in place 131
Regulators 67, 78, 95, 116–17, 119, 130–32
Relationships 4, 7, 25, 43–46, 48–50, 87, 93, 144, 184
Relative value 47, 105, 156, 183, 199
Reports, monthly 60–61, 65, 185
Residuals 46–47
Resist correlations 43–52
Resources 11, 91, 133, 145, 192, 221
– limited 11, 163
Retail price index (RPI), 75
Retailers 76, 117, 140, 168
Rethink regressions and resist correlations 43–52
Revenue 31, 41, 45, 47, 59, 62, 133–35, 141, 157
Revenue growth 46–47
– annual 47
Reversion 40–41
Risk aversion 93, 210, 229
Risk measures 203–7
Risks 30–33, 49–51, 83–84, 115–17, 152–53, 203–7, 209–10, 223–25, 234–35
– credit 83, 206
RPI (retail price index), 75
Rules 32, 82, 108, 123–24, 129–31, 139, 143, 224, 232
– regulatory 129

S
Sales 4, 14, 26, 44–46, 59–61, 69, 83, 140, 164
– level of 44, 46
Sales growth 61

Sales tax 134

Salespeople 44–45, 61

Savings 75, 77, 101, 150

SC (social capital), 111

Scale 78, 145, 149, 153, 163, 165, 174

Scandals 154, 174, 180

Securities 31–32, 38, 80, 107, 112, 159, 174, 191, 207

Securities markets 13, 55, 60, 65, 136

Seller 13, 153, 197

Service trade 184

Services 55–56, 58–60, 140–41, 163–64, 166–67, 177, 184–85, 189–91, 219–20

– international trade in 184–85

Services segment 58

Shenkman Capital 14, 69, 112

Shocks 51–52, 78, 104, 161, 171, 201, 204, 229, 231

Smith, Adam 113–14, 178, 181

Social capital (SC), 111

Social change 4, 25

Social media 123, 126, 129–30, 132, 136, 142, 155, 190

Socialism 125, 212, 215

Socialist market economy 125

Socially responsible investing. See *SRI*

Socially responsible investing 223–25

Sortino ratio 207, 234

S&P 31, 34, 38, 41, 160

Specialization 105, 180–81, 186, 215

Spending 25–26, 134, 139, 142, 171

Spread 83, 108–9, 206

SRI (socially responsible investing), 223–25

St. Louis 6, 23, 81, 84, 92, 118, 160

Stability 81, 113, 119, 126, 144, 151

– economic 108, 110, 125

– political 65, 69, 87, 97, 221

Standard deviation 49, 203–4, 207

Start-ups 117, 151, 153, 157, 163, 165, 168–69, 177, 192

Stock markets 12, 31, 61, 190

Stock price 38–40, 43, 47, 175, 205

Stock valuations 79, 157, 211

Stocks 3, 13, 30–31, 33–34, 38–41, 43, 83–85, 101, 203–5

Strategies 30, 32, 40, 48, 150, 168, 179, 209, 216

Structures 12, 25, 119, 124, 130, 150–51, 155, 210, 219

– corporate 7, 112, 150, 153, 232

Subjective value 15, 199

Subjectivity 105–6, 112, 197–98, 217

Supermarkets 164, 169

Supply 72, 76, 83, 87, 117, 125, 161, 171–72, 175

Supply chains 78, 88, 104, 107, 110, 174, 177–81, 186–87, 193

– global 20, 76, 108–10, 185–86

Supply chains and outsourcing 180, 223

Support 32, 62, 114–15, 119, 124, 131, 139, 142–43, 199

Surveys 50, 56–57, 59, 61–62, 65–66, 71, 91–93, 96, 103

– establishment 66, 71

Systems 31–32, 97, 102, 115–16, 124–26, 129, 135, 177, 179–80

– economic 80, 115, 124

– financial 29, 83, 220–21

T

Target rate 77–78

Tax changes 134, 137

Tax code 133, 135, 145

Tax Foundation 133–34, 137

Tax revenues 73, 134–36, 140

Taxation 125–26, 133, 135, 145

Taxes 62, 75, 87, 106, 129, 133–37, 139–42, 145, 198

– progressive 133–34

– regressive 133–34

Taxes and government debt pull capital 145

Technological innovations 20, 72, 77

Technology 3–4, 70, 72–73, 115–17, 149, 164–65, 171–73, 231–32, 234–35

– financial 111, 116

– innovative 163, 166

– new 3–4, 72, 78, 106, 119, 202

Technology companies 157, 216

– green 202

Technology investments 73, 151, 192

Telecommuting 73, 93, 150, 201

Television 103, 156, 167, 189

TIC (Treasury International Capital), 109

Time economies 6

Time horizon 33, 198, 203, 229
Time Magazine 9, 23
Time.com 23, 106
Tools 3–4, 43, 50, 80–81, 88, 113, 135, 206, 234
– valuable 40, 49, 60, 62, 83–84, 96, 105, 200, 204
Trade 47, 49, 85–88, 107–8, 116, 119, 126, 183–87, 193
– global 88, 178, 186
– international 68, 87–88, 183, 185, 193
– value-added 185–86
Trade data 183, 185
Trade reports 185
Trading 14, 32, 84–86
Trading volumes 32, 40, 80, 85, 205–6
Traditional balance sheet measurements of asset value 166
Training 71, 73, 112, 130
Transaction costs 32, 119
Transactions 12–13, 87, 113, 133–34, 185, 203, 205
Transforming investment economics 4
Transportation 141, 173, 178, 183–85
Treasury International Capital (TIC), 109
Trends 3–8, 13–14, 26–27, 55–56, 60–62, 73, 87–88, 92–93, 227–30
– wage 73
Trends and cycles 6–7

U
Uber 68, 73, 117, 152, 168–69
Uncertainty 11–12, 96, 195, 197–203, 207, 209–12, 229, 232, 234
– economic 160
– level of 200, 209–10, 212, 229, 234
– micro 232, 234
– true 209, 211, 234
Underappreciated law 29–34
Unemployment 60, 65–70, 93, 97, 127, 140
United Nations 58, 174–75
United Parcel Service (UPS), 179
United States 4–6, 25–26, 56–58, 65–69, 75–76, 78–80, 129–31, 133–36, 183–86

United States Postal Service (USPS), 178
UPS (United Parcel Service), 179
Usage 60, 66, 105, 172–73
USD 85, 87
USPS (United States Postal Service), 178

V
Valuations 5, 13, 94, 117, 190, 192, 197–203, 207, 229
Value 3–5, 12–13, 29–31, 86–88, 105–6, 180–81, 185–87, 197–206, 227–28
– increased 151
– intrinsic 210
Value assets 11, 199
Value-added taxes (VAT), 75
Variables 43, 45–46, 50, 228
– dependent 43, 45–46
– independent 43–47
Variations 75, 108, 184, 221
VAT (value-added taxes), 75
Vendors 153, 164–65, 224
Volatility 49–50, 162, 165, 195, 197, 203–7, 209, 232, 234
Volatility and risk measures 203–7

W, X
Wage data 69, 71, 73
Wages 65, 68, 71–73, 114
Weaknesses 66, 159, 163, 216, 221
Wealth 101, 115, 126, 133, 140, 149, 186, 201
Weighted averages 37–38, 60
Workers 37, 66–68, 72–73, 201
Workforce 71–72
Working capital 108, 180
– lower 178
– short-term 104
Working capital loan 104
Working capital, shifting 200
World Bank 89, 91, 113–14

Y, Z
Yield 6, 79, 82–83, 135, 206
Yield curve 79–80

Printed and bound by PG in the USA